"Trying to grasp the implications of financial upheavals since 2008, most commentators have drawn on a narrow range of European and American examples. *Moments of Truth* provides a crucial corrective by widening the range of comparisons. Contributors also offer insightful analyses of each, helping this book provide a much needed perspective not just on financial crises but also on their political and social implications."

—Craig Calhoun, *Director of the London School of Economics and Political Science*

"Everywhere, politicians, activists and academics are striving to make sense of a global financial and economic crisis. In this empirically rich, methodologically sophisticated and theoretically innovative book, some of the finest international scholars take a step back and ask how we make sense of such crises in the ways we do, why and with what effects. Through a series of highly illuminating case-studies, the book explores the ideas, institutions and actors that define contexts, specify options and shape choices in what is, after all political economy. It is a welcome contribution to debates in international *political* economy, comparative politics and political sociology."

—Alan Finlayson, *University of East Anglia*

Moments of Truth

The current financial and sovereign debt crisis of the European Union and the United States can be regarded as the most recent of a wave of financial and sovereign debt crises that have affected different regions of the world over the past quarter century. While there is a large and growing body of literature on the economic aspects of financial crises, their political elements remain surprisingly understudied.

Moments of Truth: The Politics of Financial Crises in Comparative Perspective fills this gap in the literature by looking at the political repercussions and policy implications of financial crises in comparative perspective, using case studies in Latin America, Korea, and Russia as well as the contemporary crises in the United States and in key European countries. Contributors to this volume look at the crises as critical junctures that generate high levels of uncertainty while calling for decisive action. The chapters emphasize structural or agency-based explanations and give relevance to the role of ideas, interests, and institutions in explaining different outcomes. The questions addressed by the case studies include how the crises were defined by key actors, the range of political and policy options available to deal with their impact, the role of ideas in policy shifts, how political and economic actors redefine their interests in contexts of uncertainty, how political institutions mediate reactions to the crises, what explains the choice of a certain option over other alternatives, and whether the crisis has (so far) resulted in significant political and policy changes or in incremental adjustments to the status quo.

The first book to comparatively analyze the political dimensions of financial crises across different global regions, *Moments of Truth* will be highly significant for any scholars interested in the contemporary debate on financial crises.

Francisco Panizza is Associate Professor in Latin American Politics at the London School of Economics and Political Science.

George Philip is Professor in Latin American Politics and Comparative Politics at the London School of Economics and Political Science.

Conceptualising Change in Comparative Politics: Polities, Peoples, and Markets

Edited by Francisco Panizza (London School of Economics) and Anthony Peter Spanakos (Montclair State University)

Conceptualising Comparative Politics: People, Polities, and Markets seeks to bring a distinctive approach to comparative politics by rediscovering the discipline's rich conceptual tradition and inter-disciplinary foundations. It aims to fill out the conceptual framework on which the rest of the subfield draws but to which books only sporadically contribute, and to complement theoretical and conceptual analysis by applying it to deeply explored case studies. The series publishes books that make serious inquiry into fundamental concepts in comparative politics (crisis, legitimacy, credibility, representation, institutions, civil society, reconciliation) through theoretically engaging and empirical deep analysis.

1. **Moments of Truth**
   The Politics of Financial Crises in Comparative Perspective
   Edited by Francisco Panizza and George Philip

Moments of Truth

The Politics of Financial Crises in
Comparative Perspective

Edited by
Francisco Panizza and
George Philip

 Routledge
Taylor & Francis Group

NEW YORK AND LONDON

"Trying to grasp the implications of financial upheavals since 2008, most commentators have drawn on a narrow range of European and American examples. *Moments of Truth* provides a crucial corrective by widening the range of comparisons. Contributors also offer insightful analyses of each, helping this book provide a much needed perspective not just on financial crises but also on their political and social implications."

—Craig Calhoun, *Director of the London School of Economics and Political Science*

"Everywhere, politicians, activists and academics are striving to make sense of a global financial and economic crisis. In this empirically rich, methodologically sophisticated and theoretically innovative book, some of the finest international scholars take a step back and ask how we make sense of such crises in the ways we do, why and with what effects. Through a series of highly illuminating case-studies, the book explores the ideas, institutions and actors that define contexts, specify options and shape choices in what is, after all political economy. It is a welcome contribution to debates in international *political* economy, comparative politics and political sociology."

—Alan Finlayson, *University of East Anglia*

Moments of Truth

The current financial and sovereign debt crisis of the European Union and the United States can be regarded as the most recent of a wave of financial and sovereign debt crises that have affected different regions of the world over the past quarter century. While there is a large and growing body of literature on the economic aspects of financial crises, their political elements remain surprisingly understudied.

Moments of Truth: The Politics of Financial Crises in Comparative Perspective fills this gap in the literature by looking at the political repercussions and policy implications of financial crises in comparative perspective, using case studies in Latin America, Korea, and Russia as well as the contemporary crises in the United States and in key European countries. Contributors to this volume look at the crises as critical junctures that generate high levels of uncertainty while calling for decisive action. The chapters emphasize structural or agency-based explanations and give relevance to the role of ideas, interests, and institutions in explaining different outcomes. The questions addressed by the case studies include how the crises were defined by key actors, the range of political and policy options available to deal with their impact, the role of ideas in policy shifts, how political and economic actors redefine their interests in contexts of uncertainty, how political institutions mediate reactions to the crises, what explains the choice of a certain option over other alternatives, and whether the crisis has (so far) resulted in significant political and policy changes or in incremental adjustments to the status quo.

The first book to comparatively analyze the political dimensions of financial crises across different global regions, *Moments of Truth* will be highly significant for any scholars interested in the contemporary debate on financial crises.

Francisco Panizza is Associate Professor in Latin American Politics at the London School of Economics and Political Science.

George Philip is Professor in Latin American Politics and Comparative Politics at the London School of Economics and Political Science.

Conceptualising Change in Comparative Politics: Polities, Peoples, and Markets

Edited by Francisco Panizza (London School of Economics) and Anthony Peter Spanakos (Montclair State University)

Conceptualising Comparative Politics: People, Polities, and Markets seeks to bring a distinctive approach to comparative politics by rediscovering the discipline's rich conceptual tradition and inter-disciplinary foundations. It aims to fill out the conceptual framework on which the rest of the subfield draws but to which books only sporadically contribute, and to complement theoretical and conceptual analysis by applying it to deeply explored case studies. The series publishes books that make serious inquiry into fundamental concepts in comparative politics (crisis, legitimacy, credibility, representation, institutions, civil society, reconciliation) through theoretically engaging and empirical deep analysis.

Moments of Truth

The Politics of Financial Crises in
Comparative Perspective

Edited by
Francisco Panizza and
George Philip

Routledge
Taylor & Francis Group

NEW YORK AND LONDON

First published 2014
by Routledge
711 Third Avenue, New York, NY 10017

Simultaneously published in the UK
by Routledge
2 Park Square, Milton Park, Abingdon, Oxon OX14 4RN

Routledge is an imprint of the Taylor & Francis Group, an informa business

© 2014 Taylor & Francis

Library of Congress Cataloging-in-Publication Data

Moments of truth : the politics of financial crises in comparative
   perspective / edited by Francisco Panizza and George Philip.
      pages cm. — (Conceptualising change in comparative politics :
polities, peoples, and markets ; 1)
   1. Financial crises—Political aspects.   I. Panizza, Francisco.   II. Philip,
George, 1951–
   HB3722.M624 2013
   338.5'42—dc23
   2013005480

ISBN: 978-0-415-83411-7 (hbk)
ISBN: 978-0-203-49950-4 (ebk)

Typeset in Minion
by Apex CoVantage, LLC

Printed and bound in the United States of America by Publishers Graphics,
LLC on sustainably sourced paper.

Contents

Figures and Tables

FIGURES

TABLES

Contributors

Edward Ashbee is an associate professor in the Department of Business and Politics at Copenhagen Business School. His publications include analyses of the culture wars (*The Bush Administration, Sex and the Moral Agenda*, Manchester University Press, 2007) as well as studies of US economic policy and comparative policy responses to the Great Recession. He is currently writing a cross-national survey, *The Right and the Economic Crisis*.

Martin B. Carstensen, is an assistant professor at the Department of Business and Politics, Copenhagen Business School. He is currently working on a comparative analysis of crisis management in Denmark, Ireland, and the Netherlands (post doc project funded by the Carlsberg Fund) and an analysis of the role of special bank resolution regimes in postcrisis financial regulation.

Mathis Heinrich is a PhD research student at the Cultural Political Economy Research Centre of Lancaster University (UK) and holds a three-year PhD scholarship of the Institute of Critical Social Analysis of the Rosa-Luxemburg Foundation in Berlin (Germany). In his thesis he is working on European monetary and financial crisis management in reaction to the current economic and financial crisis.

Jonathan Hopkin is a Reader in the Department of Government at the London School of Economics. He is the author of *Party Formation and Democratic Transition in Spain* (1999, Macmillan) and has published widely on party politics, political economy, and political corruption, with particular reference to Southern Europe and the UK. His current research focuses on the dilemma of economic reform in the context of the financial crisis and the changing role of political parties in Western democracies.

Joo-Hyoung Ji obtained a PhD in sociology from Lancaster University and is an assistant professor in sociology at Kyungnam University, South Korea. He is interested in global political economy and state theory, and his recent publications include *The Origins and Formation of Korean Neoliberalism* (in Korean).

Bob Jessop is a distinguished professor of sociology at Lancaster University and codirector of the Cultural Political Economy Research Centre. He is best known for his contributions to critical political economy, state theory, the analysis of welfare state restructuring, and the philosophy of social sciences. Two forthcoming books include *The State: Past, Present, Future* (Polity, 2013) and, with Ngai-Ling Sum, *Towards Cultural Political Economy* (Edward Elgar, 2013).

Amelie Kutter is a researcher at the Department of Sociology, Lancaster University, working on management and discourses of the current financial and economic crisis. She holds a PhD (European University Viadrina) and an MA (Diplom, Free University Berlin) in political science and cultural studies. She has lectured, researched, and published on European integration, postsocialist transformation, and transnational political communication and specialises in discourse studies and textual analysis.

Francisco Panizza is an associate professor of Latin American Politics at the Department of Government of the London School of Economics and Political Science. He is the co-editor of Routledge's *Conceptualizing Comparative Politics* Series. His main research interests are democratic politics, populism, the politics of economic reform, and the relation between ideas and institutions. He has written extensively about left-of-centre governments in Latin America. Among his main publications are *The Triumph of Politics: The Return of the Left in Venezuela, Bolivia and Ecuador* (with George Philip, Polity Press, 2011); *Contemporary Latin America. Development and Democracy Beyond the Washington Consensus* (Zed, 2009); *Populism and the Mirror of Democracy* (Verso, 2005) and 'Unarmed Utopia Revisited: The Resurgence of Left of Centre Politics in Latin America' (*Political Studies*, 2005).

George Philip has been on the faculty of the London School of Economics since 1976 and has been professor of Latin American politics since 2001. He specialises in the study of Mexico and Venezuela about which he has written several books and journal articles. His most recent book, jointly authored with Francisco Panizza, is about the return of the left in Venezuela, Bolivia, and Ecuador. He has also written a book on the Mexican presidency and a general work on oil and politics in Latin America.

David M. Woodruff is senior lecturer in comparative politics at the London School of Economics and Political Science. He is the author of *Money Unmade: Barter and the Fate of Russian Capitalism* (Cornell University Press, 1999) and articles on the political economy of money, trade, exchange rates, and legal institutions. His present research concerns the intersection of ideas and institutions in the Eurozone crisis.

Sotirios Zartaloudis is a lecturer in International Politics at the University of Manchester. He has taught extensively on the European Union (EU) (history, policies, politics and governance), comparative political economy and international politics at LSE, College of Europe (Bruges) and South-Western University of Finance and Economics (SWUFE) of China. His research focuses on four key themes: Europeanization; comparative public policy; EU economic and social policies; and the current financial crisis and its impact on public policy. He has received competitive research funding from EU and national (Greek and UK) national bodies.

Series Foreword

By Anthony Peter Spanakos

On the back cover of a book of cartoons about his travels in the United States, the British cartoonist, Simon Bond, depicted Uncle Sam reclining on a couch while a psychiatrist probingly asks 'So, how long have you thought yourself a Democracy?' (Bond 1988). Some two and a half decades later, responding to an imminent drying up of US credit markets, Henry Paulson, then Secretary of the Treasury, proposed to the US Congress, in a three-page memorandum, extensive powers for his office, powers which would be insulated from practically any oversight. There was no alternative. But there was. Roughly one week and a half later, the US Congress passed the TARP rescue plan, which did empower the Secretary of the Treasury but through a more democratic process. The move may very well have staved off a financial collapse but, half a decade later, the US economy continues to trundle fairly aimlessly with no clear indication of being able to address the pressures brought on by the Great Recession. Bond's psychiatrist could very well ask, 'So, how long have you thought yourself a developed country?'

If crisis challenged democracy and development in the US, it did far more in Europe. Traditional analysis locates the origin of the crisis in the US in 2008 (what of the Chinese government's lack of discretion in funding US deficits? Hot money fueling housing bubbles throughout the world? Incompatible monetary and fiscal architecture in Europe? Shifts in the creation, translation, and disappearance of jobs in various sectors across the world? Earlier shifts towards financialization of economic policies?), but since then, the European Union has faced tremendous challenges to its very constitutive features—including democracy and development—to say nothing of the common monetary unit, the Euro. The speed with which crisis transformed from something facing the US and its particular variety of capitalism into a problem of profligate 'swine' (the peripheral PIGS—Portugal, Ireland, Italy, Greece, and Spain) into a European Union–wide crisis (including even the UK, which opted out of the Euro) was remarkable. The lack of speed in resolution is similarly remarkable. At various points, political leaders and technocrats (whose identity qua political leaders became more clear) echoed the familiar Washington Consensus salvo: 'there is no alternative.' But there were alternatives and these are much more clearly seen in the European cases. While the US alternatives were either largely obscured within policy-making circles—periodically appearing as op-ed pieces in the *New York Times,* or appeared in the form of Tea Party or Occupy Wall Street activism—European countries saw a wider range in alternative proposals from a wider range of political actors.

Earlier crises (Mexico 1982, 1994, Venezuela 1994, Russia 1997–1998, South Korea 1998, Argentina 1999–2002, Uruguay 1999–2001) are instructive as they took place in decidedly certainly less developed (with the possible exception of South Korea) and often less institutionalized democratic regimes (with the exception of Uruguay and possibly Venezuela and Argentina). They also took place at an earlier time with different technologies and rules governing finance. In virtually each of these cases, some politicians and bureaucrats (domestic as well as international) insisted that there was no alternative to their proposals. Yet, Mexico's one-party state is now a multiparty democracy, Venezuela's two-party system was thoroughly discredited, Russia has seen a reversal in terms of political and economic liberalization, South Korea continued to liberalize and deepened its dependence on exports, Argentina defaulted and devalued its currency while remaining democratic, and Uruguay continued to be a stable democracy. Obviously, the conditions each faced were not identical, nor are they identical and, possibly even, comparable with the crises in the US and Europe, but, clearly, there were alternatives. Where there is space for comparison—and this is one of the chief contributions of this volume—is in the notion of what is a crisis and what happens during critical junctures.

Much of the scholarship on the crisis in Europe (or elsewhere) may focus on its causes and resolutions. These questions are very interesting but, as Panizza's introduction states, the chapters herein do not seek to identify causes and solutions—as though such things existed objectively—but why did one crisis narrative win out, why was one group able to silence others in declaring that there is no alternative to its prescription. Implicit in the chapters in this book are the questions: which crisis; what makes it critical; for whom? One could certainly describe any of the moments described in the books as 'critical,' but that would certainly be shorthand for a number of overlapping crises (and noncrises). The authors problematize such shorthand visions of crisis. There is a tendency to *economicize* and, particularly, to *financialize,* the notion of crisis. This is not without reason as all of these crises have occurred alongside major economic downturns, which had profound effects on the ability of the financial sector to function as an intermediary. But crises also involved challenges in the organization of state policy-making capacity, state revenue generation and spending, the organization and activity of various politically active (and inactive) sectors, the perception of how and through what mechanisms society should reconcile its diverse population, and so on. If a crisis was simply a financial crisis which could be solved by injecting liquidity into the financial sector, the authors in this volume suggest, this was not because that was a response to an empirically observable truth. Rather, it was because it was defined as a financial crisis, a product of a struggle of interpretations. It was the result of the hegemony of one particular crisis narrative, a narrative that was favored and favorable to groups that were better capable of turning their vision into *the* consensual vision.

As the book's title suggests, crises are seen here as moments of truth and, specifically, they are moments of intersubjective truth that is established through public and private contestation that aims to establish the truth about the crisis. Crisis narratives aim to understand what is the crisis, what caused and will cure it (short- and long-term, simple policy tinkering, structural changes, cultural transformations), and how the costs of the crisis and its resolution should be distributed. These narratives are partial as none can truly offer a full account, though few political accounts claim to be partial (this may be easier for scholars to accept than for politicians and citizens). When one account becomes hegemonic (sometimes very quickly, sometimes only after many years), this reflects not only the accuracy of the account but also the nature of power relations and the way that discourse is communicated in political spaces. As the critical junctures literature highlights, political spaces become more porous and flexible during crisis—they are moments in which what is envisionable as a truth expands and during which there may be wide shifts in what might be perceived as desirable. Nevertheless, they do not seem to generate ex nihilo, but build on previous ideas, are communicated through extant socio-political structures through actors who, in some form, predate the crisis. Certainly shifts occur within the crisis but, as Carstensen's chapter on the Danish bailout suggests, there is an identifiable linkage between pre- and postcrisis conditions.

Thinking of crises through dueling notions of truth does not mean that crises are reducible to words or that changes in unemployment, purchasing power, the range of political alternatives for citizens, or the amount of security—however defined—experienced by residents of a given political space are empty of empirical content. A political movement responding to a crisis may aim (and succeed) at fundamentally shifting how resident foreign nationals are treated or how citizenship is experienced. Similarly, banks have only so much money and there are limitations to how much a central bank or treasury can issue debt to produce more money (one may contest where the limits are, how much monetization is feasible, morally acceptable, and so on, but there are still limitations, partially because money is a sociocultural phenomenon depending on expectations, promises, symbolism, and enforcement mechanisms) without severe consequences. The latter issue is especially the case for countries with currencies whose value depends on their stock of another country's currency (such as Argentina and Uruguay, or Russia and Venezuela when petroleum prices are low) or is a non-decision-making part of a monetary union (such as Greece and, to a lesser extent, Spain and Italy), but it was also true of the United States in 2008 and, because of the complicated net of intra-European sovereign debt holdings, it was a possible threat for Germany, France, and the United Kingdom.

Crisis narratives are also "real" in that they are understood within the conflict of group interests and through institutional structures. The emphasis on the relationship between the political agency of human beings and the institutional structure they encounter, aim to change, and which aims to modify their behavior, is a fundamental element in knowing and understanding crises. Rather than abstracting into a definition of crisis that may lend itself to more variable-oriented research, the authors of this book suggest that crises are not only highly contested but also highly contexted. That is, they are embedded in texts (narratives of different sorts) and contexts (the conclusion contrasts the effects on democracy of different crises in Latin America and Europe, highlighting different time periods, institutional environments, legacies with authoritarianism, extragovernmental actors, and institutions). Again, the aim is not to compare the crises but, through probing the way crises were enacted, interpreted, and experienced in different contexts, the authors examine the tensions within which scholars may understand crises and critical junctures. In so doing, this book exemplifies conceptual, comparative political inquiry and is typical of what this book series aims to offer to the field.

In some ways, the best way to introduce what is meant by "conceptual comparative politics" is to read this book (or forthcoming books in the series) as it *does* conceptual comparative politics, rather than tries to identify conceptual comparative politics as a thing. But, for pragmatic reasons, it is worth briefly explaining what conceptual comparative politics is (see Spanakos and Panizza forthcoming) so that the claim that this is a book that fits in the series is more credible. Conceptual comparative politics aims to recover and update traditions within the field of comparative politics, which draw on other disciplines (political theory, history, sociology, anthropology, economics, literary theory, etc.) to reflect on concepts that are used (rather than specifying a concept for the sole purpose of testing a set of hypotheses) in explaining and understanding deeply contextualized empirical phenomena (rather than somewhat distant and unproblematized data sets). What emerges in the current study is the role of judgment and decision (linking *crisis* to the ancient Greek verb κρίνω) of organized political actors in identifying and communicating crisis narratives in institutionalized spaces, made somewhat more permissive and visible at specific moments. The authors are not interested in composing linear explanations with simple causality to explain the crises, cases, and aftermaths. *Crises* and *critical junctures* are not abstractions to be applied but terms that the authors approach after deep reflective engagement with their subjects. None of that engagement leads to the endorsement of a singular hypothesis, but all seem to endorse a broad way of approaching crisis conceptually, methodologically, and empirically. The interpretavist and qualitative orientation of this book is indicative of a particular way of doing conceptual comparative politics (see Schwartz-Shea and Yanow 2012; Brady and Collier 2004). Conceptual comparative politics may also embrace more positivist and quantitative approaches. Such work would similarly probe the concepts that will serve as variables and would recognize that the concepts and theories are intimately connected to the empirical phenomena they study (see Hawkins 2010). The goal is to rethink comparative politics and to open a conversation about how to do comparative politics.

Sources Cited

Bond, Simon, 1988. *Totally U.S.* Topsfield: Salem House.

Brady, Henry E., and David Collier. 2004. *Rethinking Social Inquiry: Diverse Tools, Shared Standards.* Rowman & Littlefield.

Hawkins, Kirk A. 2010. *Venezuela's Chavismo and Populism in Comparative Perspective.* New York: Cambridge University Press.

Spanakos, Anthony Peter, and Francisco Panizza, eds. Forthcoming. *Conceptual Comparative Politics.* New York: Routledge.

Schwartz-Shea, Peregrine, and Dvora Yanow. 2012. *Interpretive Research Design: Concepts and Processes.* New York: Routledge.

Introduction
Crises as Moments of Truth[1]

Francisco Panizza, The London School of Economics

The financial crisis of the United States and the Eurozone, whose fully blown materialization can conventionally be dated to 15 September 2008 (the date Lehman Brothers filed for Chapter 11 bankruptcy protection), and yet to come to an end at the time of writing this introduction, it is the most recent of a series of financial and sovereign debt crises that have affected different regions of the world over the past quarter century. Financial crises have political repercussions that vary considerably across regions and countries. Financial and sovereign debt crises cut across international and domestic politics and involve intense interactions between international and regional actors, governments, and citizens. While the economic factors behind financial crises are often similar, political responses tend to differ considerably. How a country responds to and manages a financial crisis is shaped by a number of political actors—domestic and international—whose objectives may be not only in conflict but also, as they try to understand the causes and consequences of the crisis, in flux. Their interactions shape both the immediate policy responses and the medium- to long-term policy and political consequences of the crisis. This book seeks to contribute to our understanding of the politics of financial crises by looking at their political repercussions in a comparative perspective. It includes single and comparative case studies across different regions, covering financial and sovereign debt crises in Asia (South Korea 1997), Latin America (Mexico 1982 and 1994–1995; Venezuela 1994; Argentina and Uruguay 2001–2002), and Russia (1998), as well as the contemporary crises in the US and some key European countries (UK, Germany, Greece, Italy, Spain, and Denmark).

Financial crises provide a wealth of empirical material to reflect on key concepts of comparative analysis: ideas, interests, institutions, democracy, change, and—last but not least—political power. By their very nature, financial crises also go to the heart of the relation between politics and economics. While this book adopts a pluralist theoretical approach to the understanding of the politics of financial crises, a useful conceptual approach for looking at financial crises is to regard them as critical junctures. This approach is in line with classical as well as more recent studies of financial crises (Gourevitch 1986; Bermeo and Pontusson 2012). It is appropriate, therefore, to outline what we mean by critical junctures and how it relates to the theme of this book—the politics of financial crises.

The term *crisis* is closely associated in our understanding of critical junctures to its original Greek meaning. Rooted in the Greek verb *krienein* (to decide), the noun *krises* was infused with a broad spectrum of meaning, including to "separate," to "choose," to "judge," and to "decide"; as means of "measuring oneself," to "quarrel," or to "fight." It meant not only "divorce" and "quarrel" but also "decision," in the sense of reaching a crucial point that would tip the scales (Koselleck 2006, 358). Drawing from its Greek meaning, a crisis can be understood as a chain of events culminating in a situation calling for urgent and decisive action (Koselleck, cited in Ritcher and Ritcher 2006, 356). As such, as the title of this book suggests, crises are moments of truth.

Financial crisis is a broad term that covers different types of crises, which are often but not always causally related: it can refer to sovereign debt crises, understood as the inability or unwillingness of a sovereign state to serve its debts or serious fears of it (*Oxford Dictionary of Economics* 2003, 109). These are sometimes triggered by banking crises when a significant part of a nation's banking sector becomes insolvent, requiring a bailout from the state, as has been the case of the crisis of the Eurozone and the US. Another important variation of crises consists of exchange-rate crises, when the value of a country's currency falls precipitously, often despite a government's "guarantee" that it will not allow this to happen under any circumstances (Reinhart and Rogoff 2009, xxvi).

There is something particular to sovereign debt crises that distinguish them from the debt crises of private actors. Countries do not go bust in the same way that a private company runs out of money. Most countries' defaults happen long before the country actually runs out of resources. In these cases, a determined debtor country can usually repay foreign creditors with enough pain and suffering. Country defaults are often the result of a complex cost-benefit calculations involving political and social considerations—not just financial ones (Reinhart and Rogoff 2009, 51). Decisions on whether or not to default involve political and moral dilemmas of the highest order and are often made in conditions of high uncertainty, with imperfect information about the consequences of the decision. These characteristics are what often turn financial crises into critical junctures.

In line with the more general meaning of *crisis*, critical junctures (Collier and Collier 1991) are regarded as moments of choice and decision. As put by Capoccia and Kelemen:

> In institutional analysis critical junctures are characterized by a situation in which the structural (that is, economic, cultural, ideological, organizational) influences on political action are significantly relaxed for a relatively short period, with two main consequences: the range of plausible choices open to powerful political actors expands substantially and the consequences of their decisions for the outcome of interest are potentially much more momentous. Contingency, in other words, becomes paramount. (2007, 343)

The previous claim merits further examination. In public life, choice and decision making involve the exercise of power. Both Collier and Collier (1991) and Mahoney (2002) emphasize the importance of power and choice in characterizing critical junctures. In order to make a meaningful decision, one must have the power to choose between alternatives: "[C]hoices demonstrate the power of agency by revealing how long term development patterns can hinge on distant actor decisions of the past" (Capoccia and Kelemen 2007, 347). Yet, as national governments often appear impotent against the speculative attacks of market forces, financial crises seem to drain power away from national governments and leave them exposed to the whims of the market and at the mercy of supranational financial and political actors. As a politician at the vortex of the political turmoil caused by a financial crisis expressed to one of the co-editors of this book: "Crises both drain power away from you and empower you" (Atchugarry, Minister of Economy of Uruguay 2002–2003, personal communication).

Financial crises drain power away from governments because they place huge constraints on governments' financial resources and undermine ruling parties' bases of support. They empower politicians because they have the potential to transform leaders into "storm riders" by enabling them to change courses of action, sweep away institutional constraints, and take extraordinary measures to prevent economic and, ultimately, political wreckage. The case studies of this book confirm the two-faced "power-draining" and "power-augmenting" nature of financial crises. The cases of Argentina in 2001 and Greece since 2010 are prima fasciae examples of a government's inability to withstand the attack of the markets on the economies and, in the case of Greece, of its submission to the dictates of "The Troika"—that is, the European Union (EU), the European Central Bank (ECB), and the International Monetary Fund (IMF). In both cases, the financial crisis led to the near collapse of the countries' political systems and to mass popular protests (see Chapter 2 by Panizza and Chapter 9 by Zartaloudis). Argentina and Greece are the most extreme examples of market forces forcing the hands of governments to take unpopular measures that they would not have taken if they had any meaningful choice. Office holders not only have unpopularity to fear, but also a likely election defeat—if not a loss of legitimacy and a crisis of representation. Thus, rather than choice and agency, financial crises appear to reinforce structural constraints and narrow alternatives. Most governments have justified austerity measures by reviving the acronym TINA (There is No Alternative) made famous by the Thatcher government in the UK in the 1980s. Yet, one of the most often quoted quips about the current crisis is the remark by President Obama's former chief of staff, Rahm Emanuel: "You should never let a serious crisis go to waste. What I mean by that is it's an opportunity to do things you couldn't do before" (see Chapter 5 by Ashbee).

Our case studies suggest at least three dimensions of choice in the politics of financial crises. First, the policies adopted by governments were not the consequence of a lack of alternatives but the choice of an alternative more in line with the political preferences of powerful actors. By presenting the policies as the product of necessity, choice is concealed and change is made possible. Second, elections at time of crisis can and often do give citizens significant political and (to a lesser extent) policy choices. The 2012 election in the US offered citizens a choice between two starkly different visions of America. In the case of Greece, the country's submission to the conditions of the Troika must not overshadow the fact that in the elections of 2012 Greek citizens chose the option most likely to keep the country in the Eurozone and voted against the uncertainty of a more radical alterative (see Chapter 9 by Zartaloudis). Third, crises open windows of opportunity for far-reaching structural reforms ranging from sectoral reforms to wholesale changes in economic models. Examples of the former include the reforms of financial sector regulation in the US and the Eurozone (see Chapter 5 by Ashbee and by Chapter 7 by Heinrich and Kutter); examples of the latter include the reforms of the models of economic development in Mexico in the 1980s, Russia in the 1990s, and Argentina and Venezuela in the 2000s (see Chapter 1 by Philip and Chapter 3 by Woodruff).

Choice and change, however, are not the same and the relation between critical junctures and change requires further elaboration. Many scholars define critical junctures on the basis of their outcome—namely, change. However, as Capoccia and Kelemen (2007, 352) argue, while it is tempting to equate critical junctures and change, this outlook is not commensurable with the emphasis on structural fluidity and heightened contingency (the defining traits of critical junctures). Moreover, even when change takes place as a result of a critical juncture, it may follow different patterns ranging from a radical rupture with the status quo to the acceleration or reversal of already existing trends.

Contributors to this book look at financial crises as key moments in time for understanding political change. It is tempting to associate the scope of change to the gravity of the financial crisis. However, this begs the question of how to measure the impact of financial crises across a battery of financial and economic and political indicators. Moreover, our case studies give no evidence of a one-to-one correlation between the gravity of the crisis and the scope of political change.

The case studies of this book suggest that we need a more sophisticated understanding of critical junctures and the nature of change itself. Philip's comparative study of Mexico and Venezuela shows how a limited banking crisis in Venezuela set in motion a radical process of political and economic change while the more substantial 1995 financial crisis in Mexico reinforced the existing economic model. Panizza's analysis of the 2001–2002 financial crises in Argentina and Uruguay is a further example of a crisis leading to substantial changes in the political system and economic model in Argentina and to significant continuity in economic policy and the political system in Uruguay. The case studies of Greece, Italy, and Spain demonstrate how the political impact of the Eurozone crisis has been very different in the countries of the European semiperiphery, as it has been in Britain and the US. Change, therefore, is not a necessary outcome of a critical juncture and lack of change does not denote the absence of choice or makes the juncture any less critical. If change was possible, plausible, considered, and ultimately rejected in a situation of high uncertainty, there is no reason to discard these cases as "non-critical" junctures (Capoccia and Kelemen 2007, 352).

When it takes place, change can be incremental and uneven rather than radical or revolutionary, as it incorporates past institutional and ideational aspects into the new arrangements. As such, one can derive important insights about how critical junctures may or may not counterweight long-run path dependency. Martin Carstensen's study of the handling of the banking crisis in Denmark shows how, by drawing on ideas and institutions developed since the banking crisis of the 1980s to address the 2008 banking crisis, Danish authorities introduced a number of incremental changes to the financial system that resulted in a distinctive solution to the banking crisis that combined elements of innovation with the reinforcement of the status quo. Also on the question of incremental change, Edward Ashbee's study of the impact of the financial crisis in the US demonstrates how expectations that the financial crisis would lead to the reconfiguration of the US political process and reshape the role of the state proved unfounded. Ashbee argues that most of those who sought reform did not attempt to replace established institutional structures. Instead, they accepted the need to seek less direct forms of change that took the form of processes of conversion, layering, and drift. Last but not least, while certain elements of a polity can change as a result of a crisis, other may become more entrenched. Philip argues that while the 1994–1995 crisis contributed to the defeat of the Partido Revolucionario Institucional (PRI—The Revolutionary Institutional Party) in the 2000 election and thus the end of Mexico's dominant party system, in the economic realm it reinforced macroeconomic orthodoxy.

Explanations of the differences in the pace and nature of change at times of crises should give greater emphasis to political, rather than financial dimensions. Policies need politics, because only political mobilization can give support and power to those that ultimately select certain economic solutions among all those available. The dominance of politics in the choice of economic policies should generally hold true, but the argument is that we become more aware of it in times of crisis, "when patterns unravel, economic models come into conflict, and policy prescriptions diverge" (Gourevitch 1986, 17, cited in Schelke 2012, 131).

Is difficult to make empirical generalizations about the depth and direction of change at times of crises, as outcomes are highly contingent, context dependent, and unfold over relatively long periods of time. Financial crises provide a "stress test" (Lachapelle, Way and Levitsky 2012) that allows us to better understand how political systems cope, or fail to cope, with their political impact. As several of our case studies indicate, institutional factors play an important role in determining the ability of governments to promote the necessary changes to overcome crises. In some countries, effective political management of the crisis has led to the reorientation of the economy and the strengthening of state capabilities. David Woodruff's analysis of Russia's sovereign debt and exchange-rate crisis of 1998 shows how the then new president, Vladimir Putin, won widespread legitimacy by spearheading a strengthening of the national state and a shift toward a more *etatiste* economic policy. President Néstor Kirchner of Argentina also took advantage of the 2001 crisis to "bring the state back in" and use state power to consolidate his power and control market forces. Through a very different strategy of crisis management and resolution than that of Argentina, Uruguay's political system came out of the crisis with enhanced legitimacy (see Chapter 2 by Panizza). On the other extreme of the spectrum, Greece and Venezuela have exposed the limited ability of a political system dependent on clientelistic forms of political representation to respond to crisis effectively when its base of support is undermined by the need to cut public spending.

While institutional analysis is an important aspect of the study of financial crises, a narrow focus on institutions fails to address the question of why certain institutions are more resilient than others and to take into account the argument that critical junctures weaken the hold of institutions on political actors. While this book borrows the notion of critical junctures from historical institutionalism as key for understanding financial crises, it places a significant emphasis on financial crises' ideational elements. Financial crises are more often than not moments of intense ideological struggle. Moreover, they generate high levels of uncertainty while calling for decisive action. While it can be assumed that actors will seek to impose their interests in times of crisis, the heightened uncertainty and greater incidence of imperfect information that characterize decisions in critical junctures make the following general argument particularly relevant: what actors seek to impose is not a direct reflection of their material self-interest but rather a reflection of particular *perceptions* of their self-interest (Hay 2011, 70; see also Blyth 2002; Wendt 1999). This is especially pertinent in crisis situations in which, by definition, asymmetry of information and heightened uncertainty severely limit the assumptions of rationality of economic theory (Barthalon 2003; Kindleberger and Aliber 2011).

Ideas reduce uncertainty and give content to interests, for under such conditions it is not obvious where agents' best interests lie and therefore what type of policies would best serve those interests (Blyth 2001, 3–4). Martin Carstensen's study of the Danish crisis (Chapter 10) exemplifies how one of the ways by which actors overcome uncertainty to enable collective action at times of crisis is by using the ideas of the precrisis discursive regime and through processes of rearticulation of the old ideas to new ideational elements fit them to new circumstances. Decisions taken under conditions of high uncertainty are more than usually shaped by psychological factors, thoughts, habits, and by ideological shortcuts, perceptions, and unexamined assumptions. As the IMF's chief economist, Olivier Blanchard, put it:

> The world economy is pregnant with multiple equilibria—self-fulfilling outcomes of pessimism or optimism, with major macroeconomic implications. Right or wrong conceptual frames change with events, and once markets turn [in favour of or] against a country, perception shapes reality (Blanchard 2011, 3)

When we enter the realm of perceptions, contingency, and the construction of interests we join the domain of ideas, rhetoric, symbols, narratives, and other accounts of the social production of intersubjective meaning. A crisis is a moment for contestation and struggle, to make sense of it and inform individual and collective responses (Jessop, 2013). Competing crises narratives are attempts to make sense of crises and shape perceptions of causality, responsibility, and interests. The importance of crisis narratives is not limited to the apportioning of blame. Narratives are also crucial for strategies of economic recovery, the formulation of which implies particular conceptions of what is considered politically and economically feasible, possible, and desirable—and, therefore, of the ability to shape and reshape the ideational parameters that circumscribe what governments can and should do to solve the crisis (Hay 2001, 199).

A number of the chapters in this book look at the narratives that have shaped dominant interpretations of the financial crises (see particularly Chapter 7 by Heinrich and Kutter, Chapter 2 by Panizza, and Chapter 4 by Ji). But even contributors that adopt a more classical political economy approach to the analysis of financial crises give particular attention to their interpretative dimensions. The reasons for this awareness are easy to understand. Financial crises have multiple dimensions and can be seen from different angles. Crises narratives are complexity-reducing devices that attribute relevance to some elements of a crisis and on this basis promote certain solutions to the detriment of others. As Craig Calhoun put it:

> It is also that different empirical accounts of this crisis—different stories— reflect distinct underlying concepts of capitalism, of finance, and of crisis itself and distinct ideas about whether to focus more on financial markets as such or more on the lives or ordinary people (Calhoun 2011, 19)

In line with this view, 't Hart affirmed: "Those who are able to define what the crisis is all about also hold the key to defining the appropriate strategies for its resolution" (cited in Hay 1996, 255). Analyses of the Eurozone crisis in this book look at the consequences of dominant interpretations of the crisis for strategies of crisis resolution. Heinrich and Kutter argue that by emphasizing national homemade problems of public expenditure, lack of competitiveness, and labor market policies as common causes of the Eurozone crisis, the European Commission and other EU representatives established a generalized story which implied that problems were endogenous and could be tackled within established policy frameworks of austerity and increasing competitiveness. By blanking out the larger implications of the crisis that are related to structural imbalances of the Eurozone model of capital accumulation, these views have effectively blocked entry points for alternative solutions. Jonathan Hopkin's study of the politics of financial crises in Italy and Spain challenges Northern European politicians and EU leaders' focus on the alleged fiscal irresponsibility and inflationary wage rises in Southern Europe as causes of the crisis. He argues that by failing to take seriously the role of financial flows within the Eurozone as the real cause of the problem, the Eurozone leaders have pre-scribed liberalizing structural reforms that will not only be difficult to enact when combined with financial austerity but that are also likely to further un-dermine support for the European integration project within the "crisis coun-tries" of Europe's semiperiphery.

The argument that crises are a matter of interpretation and that uncertainty permeates perceptions of interests does not mean that all interpretations carry equal weight. The interests of powerful actors have a disproportionate weight in determining the strategies of crisis resolution (see Chapter 1). This point is brought home by the contributions of Ji and Jessop, both of whom use a cultural political economy approach. Ji claims that the discursive reduction of complexity as a primary basis for action at times of crises is not merely episte-mologically bounded but also—and more importantly—politically bounded. In his study of the Korean crisis he explores how the government's discourse of "equal pain sharing" and *chaebol* reform masked an uneven distribution of the costs of the crisis in which labor was the main loser and the *chaebols* were able to protect their core interests. Explaining why the crisis of finance-dominated accumulation regimes in the UK and the US did not produce a crisis of neo-liberalism, Jessop (Chapter 6) argues that in the two Anglo-Saxon economies' financial capital may have lost some credibility but remained dominant in the accumulation regime, the state apparatus, and (for the US) in the legislature. It was therefore able to exploit the crisis to further entrench neoliberal reforms, making sure that it did not, in Rahm Emanuel's words, "go to waste."

Last but not least, the relation between financial crises and democracy un-derlies most of the analysis in this book. As the issue is addressed at length in the concluding chapter, a brief discussion suffices in this introduction. Fi-nancial crises test the resilience of democracy in several ways. They call for swift decisions in face of highly volatile market reactions, which are difficult to take in a political system that requires deliberation and consensus building among contending interests and multiple veto players (as seen both in the US and the Eurozone). Financial assistance from multilateral financial organiza-tions and the EU implies substantial losses of sovereignty in terms of not only policy decisions but also by the imposition of technocratic administrations in Greece and Italy. Moreover, financial crises can delegitimize governments as well as entire political systems. Loss of legitimacy is manifested in the rise in popularity of extreme right and extreme left parties and the emergence of populist challengers, as witnessed in the cases of Greece, Argentina, and Ven-ezuela. The economic costs of financial crises are seldom born by those most responsible for the crisis but by those that can less afford them: the young, the unemployed, immigrants, and those who depend on public services. All of the case studies in this book confirm this trend. Yet, as Laurence Whitehead (2012, 79) points out, democracy has a built-in error-correction mechanism: it holds failed governments into account and, through changes in leadership, re-news public authority and reinvigorates political responsiveness to economic challenges. With the exception of Germany (which will hold elections after the writing of this introduction) and Russia (which does not qualify as a full democracy), all the country cases included in this book have seen democratic electoral alternations largely driven by the fallout from financial crises. Democratic change at times of crisis should be reassuring, as it suggests that contemporary democratic institutions are more robust than those of the 1930s, although (as the concluding chapter of this book points out) the current financial crisis, particularly in the Eurozone, has yet to be resolved, and it is too soon to determine its long-term political and economic implications.

Note

1. We would like to thank Ursula Durand for her contribution to the editing of this book.

References

Barthalon, Eric. 2003. "From Here to Eternity." *International Political Science Review* 24 (3): 285–319.

Bermeo, Nancy, and Jonas Pontusson. 2012. *Coping with Crisis: Government Reactions to the Great Recession.* New York: Russell Sage Foundation.

Blanchard, Olivier. 2011. "2011 in Review: Four Hard Truths". Posted 21 December 21. *IMF Direct, The International Monetary Fund's Global Forum* (blog). http://blog-imfdirect.imf.org/2011/12/21/2011-in-review-four-hard-truths/. [accessed 2 April 2012]

Blyth, Mark. 2001. "The Transformation of the Swedish Model: Economic Ideas, Distributional Conflict and Institutional Change." *World Politics* 54: 1–26.

Blyth, Mark. 2002. *Great Transformations: Economic Ideas and Institutional Change in the Twentieth Century.* New York: Cambridge University Press.

Calhoun, Craig. 2011. "From the Current Crisis to Possible Futures." In *Business as Usual: The Roots of the Global Financial Meltdown,* edited by Craig Calhoun and Georgi Derlugugian, 9–42. New York: New York University Press.

Capoccia, Giovanni, and R. Daniel Kelemen. 2007. "The Study of Critical Junctures: Theory, Narrative, and Counterfactuals in Historical Institutionalism." *World Politics* 59: 341–69.

Collier Ruth B., and David Collier. 1991. *Shaping the Political Arena.* Princeton, NJ: Princeton University Press.

Gourevitch, Peter. 1986. *Politics in Hard Times.* Ithaca, NY: Cornell University Press.

Hay, Colin. 1996. "Narrating Crisis: The Discursive Construction of the 'Winter of Discontent.'" *Sociology* 30: 253–77.

Hay, Colin. 2001. "The "Crisis" of Keynesianism and the Rise of Neoliberalism in Britain: An Ideational Institutionalist Approach." In *The Rise of Neoliberalism and Institutional Analysis,* edited by John L. Campbell and Ove K. Pedersen, 193–218. Princeton, NJ: Princeton University Press.

Hay, Colin. 2011. "Ideas and the Construction of Interests." In *Ideas and Politics in Social Science Research,* edited by Daniel Béland and Robert H. Cox, 65–82. Oxford: Oxford University Press.

Jessop, Bob. 2013 "Recovered Imaginaries, Imagined Recoveries: A Cultural Political Economy of Crisis Construals and Crisis-management in the North Atlantic Financial Crisis." In *Before and Beyond the Global Economic Crisis: Economics and Politics for a Post-Crisis* Settlement, edited by Mats Benner, Cheltenham: Elgar.

Kindleberger, Charles, and Robert Aliber. 2011. *Manias, Panics and Crashes*. New York: Basic Books.

Koselleck, Reinhart. 2006. "Crisis." Trans. by Michaela W. Ritcher. *Journal of the History of Ideas* 67 (April): 357–400.

Lachapelle, Jean, Lucan A. Way and Steven Levitsky. "Crisis, Coercion, and Authoritarian Durability: Explaining Diverging Responses to Anti-Regime Protest in Egypt and Iran." Presentation prepared for the annual meeting of the American Political Science Association, New Orleans, Louisiana, 31 August.

Mahoney, James. 2002. *The Legacies of Liberalism: Path Dependency and Political Regimes in Central America*. Baltimore: The Johns Hopkins University Press.

Oxford Dictionary of Economics. 2002. Oxford: Oxford University Press.

Reinhart, Carmen M., and Kenneth S. Rogoff. 2009. *This Time Is Different: Eight Centuries of Financial Folly*. Princeton, NJ: Princeton University Press.

Ritcher, Melvin, and Michaela Ritcher. 2006. "Introduction. Translation of Reinhart Koselleck's 'Krise' in Geschichtliche Grundbegriffe." *Journal of the History of Ideas* 67 (2): 343–56.

Schelke, Waltraud. 2012. "Policymaking in Hard Times: French and German Responses to the Eurozone Crisis." In *Coping with Crisis: Government Reactions to the Great Recession*, edited by Nancy Bermeo and Jonas Pontusson, 130–61. New York: Russell Sage Foundation.

Wendt, Alexander. 1999. "The Agent-Structure Problem in International Relations Theory." *International Organization* 41 (187): 335–70.

Whitehead, Laurence. 2012. "Democracy, Error Correction and the Global Economy." In *Democracy under Stress: The Global Crisis and Beyond*, edited by Ursula van Beek and Edmund Wnuk-Lipinsky, 79–96. Opladen-Berlin: Barbara Budrich.

1 Crises and Their Consequences in Latin America

Mexico in 1982 and 1994 and Venezuela in 1994

George Philip, The London School of Economics

INTRODUCTION

The year of 1982 is writ large in the economic history of Latin America for all the wrong reasons. In 1982, a long period of economic growth came to an abrupt end and ushered in the so-called lost decade, which featured economic stagnation and in some cases hyperinflation. A number of factors contributed to this depressing transition, which continued in many countries until the adoption of so-called Washington Consensus economics at the end of the 1980s (Williams 1990).

For a short period in 1982—and lasting no more than a few months—it looked as though Mexico's president Lopez Portillo was contemplating leading a revolt against the world's international financial institutions. In the end, the character of Mexico's authoritarian system—with its strictly observed term limits—ruled out this option. With the inauguration of Miguel de la Madrid as president in December 1982, economic management in Mexico became one of the most orthodox in the region and has remained so ever since. This market reforming orientation later survived a further fiscal upheaval in 1994–1995—the so-called tequila crisis—with surprisingly little political drama.

Venezuela, like most of the rest of the region, experienced economic problems after 1982. Despite having to devalue in early 1983, it would be too much to say that the country experienced a full-scale crisis in a way that Mexico clearly did. However, both the political system and the economy ran into increasing trouble at the end of the 1980s. A series of crisis events, including the collapse of the Banco Latino in 1994, shook the status quo over a period of several years and led to the election of Hugo Chavez to the presidency in 1998.

For Latin America as a whole, the long-term consequences of the region's lost decade were not wholly negative. The 1982 crisis played a major role in discrediting the authoritarian regimes that were then in power in most of the region. As it turned out, the subsequent democratization proved to be much more thorough and durable than most observers expected at the time. Mexico was part of the general Latin American trend toward democratization during the 1980s, though it had some specific features of its own. Ironically, despite its reluctance to democratize, Mexico proved to be more politically robust than economically successful until it suffered a further economic crisis in 1994. This crisis, painful though it was, enabled a decisive rebalancing of the economy to take place and led to even closer integration with the US.

Democracy and free-market economics had become widespread across Latin America by 1994, and its economic prospects seemed to be improving markedly in consequence (Edwards 1995). Yet, 1994 also proved a year of crisis—not across the whole region, but in two important countries. In Venezuela, the collapse of Banco Latino was followed by a domino effect across the whole national financial sector. Then, at the end of 1994, the Mexican economy suffered yet another setback (the "tequila crisis") that forced the economy back into recession. The 1994 crises in Venezuela and Mexico should have dispelled any naïve belief that democratization, fiscal orthodoxy, and market reform were proof against crises in Latin America, though it is fair to say that the effect of the 1994 crises was more localized than was the case in 1982.

The consequences of the 1994 crises were mostly less than those of 1982. Mexico continued with its process of democratization and market reform, and by the end of 1996 its economy was well on the road to recovery. Mexico has not suffered another major financial crisis since then, though it has experienced "normal" recessions. If anything, the effect of the tequila crisis was to speed up the process of market reform and political democratization rather than change the direction of policy as such.

Although Venezuela was a market-reforming democracy in 1994, its public opinion was far more skeptical about its political system—with good reason—than most other countries in the region. The Banco Latino crisis further weakened popular attachments to existing institutions. Venezuela was already in the process of moving closer to twenty-first-century socialism and plebiscitary democracy. There is at least something in the notion that the rise of Chavez was a consequence of the Banco Latino's failure. Moreover, the Banco Latino's failure illustrates much of what was wrong with the whole pre-Chavez *partidocratic* Venezuelan system. We now look at these three cases in more detail.

THE MEXICAN CRISIS OF 1982

The Mexican crisis of 1982 came as a real shock, and not only in Mexico. What made it particularly surprising was that Mexico was in the process of becoming a major oil exporter while oil prices, though by then generally on the decline, were still historically high. Mexican oil output had risen dramatically in the 1970s. During the course of the Lopez Portillo presidency (1976–1982), petroleum exports rose from $600 million to $16,500 million (Luke 1988, 60). The fact that this degree of export expansion did not protect Mexico from a balance of payments crisis made for a real paradigm shift, not least because the government was as surprised by this turn of events as everyone else. President Lopez Portillo, in office during the most expansive years of the oil boom, was personally convinced that Mexico's economic future lay with its oil, famously remarking on one occasion that 'our task is to manage abundance.'

There had been an enforced devaluation in Mexico in 1976, but the 1982 crisis was deeper, more durable, and more significant. Many policymakers believed that the discovery of large oil reserves would cure the balance of payments weaknesses that seemed responsible for the 1976 setback. There was a real sense of shock when this turned out not to be the case. Initially, observers tended to blame the government for the debacle, and there was certainly a degree of macroeconomic mismanagement involved (Chislett 1985; Kraft 1984; Duran 1988; Luke 1988). For example, public sector prices were kept low and there was little serious tax effort.

However, in hindsight, research has tended to give more importance to the existence of an unresolved ideological conflict in Mexico between structural and monetarist economists, both of whom were represented at high levels in the government. President Lopez Portillo arbitrated but did not seek to homogenize economic policy. Some of Mexico's most prominent economic policymakers (including cabinet ministers) took what was in effect a Keynesian position, with the claim that public-sector deficits could be financed so long as there was enough demand within the economy.

In 1982, the Mexican government learned the hard way that deficits mattered as inflation led to several devaluations of the peso. After one of them, President Lopez Portillo ruefully admitted that 'a president who devalues is a devalued president.' What added a further dimension to this crisis was its regional, and indeed global, dimension: Mexico was not alone. Many other Latin American countries found themselves in a similar predicament. The region as a whole had built up dangerously high levels of foreign debt, allowed its currency to become overvalued, and failed to deal effectively with the problems caused by capital flight. Meanwhile, the global economic environment was changing in an ominous way for Latin America. Neoclassical economics was tending to replace Keynesianism as the dominant paradigm in US and European government thinking. Bringing down inflation rather than achieving global macroeconomic balance was increasingly seen as the primary aim of policy. When US interest rates moved up sharply at the beginning of the 1980s, many Latin American countries found themselves exposed by their excessive levels of debt. What made things worse was large-scale capital flight, as private wealth holders proved quicker on the uptake than governments and sought to protect their assets by moving their local currency holdings into dollars.

The Mexican crisis deepened further when the government finally responded to its policy dilemmas by moving in the direction of aggressive nationalism. It nationalized the banks in September 1982, forcibly converted dollar accounts held by Mexicans into pesos at unfavorable rates, imposed exchange controls, and began to consider the possibility of a debtor cartel covering the major Latin American borrowers. These steps encountered popular approval at the time (Basáñez 1990), but they were viewed with dismay by Mexico's economic elite and even the middle class.

NEOLIBERALISM TRIUMPHANT IN MEXICO

At the end of 1982, however, Mexico decisively rejected nationalist economic policies and moved in the direction of fiscal orthodoxy and market reform. The immediate factor that enabled this to happen was the unusually institutionalized character of Mexican authoritarianism. Authoritarian Mexico was commonly described as a six year dictatorship and, by the Peruvian novelist Mario Vargas Llosa, as a perfect dictatorship. One thing that it did perfectly was to organize presidential successions. The Mexican presidential term was six years, and no reelection (to anything) was permitted. The outgoing president chose his successor, subject to a few restrictions, theoretically after consultation with his close colleagues. The cabinet, however, had been appointed by the incumbent, whose power to decide upon the succession was therefore largely unlimited.

This institutional arrangement meant that what might have been the decisive battle in late-twentieth-century Mexican history between the statist nationalists and the market liberals was largely over before it was fought. The statist-nationalist response to the 1982 debt crisis was undermined by the political calendar, because, in October 1981, Lopez Portillo had nominated his planning minister, Miguel de la Madrid, to be president. The two men were not particularly close (Zarate 1995; Torres 1999), but the Planning Ministry was a key power center from when it was set up in the late 1970s until its abolition in the early 1990s (Torres 1999). De la Madrid's achievements as planning minister included the publication of the national plan, a project that was dear to the president's heart. De la Madrid also proved a good planning minister. He was a capable administrator and a man with relatively few enemies. He was also expected to stabilize Mexico's financial markets, which were just starting to become jittery in late 1981. Even so, it is widely believed that Lopez Portillo would have preferred to nominate the head of Pemex, Jorge Diaz Serrano, but the latter blundered by cutting the export price of oil at a time of market weakness without presidential permission. This permitted Diaz Serrano's many enemies within the cabinet to come together against him and make his position untenable. In the end, de la Madrid was nominated because he was believed to be an economic technocrat (which he was) and not because he was an ideologically committed market-reforming economist (which he was as well, though he mostly concealed the fact).

De la Madrid was nominated before the full economic crisis broke. When it did break, the president and the presidential nominee reacted quite differently. Lopez Portillo, after vacillating to a degree, eventually reacted as a nationalist. De la Madrid reacted as an orthodox economist, seeking debt renegotiations and a deal with the IMF. De la Madrid also put together a mainly orthodox transitional economics team that included many future members of the cabinet. This made it feasible for the US government and the international financial institutions to bypass Lopez Portillo in his last few months in office and deal directly with de la Madrid (Kraft 1984). When de la Madrid was inaugurated in December 1982, a period of market-reforming government began that has persisted to this day.

Once de la Madrid was safely in office, presidential patronage power played a major part in reorienting the state as a whole in the direction of market reform (Centeno 1994). In theory, the president appointed virtually the whole public sector, and in practice he controlled the careers of several thousand top officials. This was more than enough to reorient the state. Whereas there had been a degree of ideological pluralism in most Mexican cabinets before 1982, this was less true thereafter. Post-1982 cabinets have all had a significant market-reforming orientation. Such were the powers of the Mexican presidency that de la Madrid could appoint a cabinet full of market-reforming technocrats despite the fact that in 1982, at every level of politics within Mexico (including the general public), the rank and file of the PRI, the trade unions and most of the government bureaucracy there would almost certainly have been a majority in favor of adopting a more nationalist orientation. However, the presidential system gave the nationalists nowhere to engage except by taking on the PRI colossus in a doomed electoral undertaking—as they did without success in 1988.

Near the end of his term, de la Madrid nominated Carlos Salinas, another market liberal, as his successor. This choice was made essentially on ideological grounds, though Salinas' experience as planning minister during 1982–1987 would have helped him. Things did not run smoothly on this occasion due to what was in effect a split in the PRI, but in the end Salinas was declared elected and was inaugurated in December 1988. The general perception that the 1988 election results were doctored only reinforces the argument being presented here, which is that market reform in Mexico was essentially an elite project that was unpopular among the broader public. This did not bother Salinas, who continued with market-reform policies more aggressively than did de la Madrid and still (until 1994, at least) enjoyed considerable personal popularity.

It may seem surprising that there was not more political fallout from the economic crisis of 1982, but the Mexican state elite was both organizationally impressive and utterly ruthless. Until the system democratized at the end of the 1980s, the PRI continued to deliver electoral victories to order, and Fidel Velazquez of the Confederation of Mexican Workers (Confederación de Trabajadores Mexicanos) kept organized labor in line. The PRI did split in 1987–1988, but the market liberals retained control of the electoral machinery and were also responsible for counting the votes.

One key to the victory of Mexico's market reformers, therefore, is that Mexico had a disciplined state elite, which was embedded within civil society, institutionalized in its own way, on good terms with the United States, and capable of fighting to win (Centeno 1994). Many of the younger members of this elite had studied economics at US (in some cases UK) universities. They broadly accepted the need for market reform and were capable of managing it, if asked. A common educational and to an extent cultural background also made it easier for members of this state elite to communicate meaningfully with each other and with their US counterparts.

Meanwhile, the inflation and recession that hit Mexico in the years after 1982 had a powerful inoculating effect on the Mexican public, which by the end of that decade had shown every sign of changing its mind about the merits of debts, deficits, and nationalization (Basáñez 1990). Still, the extent to which these hard times generated civil unrest was limited by elite cohesion.

Apart from a combined commitment to market-reforming economics, there is a plausible historical explanation for this elite cohesion. At least until Mexico democratized, the key event in twentieth-century Mexican history was the Mexican Revolution. While schooled in its official values, successive Mexican authorities nevertheless did everything possible to avoid a repetition of its anarchy and economic hardship. The Mexican state—notwithstanding its revolutionary past—had by the 1970s acquired a pronouncedly counterrevolutionary character. The country's powerful trade union confederation was in the hands of authoritarian anticommunists supportive of the regime. The student unrest of the 1960s had been shot down by the army. The PRI routinely submitted election results demanded by the regime. Not only was political repression pervasive, but the government's at times ruthless mechanisms of social control were seen by much of the Mexican population as legitimate. Thus, the army was simultaneously obedient, violent, and reasonably popular (Lopez 2012). Meanwhile, despite not being exactly a members' party, the PRI had an impressive capacity for mobilization and, indeed, demobilization. While less personally authoritarian than their predecessors, presidents Lopez Portillo and de la Madrid were in a position to impose order if they so desired, and this was known to be the case. Potential dissidents needed to tread carefully.

The authoritarianism of Mexico's political system was not invented purely to oppress the population—though it certainly was capable of this—but to facilitate social peace and economic growth. The PRI's investment in social control paid off throughout the 1940–1970 period, when the economy mostly performed well, and only gradually attenuated thereafter. When financial crises struck in 1976 and 1982, the first instinct of the majority of the population was to support the government. It is true that ballot rigging and the organizational weakness of the opposition limited the electoral challenge that could be mounted against the dominant PRI, but 1980s' polls showed that the PRI remained surprisingly popular (Basáñez 1990). This degree of deference toward the PRI gave its leaders an additional margin of autonomy when embarking on an uncertain and difficult economic pathway.

MEXICO IN 1994

The Mexican economy eventually showed some signs of recovery. The export of manufactured goods increased rapidly during the 1980s, albeit from a low base. Meanwhile, the Mexican bailout of 1982 was followed by the Baker Plan (1986), the Brady Plan (1989), and finally Mexican membership of NAFTA (at the beginning of 1994). The general consequence was to improve Mexican budgetary stability, its economic openness, and its resilience during a period of lower oil prices. Furthermore, the end of the Cold War increased the general prestige of the US and reduced the political weight of Mexican nationalism. It seemed for a time as though Mexico was back on track for export-led progress.

Unfortunately, Mexico experienced another financial crisis in 1994. Its causes were similar to some others in that the authorities tried to maintain an uncompetitive exchange rate (in this case involving a crawling peg system) with the purpose of holding down inflation. This led to an increased vulnerability to capital flight. New financial instruments, sometimes no more than half understood by those who operated them (Parker 2000), allowed the shifting of billions of dollars in short-term capital movement. Making matters worse was a low Mexican savings rate that in turn led to a dangerously high current account deficit and a fresh buildup of debt (Santin Quiroz 2001).

What fatally undermined the crawling peg strategy was a series of untoward political events during the course of 1994. These included the Zapatista rebellion at the beginning of the year, the assassination of the PRI's presidential candidate in March, and the murder of the president's brother-in-law (seemingly for family reasons) in September. Taken as a totality, these events spooked the markets and forced the authorities to draw down their foreign exchange reserves to cope with speculation against the peso. Meanwhile, rising US interest rates during 1994 added to the pressure. The cupboard was almost bare when the new government came into office at the beginning of December.

The final step toward crisis occurred when the incoming finance minister—who had previously served in an earlier government as commerce minister—allowed the value of the peso to fall. He was worried about the costs to growth of maintaining an uncompetitive exchange rate but in retrospect underestimated the damage to confidence that could follow an unexpected devaluation. When he announced the devaluation, markets feared that the new rate might be unsustainable and followed by further devaluation, and this led to furious selling of the peso. This, in turn, undermined the balance sheet of many companies—including most of the banks—which had large debts in dollars that they could no longer afford to service.

The crisis was eventually resolved when an international consortium led by the US agreed to make a very large dollar loan to Mexico. This decision was not uncontested in the US, but in the end it marked a further strengthening of Mexican–US relations. By 1996, Mexico was growing again. One reason why the 1994 crisis was relatively short in duration—though acutely painful while it lasted—was that the Mexican economy was much more open than it had been in 1982, and it was now capable of rapid export growth.

Unlike in 1982, in 1994 there was a broad consensus within Mexico around the desirability of fiscal orthodoxy and free markets. The US government was also seen as a lender of last resort when the Mexican economy got into difficulties. There was an exception to the generally pro-American orientation of political society in the shape of the Zapatista movement, which launched a rebellion in the southern state of Chiapas at the beginning of 1994 and generated a considerable amount of excitement at the time. However, the Zapatistas were outsiders with few allies who could be marginalized, as indeed they eventually were. There was no 1982-style division within the elite in 1994. Membership of NAFTA was broadly popular at all levels of society, and the Mexican public tended to blame political corruption and other forms of criminality for the crisis rather than the development model. What gave this view some plausibility was the fact that the outgoing government of Carlos Salinas had privatized a lot of state assets with insufficient diligence regarding the purchasers and insufficient regulation. When the crisis struck, it turned out that some of the beneficiaries of the privatization process were at best inexperienced operators and at worst drug traffickers and criminals.

The 1994 crisis did not exactly condemn the PRI to defeat in 2000—under different circumstances the PRI might have won, notwithstanding its problems—but it did make the PRI's defeat possible. Economic nationalism by 1994 was mostly a thing of the past. Mexico was in NAFTA, its trade with the US was booming, and nobody wanted a return to protectionism. Even Cuauhtemoc Cardenas, the leader of the social-democratic Party of the Democratic Revolution (Partido de la Revolución Democrática) at the time, supported the idea of NAFTA membership. The Mexican political elite had also come to accept the idea of democracy.

VENEZUELA'S BANCO LATINO CRISIS OF 1994

Whereas Mexico's 1982 financial crisis pushed it decisively down a market path (and the 1994 crisis reinforced this), Venezuela's 1994 financial crisis had a different effect. The crisis marked the end of what may have been Venezuela's last chance to enact significant market reform before the triumph of Chavez and his form of socialism changed everything. The circumstances leading up to the collapse of the Banco Latino—then Venezuela's second largest bank—also illustrates much of what was wrong with Venezuela's institutional system at that time.

The period between 1989 and 1998 was one in which elected governments sought to push Venezuela in the direction of market reform. President Perez (1989–1993) was at this time a market reformer, albeit a politically insensitive one, while Caldera (1994–1999), though aspiring to be something of a European Christian Democrat, in the end looked for market solutions to some of Venezuela's problems. These included the partial denationalization of Venezuela's oil industry. The conditions facing the country, however, were not favorable to reform. Public opinion had been seriously alienated for good reasons and was likely to reject further change (Templeton 1995).

One reason for popular alienation from Venezuela's seemingly strong parties was that the proceeds from the previous period of high oil prices (1974–1981) had mostly been wasted amid complaints of much increased corruption (Gelb 1988). Oil prices had then fallen back a long way during the 1980s, and this left many Venezuelans with unrealizable expectations (Romero 1997; Naim 2001). There was also a problem with the provision of basic public services, which were much worse than most Venezuelans had a right to expect.

President Perez's insensitively imposed austerity measures led to major rioting in Caracas in 1989, and the political crisis deepened when Hugo Chavez launched a broadly popular but narrowly unsuccessful coup attempt in

February 1992. The collapse of the Banco Latino in 1994 therefore came a time of acute political difficulty, to which it added difficulties of its own.

President Caldera (1994–1999) was genuinely worried by the prospect of a fresh military coup (Luis Castro Levya, personal communication, April 1997). He had already sacked and replaced the entire military establishment upon taking office. When asked in private why had appointed his son-in-law to be head of the army, he replied "so I can sleep at night" (ibid). In fact, there were public calls in the crisis year of 1994 for Caldera to close Congress and govern by decree, as Fujimori had done in Peru in 1992. Caldera rejected any idea of open illegality, probably on the entirely reasonable ground that if he broke the national constitution he risked losing control over the army. He nevertheless thought it necessary to impose a state of economic emergency, which was legal under Article 240 of the Constitution (Crisp 1997, 180). When Congress voted to lift the emergency, Caldera reinstated it the same afternoon. Congress then backed down.

The Banco Latino was a perfect example of a politicized bank in a politicized environment. It had for years been closely associated with the fortunes of Carlos Andres Perez. The first Perez presidency (1974–1979) had already marked a significant change in Venezuela's political economy. In the early years of democratization after 1958, Venezuela's political system had been based mainly on disciplined party political organizations and interelite negotiations—a quasi-corporatist system not unlike that prevailing in some European countries. Under Perez, however, big money and big business came to count for more, and by general consensus there was also an increase in corruption at this time. The president openly associated with a group of businessmen who popularly became known as the twelve apostles. The Banco Latino soon came to be dubbed the Bank of the Twelve Apostles, with its president, Pedro Tinoco, being one of the twelve (Jones 2008, 182). As a measure of its political influence, Tinoco—a man with right-wing political connections—combined his Banco Latino role with a position as head of the legislative section of an important commission of the Chamber of Deputies in the 1970s (Karl 1990).

Perez was reelected to the presidency in 1988 for a second five-year term. He then surprised most Venezuelans by redefining himself as a market reformer. One of his first acts in this reincarnation was the deregulation of the banking system, though Perez did not take the final neoliberal step of permitting foreign financial agencies to set up in Venezuela. Such a step would have allowed the Banco Latino to be sold to a US or other foreign bank with windfall profits.

Meanwhile, regulation continued to be weak, and Perez continued to appoint his friends to such regulatory positions as there were. For example, according to one press report, the head of Venezuela's equivalent of the Federal Deposit Insurance Corporation was said to have been employed because she was married to Perez' chief bodyguard (New York Times 1994). Meanwhile Perez's connections with the Banco Latino remained in place. Upon being reelected, Perez nominated Pedro Tinoco to be head of the central bank.

There was, however, a growing problem of profitability. The coup attempts of 1992 imparted a considerable shock to business confidence and capital flight increased (Casas 1999). The authorities sought to protect the Bolivar, the national currency, by raising interest rates, but this put the whole banking system under pressure. The Banco Latino responded by offering unsustainably high interest rates to compete. It also offered financial help to a variety of different political figures and even military officers in return for political favors (Buxton 2001).

When Perez was impeached in 1993, the Banco Latino lost its most important friend, and it responded by adopting desperate measures. It is even believed to have manufactured an incident in 1993 in which a bystander was accidentally killed in a bomb outrage designed to look like an act of terrorism. It was also believed to be preparing to finance a coup attempt (Buxton 2001).

Rafael Caldera, who won presidential elections in December 1993, was no friend of the Banco Latino. Within days of Caldera's inauguration, it collapsed and took with it around two-thirds of the national banking system (Casas 1999). The government issued arrest warrants for some 322 bankers, but all of them escaped (Jones 2008, 183), many of them with substantial amounts of public money

According to several of Caldera's allies, the Venezuelan military hierarchy quietly warned Caldera in 1994 that their subordinates could not necessarily be relied on if there was a repetition of the riots of 1989. This warning was taken seriously, and it influenced the government's response to the Banco Latino collapse. This provides a clear contrast with Mexico. Mexico's political hierarchies operated institutionally during the crisis years in a way that Venezuela's did not. It is difficult to imagine the Mexican military failing to give full support to the president, no matter what the circumstances

NEOLIBERALISM DEFEATED IN VENEZUELA

There is never a good time for a banking system to fail, but the Banco Latino failure may well have destroyed the last chance for the old system (which was already somewhat discredited) to reform itself. From an economic point of view, the rescue was poorly handled by the government, which had only been in office for a few days and was taken completely by surprise. The doors simply closed, leaving thousands of angry depositors completely bereft. It did not help that, when the Banco Latino collapsed, Venezuela's superintendent of banks was in Argentina buying racehorses. He did not respond to an invitation to return to Venezuela (*New York Times* 1994).

Caldera, himself no economist, saw the real problem as political (Luis Castro Levya, personal communication, April 1997). He saw an ominous parallel between the inauguration of Carlos Andres Perez at the beginning of 1989 and that of Caldera in 1994. In 1989, increases in bus fares in large part triggered the rioting. During the first weeks of the Caldera presidency, bank failures sparked civil unrest. Whereas the 1989 riots mainly involved the lower classes, the victims of bank failure mainly came from the middle class. The government felt that this made the situation even more dangerous because of the middle-class outlook of the military (Luis Castro Levya, personal communication, April 1997).

The Caldera government therefore resorted to an inflationary policy of printing money to preempt fears of unrest. It agreed to compensate depositors and attempted to offset the resulting inflation by controlling prices. Ironically, Caldera also used his emergency powers to pass a law that finally allowed foreign interests to buy domestic banks, and a number of transactions occurred. The authorities missed both targets as a result. They neither changed the law in time to help the Banco Latino, nor did they effectively pursue law breakers in the banking system. They got the worst of both worlds. This therefore came to be seen as another case of unpunished corruption on a massive scale, rivaling the multiple exchange rate scandal of the 1980s, which also did great damage to Venezuela's political system.

What ultimately went some way toward resolving the situation—albeit at a cost—was the fact that Venezuela still had some spare oil producing capacity that was supposedly being curtailed to meet OPEC quota restrictions. In order to avoid utter disaster, Caldera gave the word for Venezuela to ignore OPEC and produce all the oil it could. This decision seemed vindicated for a time since Venezuelan oil production did increase considerably, but then several Middle Eastern countries responded by raising output themselves and the oil price suffered. It was in 1998 that *The Economist* magazine notoriously predicted that oil might fall to $5 a barrel, which would have been below cost for the majority of the Venezuelan industry. Even as it was, the government had to invoke yet another austerity package in 1998 to deal with the effects of unexpectedly low oil prices. This election year package proved of great help to Chavez, who was then running for president.

While not the only factor, the Banco Latino failure played its part in Venezuela's political and economic unraveling. The resulting unpopularity of the main parties can be gauged from a poll taken in 1997 relating to the presidential candidacy of Irene Saiz, a former beauty queen and media celebrity. She was at that point considering whether to run independently or with the leadership of the Christian-Democratic party (Comité de Organización Política Electoral Independiente—COPEI). Polls suggested that any alliance with COPEI would reduce her electoral appeal. She nevertheless made the mistake of allying herself with COPEI and lost badly.

In fact, both the centrist party Democratic Action (Acción Democrática) and COPEI polled very badly in the 1998 elections—much worse than in 1993—and then declined to the point that they ceased to be a major electoral force. In 1998, around 80 percent of the votes cast went to independent candidates. Over the subsequent half-decade Venezuelan politics metamorphosed into a left-versus-right struggle with Hugo Chavez playing an unchallenged role as leader of the left. The Banco Latino scandal therefore played a significant role in causing Venezuela's system of multiclass parties to be replaced by a politics of class.

When comparing the experiences of Venezuela and Mexico, we need to turn again to the mentality of the political elites. The Venezuelan *partidocracy* was essentially designed, not for social control or to provide good government, but to organize the allocation of oil rents and avoid any kind of ideological polarization that might bring in the military. It did a reasonably good job in these respects for some years. Venezuela successfully avoided the kind of democratic breakdown that occurred in Chile, Uruguay, or Argentina—though it did come close in 2002, by which time the *partidocracy* had already collapsed. During its heyday in the 1960s, a kind of multiclass party politics developed (Dunning 2008), and there is evidence that such a system appealed to the majority of Venezuelans (Templeton 1995). When the economy went into decline, however, negative-sum politics replaced consensual ones. Venezuelans with business advantages or political connections then proved better able to protect their interests than the poor, who became more and more excluded, marginalized, and resentful. The middle class, too, was increasingly squeezed, and many middle-class people fell into poverty.

Another shortcoming was that the Venezuelan state was (with the exception of the state oil corporation) poorly and corruptly run. Striking evidence for the shortcomings of the Venezuelan state comes from a US State Department memo dated December 1991, when the *partidocracy* was in the process of unraveling (US Department of State 1991). It contained a devastating critique of the poor quality of public spending in Venezuela. It pointed out that "despite having 1.2 million civil servants, it [Venezuela] does not educate the population adequately, or treat its illnesses, or maintain public security, or even provide water reliably." So inefficient was the economic system that the marginal productivity of labor was—for a time at least—actually negative (see also Marquez 1988). Low oil prices during the 1990s would have led to some decline in Venezuelan living standards, no matter what, but the way in which the *partidocracy* failed to reform itself and continued to operate as it always had made things much worse than they needed to be.

It remains puzzling why the executive performance of the Venezuelan state should have been as bad as it was. Some authors (notably Karl 1990) have blamed the so-called oil curse. However, this is plausible only up to a point. Oil-exporting least-developed countries do not invariably fail. Indeed, if we consider the long run, development indicators in both Venezuela and Mexico showed a consistently improving trend between the 1930s and the 1970s.

AFTERMATH

Financial crises are likely to produce a sense of failure and a willingness to blame. They are also likely to produce a desire not to return to the "bad old days." This does not mean that crises will not recur, but it does mean that those who have experienced them are likely to be sensitized against policies that seem likely to produce recurrence—for example, German sensitivities about inflation are often attributed to the hyperinflation of 1923. Of course, there is a problem with drawing conclusions from history because historical events are inherently subject to conflicting interpretations. For this reason, debates about the kind of postcrisis change that may be desirable are likely to be won by the powerful. This matters, because the questions "what went wrong" and "what to do now" are intimately linked. They are also likely to be resolved differently in different countries. In our case studies, Mexico democratized, adopted market reform, and joined NAFTA, while Venezuela elected Chavez.

After 1982, Mexican president Miguel de la Madrid and his close allies mostly blamed what they called fiscal populism for the earlier crises, whereas some intellectuals blamed overmighty presidentialism (Zaid 1987) or an absence of democracy (Newall and Rubio 1984). All of these interpretations were potentially tenable, but the Mexican government privileged economic over political reform. Mexico did not choose to democratize until it had gone a long way with its trade reforms and, as a result, locked in economic change before it could be tested at the ballot box.

In 1994, the Mexican tequila crisis was mostly blamed on corruption and high-level misconduct rather than a wrong economic strategy. Although a case could be made that macroeconomic error was mainly responsible (Salinas 2000), the blaming of corruption meant that President Zedillo was given enough political breathing space to continue Mexico's slow transition to democracy. The partial discrediting of the corrupt incumbency did, however, make the PRI vulnerable to its landmark defeat of 2000.

For their part, most Venezuelans quite plausibly saw the Banco Latino failure as the result of corruption and mismanagement. The *partidocratic* system had for years allowed politics and money to mix too carelessly and was repeatedly found wanting when real crises developed. None of this is false. However, poorer Venezuelans also tended to exaggerate the extent to which oil abundance could protect them from the rigors of the international marketplace. Meanwhile, wealthier Venezuelans tended to be economic liberals, whose sense of economics (however sound) tended to blind them to social issues. Most Venezuelans in the 1990s were poorer than they had been a decade earlier, and the result was an accumulation of resentment. Chavez tapped into this discontent, and identified his country's enemies as being the economic elite and the old political establishment. In terms of how they interpreted their countries' financial crises, Chavez and de la Madrid were extreme opposites. De la Madrid blamed everything on economic mismanagement, whereas Chavez blamed everything on politics.

Changing attitudes toward the US were also significant in the Mexican and Venezuelan cases. Mexican Presidents Echeverria (1970–1976) and Lopez Portillo (1976–1982) only barely disguised their suspicion of the US. Conversely, Venezuelan presidents of a slightly earlier period—notably Betancourt (1958–1963) and Leoni (1963–1968)—were pro-US. Today, Venezuela and Mexico have largely changed places. Mexico seeks a closer union with the US; Venezuela under Chavez is pro-OPEC and uses a populist form of anti-Americanism to win popularity.

CONCLUSION

If we return to the central idea that a financial crisis is a stress test for the entire political and economic system, then Mexico passed its tests (albeit at a high social cost) while Venezuela mostly failed. Evidence for this judgment comes partly from the contrasting outcomes of the financial crises. Mexico reoriented its economy in the direction of manufactured exports while Venezuela remains dependent on oil. It is also a political judgment, based on Mexico's ultimately successful democratization in contrast to the collapse of the Punto Fijo system in Venezuela. Venezuela's *partidocracy* has gone and will not return; Mexico's PRI remains very much in business. The election of Hugo Chavez in 1998 was certainly not a defeat for democracy, but it was a defeat for a particular type of democratic system. The Mexican PRI, despite losing presidential elections in 2000, retained control of most national power centers and made a triumphant return to power in 2012.

This is not a particularly surprising outcome. The Mexican system in the 1970s and 1980s was built for stability, while Venezuela's Punto Fijo pact was built to regulate redistribution. When hard times arrived, it became clear that the Venezuelan constitution builders had asked the wrong question.

Mexico benefited significantly from its close relationship and support from US. Venezuela, however, received a much lesser degree of support from the US when the Banco Latino collapsed. This difference had political consequences in both directions. To say that Venezuela is today a keen member of OPEC while Mexico is a willing member of NAFTA makes the point. It could be argued in respect to Venezuela that the US did enough to become associated with its ancien régime, but not enough to defend it effectively. There were no similar half-measures in US–Mexican relations.

What is still worth asking is not so much why, but how, Mexico survived its crises. We return to Vargas Llosa's assertion that Mexico was a perfect dictatorship—if what is meant by perfect is that the iron fist was mostly concealed within a velvet glove. Power mattered to authoritarian Mexico, but ideas and institutions did as well. Dissent could express itself (at least most of the time), but a popular desire for peace and order—backed up by powerful state dominated organizations—ensured that presidents were able to maintain control even when their policies were leading toward disaster.

One also has a sense that economic issues were of fundamental importance to the Mexican elite. The key political fault line was between market reformers and economic nationalists. Thus, de la Madrid was nominated to the presidency in 1981, with decisive effects for the future of Mexico, because he had shown himself to be a competent planning minister. De la Madrid subsequently chose Salinas because he regarded him as a successful minister. He rejected several other plausible contenders because he saw them as fiscal populists. He might as well have referred to fiscal populism as devilry incarnate.

Meanwhile, there was a great extension of elite university education for talented young Mexicans starting around 1970. This occurred mostly in economics or economic-related subjects and mostly in the US and European universities. It provided the necessary strength in depth for a series of market reforming presidents to use their powers of patronage to build a market reforming state. For example, in the 1970s, the Ministry of Commerce was responsible for enforcing the many economic controls imposed on Mexican business. A decade later it was the main agency responsible for negotiating the terms of NAFTA. Moreover, not only was the Mexican state much more market oriented after 1982, but it was also more technically proficient.

While the most important factors in Mexico's change of economic direction were internal, one should not ignore the role of the US. While it is tempting to postulate a tradeoff between Mexico's acceptance of democratization and US economic support for Mexico, any such bargain was indirect at most. It seems much more plausible to claim that elites in both countries were forced closer together as the result of a set of circumstances. The US needs a stable Mexico. The title of a book by Sol Sanders, *Mexico, Chaos on our Doorstep*, perfectly underlines what might have happened in Mexico without US involvement at key points (Sanders 1986).

In Venezuela, one sees a similar conflict between market reformers (or "neoliberals") and economic nationalists, but with a different result. In Venezuela's case, the outcome was a decisive victory for Chavez and the nationalists. The main reason for this is that political authority was not secure in Venezuela, whereas it clearly was in Mexico. Despite the fact that they were legitimately elected, successive Venezuelan presidents had to govern with the prospect or reality of riots, corruption, and coup attempts. It is likely that Venezuela's oil wealth created too many expectations and too many opportunities to show disappointment when things went wrong. In fact, there seems to have been something of a vicious circle in which policy failure and evidence of large-scale corruption discredited the political elite and so weakened it, thereby making further failure more likely. The Banco Latino failure was just another of many setbacks to governability.

References

Basáñez, Miguel. 1990. *El pulso de los sexenios*. Mexico City: Siglo XXI.

Brooke, James. 1994. "Failure of High-Flying Banks Shakes Venezuelan Economy," *New York Times*, 16 May

Buxton, Julia. 2001. *The Failure of Political Reform in Venezuela*. London: Ashgate.

Casas, Antonio. 1999. *El Banco Central de Venezuela: Desafios y soluciones*. Caracas: CV.

Centeno Miguel. 1994. *Democracy within Reason: Technocratic Revolution in Mexico*. University Park: Pennsylvania Press.

Chislett, William. 1985. "The Causes of Mexico's Financial Crisis and the Lessons to Be Learned." In *Politics in Mexico*, edited by George Philip, 1–14. London: Croom Helm.

Crisp, Brian. 1997. "Presidential Behavior in a System with Strong Parties: Venezuela, 1958–1995." In *Presidentialism and Democracy in Latin America*, edited by Scott Mainwaring and Matthew Soberg Shugart, 160–198. Cambridge: Cambridge University Press

Dunning, Thad. 2008. *Crude Democracy: Natural Resource Wealth and Political Regimes*. Cambridge: Cambridge University Press.

Duran, Esperanza. 1988. "Mexico's 1986 Financial Rescue: Palliative or Cure." In *The Mexican Economy*, edited by George Philip, 95–109. London: Routledge.

Edwards, Sebastian. 1995. *Crisis and Reform in Latin America: From Despair to Hope.* Oxford: Oxford University Press.

Gelb, Alan. 1988. *Oil Windfalls: Blessing or Curse.* Oxford: Oxford University Press.

Jones, Bart. 2008. *The Hugo Chavez Story: From Mud Hut to Perpetual Revolution.* London: The Bodley Head.

Karl, Terry Lynn. 1990. "Dilemmas of Democratization in Latin America." *Comparative Politics* October: 1–21.

Kraft, Joseph. 1984. *The Mexican Rescue.* New York: The Group of Thirty.

Lopez, Jesus. 2012. "Civil-Military Relations and the Militarization of Public Security in Mexico 1989–2010: Challenges to Democracy." In *Mexico's Struggle for Public Security*, edited by George Philip and Susana Berruecos, 71–98. New York: Palgrave Macmillan.

Luke, Paul. 1988. "Debt and Oil-led Development: The Economy under Lopez Portillo." In *The Mexican Economy*, edited by George Philip, 41–77. London: Routledge.

Marquez, Guillermo. 1988. *La economia venezolana en la decada de los setenta: 1970–83.* Caracas: Monte Avila.

Naim, Moses. 2001. "The Venezuelan Story: Rewriting the Social Contract." Journal of Democracy 12: 2.

Newall, Roberto, and Luis Rubio. 1984. *Mexico's Dilemma: The Political Origins of Economic Crisis.* Boulder: Westview Press.

Parker, Charles. 2000. "The Political Economy of Emerging Market Investment: US Private Creditor Influences on the Mexican Financial Crisis of 1982." PhD diss., London School of Economics.

Romero, Anibal. 1997. "Rearranging the Deckchairs on the Titanic." *Latin American Research Review* 32: 7–36.

Salinas, Carlos. 2000. *Mexico: Un peso dificil a la modernidad.* Mexico City: Janes.

Sanders, Sol. 1986. *Mexico, Chaos on our Doorstep.* Ontario: Madison Press Books.

Santin Quiroz, Osvaldo. 2001. *The Political Economy of Mexico's Financial Reform.* Basingstoke: Ashgate.

Templeton, Andrew. 1995. "The Evolution of Public Opinion." In *Lessons of the Venezuelan Experience*, edited by Louis Goodman, 79–114. Baltimore: Johns Hopkins University Press.

Torres, Eduardo. 1999. *Bureaucracy and Politics in Mexico: The Case of the Secretariat of Programming and Budgeting.* Aldershot: Ashgate.

US Department of State. 1991. "Tough Times for President and More to Come." Declassified document. Doc. 13152 O121928 X, December.

Williamson, John, ed. 1990. *Latin American Adjustment: How Much Has Happened?* Washington DC: Institute for International Economics.

Zaid, Gabriel. 1987. *La economia presidencial.* Mexico City: Vuelta.

Zarate, Alfonso. 1995. *Los usos del poder: Mecanismos de la sucesión presidencial.* Mexico City: DR.

2 "Everybody Out," "We Are Fantastic:"

The Politics of Financial Crises in Argentina and Uruguay 2001–2003

Francisco Panizza, The London School of Economics

INTRODUCTION

There are a number of reasons that make the comparative study of the 2001–2003 financial crises in Argentina and Uruguay particularly relevant as a contribution to the broader understanding of the political dimensions of financial crises. While the international significance of the 2001–2003 crises in Argentina and Uruguay paled in comparison to the 2008 crisis in the US and the Eurozone, they were arguably the worst financial crises in the modern history of the two countries (Argentina's default was the largest in the world at the time) and by several measures they were among the worst in the modern history of Latin America (Sturzenegger and Zettelmeyer 2006; Roubini and Setser 2004; Wylde 2011). The upturn has been as remarkable as the downturn. Since their nadir in 2002, the economies of the two countries have recovered faster and more vigorously than predicted. This led some commentators to present the two countries' very different crisis resolution strategies as examples of how to come out of a crisis, particularly for small peripheral European countries such as Greece.[1]

While the financial elements of the crises in the two countries were closely interlinked and the economic recoveries followed broadly similar trajectories in terms of GDP growth, the management of the crises and their political repercussions could hardly have been more different. Concerning strategies of crisis resolution, Argentina defaulted and subsequently imposed hostile debt restructuring. It then broke with the neoliberal economic model of which it had been the poster boy in the 1990s during the recovery. In contrast, Uruguay negotiated a creditor-friendly restructuring of the debt in 2003 with no cuts in the principal. The Frente Amplio (FA—The Broad Front), the center-left government that came to office in 2005, maintained key elements of previous macroeconomic policies, including a collaborative relationship with the International Monetary Fund (IMF) financial integration, an open economy, and policies aimed at attracting foreign direct investment. Politically, the unfolding of the crisis in Argentina was characterized by intense civil disorder, a crisis of political legitimacy, and heightened elite factionalism (Auyero 2007). The crisis brought the country's political system to the verge of collapse between late 2001 and early 2002, a period in which Argentina saw five presidents in the space of fifteen days (Wylde 2011). In contrast, the politics of the economic crisis in Uruguay was characterized by collaboration and limited dissent among the political elite and low levels of social disorder. Political parties and Parliament played a key role in the political management of the crisis and, arguably, the political system came out of the crisis with its legitimacy strengthened.

While a complete match between two case studies is not possible in the real world, there are enough common elements in the cases under consideration to make the comparison meaningful. Argentina and Uruguay are neighboring countries with highly correlated business cycles and similar levels of GDP per capita. They are both agricultural commodities exporters, although Argentina is more industrialized and has a much larger internal market and a more diversified economy. By the time of the crisis in 2001, Argentina and Uruguay were into their third consecutive year of negative growth, a recession that coincided with the repercussions of the devaluation of Brazil's real in 1999 on their international competitiveness. In both countries the financial crisis comprised a banking crisis, an exchange rate crisis, and a sovereign debt crisis (although the precise effects of each type of crisis varied considerably between the two countries) (Hatchondo and Martínez 2010, 312; Sturzenegger and Zettelmeyer 2006).

Important differences between the two countries are found at the political and institutional levels. Historically, Uruguay has been politically more stable and has maintained a longer democratic tradition than Argentina. While Argentina has a history of populism, Uruguay is characterized by a consensus democracy with a strong party system (Lanzaro 2010). Accounts of the Uruguayan crisis highlight the decisive role played by Parliament in July 2002 in passing emergency legislation that was a condition for an emergency loan from the US that avoided the meltdown of the country's banking system and the collaborative role played by the opposition in the legislative process (Pérez Antón 2008). Yet, even at this level there were important elements in common between the two countries. After returning to democracy in 1983, Argentina became a robust democracy dominated by two parties rooted in Argentina's history and society, the Partido Radical (PR—The Radical Party) and the Partido Justicialista (PJ—The Justicialista Party, also known as the Peronist Party). Congress also played an important role at various stages of the Argentine crisis. It passed several fiscal adjustments during the administration of President Fernando De la Rúa (1999–2001) and made possible a constitutional solution to the institutional vacuum created by the resignation of De la Rúa in December 2001. The two governments that were in office at the height of the crisis, the administrations of presidents De la Rúa (1999–2001) in Argentina and of Jorge Batlle in Uruguay (2000–2005), were coalition governments midway through their mandates. Both were centrist governments, with the De la Rúa government leaning to the center left and the Batlle government to the center right.

This chapter argues that while institutional differences have significant weight in explaining the different ways in which the crises unfolded in the two countries, a full analysis of their political management must take into account the values and ideas that informed policy decisions and shaped actors' interests. By disrupting institutional path dependence and unsettling actors' sedimented views of the world, crises heighten contingency and make actors' identification of their own self-interest more difficult (Jessop 2013). Ideas and values reduce uncertainty and shape perceptions of interests (Blyth 2001, 3–4). As suggested in the introduction to this book, a privileged focus for the analysis of the ideas and values underlying the politics of financial crises is the study of crisis narratives. Competing narratives are attempts to make sense of crises and thus shape perceptions of causality, responsibility, and interests. Narratives are also crucial for strategies of economic recovery, the formulation of which implies particular conceptions of what is considered politically and economically feasible, possible, and desirable—and therefore able to shape and reshape the ideational parameters that circumscribe what governments can and should do to solve the crisis (Hay 2001, 199 and 203–4). In what follows, this chapter examines the crisis narratives of the two countries and their impact on the strategies of crisis management and crisis resolution.

CRISIS NARRATIVES IN ARGENTINA

By the 1999 presidential election, Argentina was in a recession and suffering from a high fiscal deficit (Sturzenegger and Zettelmeyer 2006, 166–67). However, in the electoral campaign the winning candidate, Fernando De la Rúa (PR), downplayed the country's economic problems and stressed his support for the economic model of neoliberal modernization put in place by President Carlos Menem in the early 1990s. There were several reasons for De la Rúa's reluctance to fully address the critical condition of the economy. In spite of growing popular discontent, particularly because of high levels of unemployment (Svampa 2005), De la Rúa felt particularly vulnerable to questions about his support for an economic model that had brought economic stability and prosperity to many, particularly among the middle classes that comprised his main electoral base (Llach 2004, 41). Argentina's rapid recovery from the 1995 recession caused by contagion from Mexico's "tequila crisis" reinforced the belief among the political elite about the fundamental robustness of the free market economic model. While economic recovery had been short lived, De la Rúa believed that stating his public commitment to economic orthodoxy was crucial to gaining the confidence of investors in the new government and for creating the conditions for economic recovery (Novaro 2002, 71).

Critical for understanding the limitations of De la Rúa's crisis narrative was his commitment to maintaining "convertibility," the currency board-like exchange rate policy instituted by law in 1991 that guaranteed that the central bank would exchange pesos for US dollars at the fixed exchange rate of one peso per dollar (Blustein 2005, 14). While it was never a part of neoliberal orthodoxy, the dramatic success of convertibility in lowering inflation and restoring confidence in the Argentine economy made it the fulcrum of the program of free market modernization of the 1990s. As such, convertibility became more than just a macroeconomic institution. In a country historically characterized by questions of high inflation and institutional weaknesses, convertibility played a wider political, institutional, and normative role. Domestically, it was conceived by its creator, former economy minister Domingo Cavallo, as a disciplinary device aimed at changing the ways of thinking and acting of political and economic actors. In a country with weak institutions, he saw it as an institutional barrier against the Argentinean politicians' historical tendency to constantly change the rules of the economic game. In short, it would ensure that economic rationality would trump political expediency (Amadeo 2003, 22). Internationally, convertibility aimed at restoring the reputation of Argentina as a credible actor before international financial institutions (IFIs) investors and the broader community of developed nations, particularly the US, of which Argentina was a close ally in the 1990s. Grounded on recent memories of stagnation and economic disorder (Blustein 2005, 43), convertibility became a cognitive lock (Blyth 2001, 4) that, as intended by Cavallo, transcended the agents that originally created it. As affirmed by Bonvecchi (2002, 167), the convertibility law and the political dynamic set in motion by the Menem government to implement and defend it constituted fundamental elements of the notion of economic normality held by the main economic policy making actors of the time.

Cognitive locks are almost always political locks. Convertibility did not just create a new common sense but also constituted powerful interests (Cherny 2009). In defending convertibility, De la Rúa aligned his electoral campaign with the perceived interests of both the majority of the citizens and of powerful economic actors (Llach 2004; Blustein 2005). Fear as much as love was behind the public support for convertibility (Llach 2004, 57–8). Given that almost 80 percent of all bank loans and most of the public debt was denominated in US dollars, as were many business contracts and utility prices, the cost of devaluing the currency acted as a powerful deterrent against abandoning the fixed exchange rate regime (Blustein 2005, 96; Cherny 2009). As such, convertibility generated political as well as ideational path dependency.

The cognitive lock of convertibility limited the policy tools available to the new Alianza government for bringing the country out of recession. With no possibility of an independent monetary or exchange rate policy, fiscal policy effectively became the only macroeconomic tool available to the government for dealing with the worsening economic situation. Thus, while it was clear that by the time his administration took office the Argentine economy was faltering and required substantial reforms, and that an overvalued currency was a major barrier to recovery, the De la Rúa government's economic policy concentrated almost exclusively on reducing the fiscal deficit in the expectation that reducing the deficit while maintaining orthodox economic policies would bring down interest rates and regain the confidence of investors necessary to restore economic growth (Sturzenegger and Zettelmeyer 2006, 170).

From the date of his inauguration on 10 December 1999, in which he mentioned the need to bring down the deficit eleven times (De la Rúa 1999) to the day of his resignation on 20 December 2001, the De la Rúa government played—and lost—the confidence game (Martínez and Santiso 2003) with the markets.[2] It is beyond the scope of this chapter to analyze in any detail the government's policy initiatives during the period or the consistently negative reactions that the initiatives generated among market actors.[3] It suffices to say that several rounds of public spending cuts and tax increases generated a negative feedback loop that deepened the recession and failed to meet the quantitative targets set with the IMF. The fast-deteriorating economic situation allowed the emergence of alternative discourses within both the government and the opposition that argued that cuts were making a bad economic situation worse and exposed divisions within the president's own party. When a weak and isolated De la Rúa appointed Domingo Cavallo as his finance minister in March 2001, the president tied his government's fate to that of the father of convertibility. However, Cavallo's own policy initiatives further undermined the very principles of trust and credibility that he had sought to institutionalize under convertibility. On 1 December 2000, the government almost completely froze bank accounts and fully blocked withdrawals from US dollar denominated accounts (the so-called *corralito*) in order to forestall a run on banks. This was perceived by the middle-class citizens that had voted for De la Rúa because of his promise to strengthen the rule of law as a fundamental breach of their property rights, and it became one of the main grievances that contributed to his resignation (Peruzzoti 2005, 247).

While the cognitive lock of convertibility and its core principles of trust and credibility dominated the political scene in the months leading up to De la Rúa's fall, the event that triggered his resignation on 20 December 2001 was political rather than economic. If any public statement of De la Rúa's ill-fated term in office has remained ingrained in Argentina's collective memory, it is his four-minute speech on the evening of 19 December, in which he announced that the government had decreed a state of siege to put an end to the lootings and food riots that had spread throughout the city of Buenos Aires and other main cities during the previous days.[4] Minutes after he finished his speech, thousands of Argentineans spontaneously took to the street in defiance of his orders. Many of them marched towards the Plaza de Mayo, the downtown square that is the historical place of Buenos Aires' mass demonstrations. Chants of *"que se vayan todos"* ("away with them all") became the common unifying demand of the protesters throughout the city. By 7 p.m. on 20 December, after failing to convince the *Justicialista* Party to form a government of national unity, and abandoned by his own party, De la Rúa signed his resignation and fled from the Casa Rosada (the presidential palace) by helicopter.[5] The president pro tempore of the senate, Ramón Puerta, took over as interim president until Congress chose a successor to De la Rúa in a process that would lead to four provisional presidents in a period of less than two weeks.

"Away with them all," together with the images of lootings and of the various forms of mass protests and police repression, relayed to every household in real time by television stations throughout the country, became the dominant crisis narrative of the final weeks of 2001 and the first months of 2002. The force and directness of the demand made its meaning apparently unambiguous. Significantly, it was the entire political class rather than just the government that was the target of the protesters. The disconnect between the main political parties and large sections of the citizenry had already become apparent by the large number of blank and destroyed ballots cast in the parliamentary election of October 2001 (which was won by the opposition *Justicialistas*). By December 2001, the discontent had turned into a fully-fledged crisis of representation. Yet, while there was no apparent ambiguity concerning who were the targets of the people's anger (the political class), the literality of the demand masked its nature as an empty signifier—that is, a signifier so overcoded with meaning that it becomes empty of any precise content (Torfing 1999, 301).

"Away with them all" acquired different connotations across localities (downtown Buenos Aires, the middle-class neighborhoods, the rustbelt industrial suburbs), class (shanty-town dwellers, depositors, political activists, trade unionists), and type of action (food riots, lootings, mass protests, pot banging, popular assemblies). It crystallized specific grievances with more universal demands. Concerning the former, the *corralito* prompted an unlikely natural alliance of interests between the mainly middle-class depositors that had no access to their cash and the urban poor that found themselves with no income, as the lack of cash stifled the informal economy on which most of them depended for their living (Bonasso 2002). Among the broader grievances, it is significant that the event that triggered the fall of De la Rúa was the declaration of the state of emergency. For many citizens, the imposition of the state or emergency and the repression that followed brought back the ghosts of state violence under military rule. For others, particularly those in the middle classes that had voted for him, De la Rúa had broken his electoral promises of a more honest, transparent, and accountable style of government (Peruzzoti 2005).

If De la Rúa's resignation exposed the divisions within the political elite and "away with them all" revealed the chasm between the political system and the people, the default on the external debt materialized the breakdown in relations between the Argentine government and international lenders. The default was announced on 22 December 2001, during the inaugural speech of Adolfo Rodríguez Saá, the provisional president elected by Congress to succeed De la Rúa until elections were held. Rodríguez Saá talked about the "so-called external debt" (Esteves 2003, 15) and questioned the assumption that honoring debt commitments should always be the defining principle concerning the government's obligations. He then announced that Argentina was suspending payments of the external debt (Esteves 2003). As former economy minister Roberto Lavagna (2007) noted, Rodríguez Saá's nationalist rhetoric framed the default as the voluntary decision of a populist government rather than what is really was—the inevitable consequence of previous mistakes—and, in doing so, contributed to the perception of Argentina as a country that could not be trusted to honor its obligations.

Rodríguez Saá's presidency lasted only ten days, as he was forced to resign by his own Peronist party under the suspicion that he intended to extend his presidency beyond the three-month period that Congress had appointed. On

1 January 2002, Congress elected Senator Eduardo Duhalde, the PJ's candidate defeated by De la Rúa in 1999, as the new president until the end of De la Rúa's term in office. One of his government's first measures was to end convertibility and implement a provisional dual exchange rate that was to become a unified, free-floating exchange rate in six months. The end of the cognitive and political lock of convertibility allowed the new government to use a wider toolkit of macroeconomic instruments to stabilize the economy and promote export-led economic growth. The Duhalde administration achieved this while avoiding the danger of hyperinflation associated with currency devaluations by using a mixture of orthodox (fiscal and monetary policies) and heterodox (asymmetric debt conversion, a further freezing of bank deposits) policy instruments (Mario Blejer, President, Banco Central de la Repúbica Argentina personal communication; Renes Lenicov 2008).[6] By mid-2002, the economic crisis had bottomed up (Sturzenegger and Zettelmeyer 2006, 186). There were, however, clear political, social, and economic limits to Duhalde's attempt at repairing the social and political fault lines in Argentina's society exposed by the events of December 2001. He had no popular mandate and had committed himself not to run for reelection. Politically, he represented everything that the "away with them all" demand was meant to be against: he was a career politician associated to the corrupt practices of the Menem governments (he had been Menem's vice president). His economic program was strongly criticized by mainstream economic analysts who predicted it would lead to hyperinflation (Levy Yetati and Valenzuela 2007). For the IMF, he was a populist at a time that Argentina was required to take painful economic decisions to avoid an even greater economic collapse (Amadeo 2003).

It was up to Duhalde's popularly elected successor, Néstor Kirchner (2003–2007), to elaborate a crisis narrative that resignified the meaning of "away them all," reframe the terms of political discourse, reconstitute relations of representation, and set up a new economic model and a new political hegemony. Although a member of the PJ and governor of the southern province of Santa Cruz, Kirchner was relatively unknown nationally and was more of an outsider than a member of the political class. Elected in April 2003, with just 22 percent of the votes, he set up a process of accumulation of political capital that by the time of his death in October 2010 made him one of the most dominant political figures since the country's return to democracy in 1984. Kirchner's strategy combined the preservation of the economic and political stability gained by Duhalde with a message of rupture that set up an encompassing political frontier in antagonism not just to neoliberalism but to the political and economic order of the past two decades (Barros 2006). He claimed that the neoliberal model of the 1990s had its origins in the economic policies of the military dictatorship (1976–1984). By stressing the continuity between the military rulers and the democratic administrations that followed democratization, he made both military and civilian governments responsible for the social costs of the model and ultimately for the 2001 crisis. On 21 September 2003, he made a call to "leave behind the old Argentina ... then [neoliberal] political project that unfortunately was in place mainly in the 1990s, but that started in March 1976 [the date of the military coup] until the [social] explosion of 2001" (Kirchner, quoted by Slipak n.d., 13). He also claimed that the democratic governments of the 1980s and 1990s had failed to punish those responsible for human rights crimes during the years of dictatorship, which made these administrations guilty of condoning impunity, a charge that was extended to the episodes of corruption of the Menem governments. In Kirchner's narrative, crimes against human rights and neoliberalism were now equally a part of the "old Argentina" of impunity, poverty, and marginality. The following words, delivered at the legislative assembly on 1 March 2004, highlight the strong foundational nature of his appeal:

> A deep change will mean leaving behind the Argentine that sheltered geno-cides thieves and corrupts while it condemned to misery and marginality millions of our fellow nationals. (Kircher, quoted by Slipak n.d., 14)

In claiming to give voice and recognition to both the victims of crimes against human rights of the 1970s and 1980s and to those of the 2001–2002 economic crisis, Kirchner's narrative articulated the two most traumatic events in modern Argentine history: the military dictatorship and the financial crisis that brought down the neoliberal model (Barros 2006). In doing so, he set up a new political frontier that retroactively gave new meaning to the "away with them all" demand of the streets: the political dividing line no longer stood between the citizens and their representatives, as it had in December 2001, but between the Argentinean people and those responsible for the pain inflicted on the victims of human rights crimes and neoliberal economics. The crisis of 2001 was thus resignified as both a traumatic event and as the birth of a new socially fair and morally just political and economic order.

The relevance of political frontiers is that their change changes the limits of what can be said and what can be done in a political formation. The breakdown of the cognitive lock of convertibility expressed in Cavallo's view that default and devaluation were unthinkable because they would destroy the country's credibility was now seen as the foundation of the country's new prosperity. As Damill, Frenkel, and Rapetti (2005, 191) argue, the default allowed the recovery of the economy not only because of the fiscal benefits of the suspension of debt payments but also because it liberated economic policy makers from the need to send signals to the markets to facilitate the rollover of the debt. Kirchner used the debt default to assert Argentina's financial autonomy over private and public international lenders. More broadly, he used the power of the state to assert the primacy of politics over the economy, of the government over corporate interests (particularly multinationals), of conviction over pragmatism, of states over markets, and of political leadership over institutions.[7]

Kirchner combined a foundational populist rhetoric with significant elements of political and economic pragmatism. Economic policies entailed a careful management of public finances with a retreat from the basic tenets of neoliberal orthodoxy. The government's economic strategy was based on state intervention, protectionism, selective nationalizations, social policies, and price controls (Grugel and Riggirozzi 2007). Domestic industry and the Peronists' popular base of support, which now included the unemployed and informal workers as well as the unions, were the main beneficiaries of the new model. The economic recovery that had begun before Kirchner took office accelerated due to the boom in agricultural prices and internal demand. Between 2003 and 2007, the Argentine economy grew by an average of 9 percent. This high economic growth consolidated Kirchner's popular support, legitimized the change in the model of economic development, and gave credibility to his crisis narrative.

URUGUAY'S CRISIS NARRATIVE

As noted above, the De la Rúa administration failed to produce a credible crisis narrative. Multiple crisis narratives thus competed for hegemony until the account of the crisis was hegemonized by the discourse of *Kirchnerismo*. In contrast, the center-right government of President Jorge Batlle of Uruguay (2000–2005) produced a clear and simple account of the crisis. In its view, the crisis was the result of events in Argentina for which the Uruguayan government bore no responsibility. The comparison with Argentina also allowed the government to argue strongly in favor of the need to preserve the intangible asset upon which the country's very existence as a nation was allegedly at stake: its reputation as a serious and trustworthy country that always met its international obligations. The following statements are representative of a much wider discursive output that reveals a consistent line of argument regarding the crisis and its origins.[8] In a press conference on 1 March 2002, President Jorge Batlle stated:

> I will try to summarize what was a long meeting of the council [of ministers] in which the President [i.e. himself] made an extensive reference to the events that we have been facing over the past few years and particularly during the current year, that, as it is well known, culminated with the consequences for Uruguay of what happened in Argentina. (Batlle 2002a)

To blame a foreign country for one's own economic problems is a staple element of government crisis narratives. Yet, highlighting the foreign roots of an economic problem often goes beyond the apportioning of guilt. It also seeks to reassure the citizens that "what is happening over there" is not going to happen "over here." The Uruguayan government also used this argument in the first weeks of the banking crisis to attempt to reassure the public that, in contrast to Argentina, the financial situation in Uruguay was under control. Batlle replied with the following statement to a question presented to him at a press conference:

> No sir, you should not worry about the people being worried. What would be really very grave is if the people were to find out that we haven't

maintained fiscal equilibrium or instead of having 250bp investment grade, we were in the same situation as Argentina and Brazil; that would be really worrying! (Batlle 2002b)

As the banking crisis unfolded, the grounds of comparisons with Argentina again shifted. What was supposed to be a factual statement ("there is nothing to be worried about because our economy is sound") became a normative statement ("we should not allow happening over here what is happening in Argentina"). This was the argument used by Washington Abdala, a ruling Colorado Party congressman, during a parliamentary debate on a fiscal adjustment package. In an article discussing the government's strategy to the crisis, the congressman stated the following: "What we precisely need to avoid here is that this doesn't turn up to be like Argentina and avoid following the model of Argentina" (*La República* 2002c).

The food riots, lootings, and mass protest that dominated narratives of the crisis in Argentina in late 2001 and early 2002 served to warn to the entire Uruguayan political system as well as further mark the differences between the two countries. After some episodes of looting, Interior Minister Guillermo Stirling made another comparison with Argentina to highlight social differences in the two countries. In an article in one of the national newspapers, the minister (while acknowledging that looting can take place all over the world, even Buenos Aires) played down the parallels between the disturbances in the two countries by affirming that "Uruguay is different from Argentina. It is not comparable" (*Búsqueda* 2002c).

The government's use of the contrast with Argentina as a rhetorical device to apportion blame and to present the country's financial situation in a more favorable light was to be expected, as it was in line with crisis narratives elsewhere. What is more significant is the extent to which the center-left FA's opposition shared the same discursive lock. At the beginning of the crisis in January 2002, the FA's vice president, Jorge Brovetto, expressed his belief that Uruguay would not experience the social upheavals of Argentina because "the two peoples have different characters" (*La República* 2002a). Broader parallels with Argentina were strongly dismissed by FA leaders, one whom, Senator Danilo Astori, was quoted in an article declaring the following:

> I don't agree with the parallels that have been drawn with Argentina. Our situation is very different to that of Argentina, because our different social, political, and cultural histories (*La República* 2002b)

The common discursive frame did not signify a political consensus between the government and the opposition on the best policies for solving the crisis. Rather, parallels with Argentina served to frame the terms the political debate. Political differences between the government and the opposition ran along traditional center-right and center-left lines. While the government passed two fiscal adjustments in the first half of 2002 to comply with the IMF's conditions for financial assistance, the left argued that the cuts were deepening the recession and demanded public investment to promote economic growth. The case of Argentina was used to disqualify the opponent's proposals: the left argued that by implementing fiscal adjustments, the Uruguayan government was enacting the same misguided IMF prescriptions undertaken in Argentina by the De la Rúa administration. The government in turn claimed that the opposition's demands for increases in public spending were the same irresponsible policies that led to fiscal debacle in Argentina.

Crisis narratives do not float above the interests of key actors; they define and articulate them as representations of the common good. The use by the government and the opposition of events in Argentina to mark the differences between the two countries was an expression of their shared interests in preserving social order. Throughout the crisis, events in Argentina functioned as a warning of things to come and as a marker of differences for Uruguay's political class. The government had an obvious interest in avoiding a social breakdown, as did the FA opposition (which had a good chance of winning the next election). The FA also used the contrast with Argentina to claim credit for the country's political stability. During the apex of the crisis, FA leaders repeatedly stressed that they had no intention of "setting the prairie on fire" by encouraging potentially violent social protests (*Búsqueda* 2002a).

Crisis narratives express the values and ideas of their enunciators. Yet, to become hegemonic, narratives have to resonate with values and ideas rooted in history and popular culture and with the mood of the time. In the case of Uruguay, the contrast with Argentina was used to reinforce perceptions of national identity. Particularly in the first half of the twentieth century, Uruguay saw itself as more democratic, law abiding, and socially progressive than other Latin American nations, a common perception encapsulated in the label often attached to it—"the Switzerland of Latin America." Furthermore, Uruguay maintained a sense of vulnerability as a small country sandwiched between South America's biggest nations, Argentina and Brazil. In 2002, traditional perceptions of the country's self-identity and of its vulnerability were revived and given new meaning in the context of the crisis. Key elements of this national imaginary are visible in the following excerpt from President Batlle:

> All this requires that Uruguay once again tells the world, "This is a serious country, this is a trustworthy country, it is a country that when it has a problem it faces it, it is not afraid, it does not run away. This will allow us, without the shadow of a doubt, not only to solve our problems, but [also] to take a great step forward. (Batlle, cited in Steneri 2011, 51)

Identity is integral to the definition of interests: what I am defines what I want. Preserving key values that allegedly formed part the country's national identity was presented in the dominant narrative not just as a matter of national interest but also as an existential question. The country's credibility was redefined as "intangible economic asset" that was crucial for the economic well-being of a small country with no significant natural resources other than agricultural land. The following excerpts from the memoirs of a key actor in the negotiations between Uruguay and the international financial organizations, Carlos Steneri, Uruguay's financial agent before the US and Canadian governments (1989–2010), summarizes this view:

> And finally, [Uruguay's debt exchange proposal] send the message to the financial community, both official and private, that in spite of its troubles Uruguay was seeking to keep unscathed what it considers to be one of its basic intangible assets: the respect for contracts, which is nothing more than the legal form of the principle that you should keep your word. (Steneri 2011, 143)

Uruguay's economic recovery began by the end of 2002 and gained momentum after the debt exchange of 2003. It was the beginning of one of the strongest cycles of economic growth in the country's history, as GDP more than tripled from $11.1 billion in 2003 to $40 billion in 2011. Similar to Argentina, the recovery of the economy validated the strategy of crisis resolution and the narrative that gave it meaning. The opposition FA won the 2004 elections in Uruguay for the first time in history. The victory of the center-left coalition was part of the pink tide of left and center-left parties that gained office in a number of Latin American countries in the first decade of this century. The electoral successes of the left in Latin America has been construed as resulting from a popular backlash against the neoliberal policies of the 1990s. In the specific case of Uruguay, it must be also seen as a vote against the traditional Colorado and Blanco parties' coalition that was in office during the 2002 crisis. As other center-left parties elsewhere in the region, the FA denounced the ills of neoliberalism and made political capital of the traditional parties' responsibility for the 2002 crisis. What is remarkable, however, is how the strategy of crisis resolution and the narrative that gave it meaning have shaped important aspects of the FA governments' economic policies and discourse (the FA won a second election in 2009). At the center of this strategy has been some been some core policy elements of the 2002 strategy of financial crisis resolution: a collaborative relation with the IMF (the government cancelled all debts with the Fund in December 2006), financial integration, no capital controls, openness to foreign trade and investment, orthodox macroeconomic management, and more generally market friendly and investor friendly economic policies.[9]

The links between the events of 2002 and the political and policy options made by the FA have been explicitly acknowledged by some of the FA's top leaders. In an article in which he was quoted reflecting on the events of 2002, President José Mujica (2010–2015) noted that the way Uruguay got out of the crisis was different from that of Argentina:

> The "away with them all" that they shouted over there [i.e. in Argentina] was rather difficult to understand, and it did not happen over here. . . . I think that if we compare the outcomes, it is quite reassuring. (*Búsqueda* 2010)

The management of the 2002 crisis created economic policy as well as discursive path dependency. The FA governments' discourse, particularly regarding foreign investment, is rooted on the country's so-called intangible comparative advantage that was at the center of the 2002 crisis narrative, that is, the country's reputation as serious, law-abiding country with strong institutions. Talking to Brazilian businessmen in São Paulo, Brazil, President Mujica said that Uruguay's economic growth was due to two factors: "Asia's demand [for Uruguayan exports] and the country's institutional stability and respect for contracts. Our attraction is our seriousness in honoring our commitments" (*El País* 2011). The homepage of Uruguay XXI, a government agency aimed at promoting foreign direct investment and exports, has as its main banner "Uruguay, a trustworthy country" (*país confiable*). Under the heading "Clear Rules" it states:

> The Uruguayan political system has three major parties that have alternated in government. Economic stability, adherence to general economic principles, transparency, and respect for contracts have transcended the specific programs of various administrations.[10]

CONCLUSION

While in the 1990s Argentina was the darling of the IMF and the US's closest ally in Latin America, the crisis led to an extraordinary shift in the perception of the country that drew on its history of economic mismanagement. In 2001, Paul O' Neill, the George W. Bush administration's then secretary of the treasury, was quoted by *The Economist* stating that Argentina's problems were "true to form and largely of its own making." He went on: "They've been off and on in trouble for 70 years or more. . . . They don't have an export industry to speak of. And they like it that way" (quoted by Suskind 2004, 17). What made the airbrushing of the country's conversion to neoliberalism more significant is that convertibility was conceived as a trust-building institution. When he was appointed minister of the economy in March 2001, Cavallo was well aware of what was at stake at that critical stage in the unfolding of the crisis. Former US Treasury Under Secretary for International Affairs (2001–2005) John B. Taylor recalls his meeting with Cavallo in 2001:

> He [Cavallo] spoke passionately about the importance of trust and credibility in economic policy and how the reforms he introduced in the early 1990s were meant to bring such trust and credibility to Argentina. Default and devaluation were unthinkable in his view because they would destroy the country's credibility for a long time. (Taylor 2007a, 81)

Arguably, Argentina's institutional weakness overloaded the significance of convertibility as the repository of both domestic and international trust in the country's newly found rule-bound stability. As Laurence Whitehead (2006,

31) put it, convertibility was an exceptionally powerful form of precommitment embraced as a substitute for normal political compromise and market confidence. Its collapse was therefore a particularly severe shock, destabilizing both the politics and the economics of the country. The political impact of convertibility was eloquently put to me by several key actors of the time. The following quote from Chrystian Colombo, President De la Rúa's chief of cabinet 2001–2002, is representative of several similar statements:

> Convertibility was a much broader issues that the exchange rate. To abandon it amounted to a break of the social contract, which has not yet been restored. It would have required a different electoral promise that the one made by the President [De la Rúa]. The President was brought down by his own promise. Politics, in the broad sense of the world, had disappeared. (personal communication)

The breakdown of convertibility made possible the return of politics as represented by the populist politics and policies of the Kirchner administration. As such, it radically changed the values embedded in convertibility expressed by Cavallo. As Paul Haslam (2010, 26) put it:

> In post-crisis (and post-neoliberal) Argentina, the illusion that the stability of the rules was the sole cause of prosperity was definitively dismissed. . . . Objectively speaking, the devalued exchange rate meant that dependence of FDI inflows en masse was reduced and, subjectively speaking, the fear of breaking the rules was banished.

In contrast, Uruguay had wider network of institutions (parties, Parliament, the courts) that underpinned the social contract and values attached to it that in Argentina were embedded in convertibility. Uruguay's reputation as a trustworthy country was cited by the US government as one of the reasons for providing emergency financial assistance in July 2002. At a time when the George W. Bush administration was against "using US plumbers' money" to bailout countries in crisis, this extraordinary assistance was difficult to justify in terms of either its coherence with government policy or by the strategic importance of Uruguay. Instead, the justification was made in terms that bear a striking parallel with Uruguay's crisis narrative.[11] As former Under Secretary of State Taylor put it:

> Helping Uruguay was consistent with our new policy to deal with contagion—help countries who were following good policies and who were not the cause of the crisis. Well, if there was ever a case where a country was directly hit by a crisis in another country and was also following good policies, Uruguay was it. (Taylor 2007b, 4)

Whether the claims by Taylor and the Uruguayan government that Uruguay was an innocent victim of Argentina's bad policies were entirely merited requires a detailed policy analysis that goes beyond the scope of this chapter. Still, one should note that since Uruguay's return to democracy in the 1980s, and even as far back as the 1960s, the country experienced a number of banking crises that were solved by government bailouts with no losses to depositors, which created clear moral hazard precedents. More broadly, by the time of the crisis the Uruguayan economy was suffering from chronic problems of fiscal deficits, a growing public debt, an overvalued currency, and a prolonged recession that had strong parallels with the condition of Argentina. As Roubini and Setser put it: "Uruguay had many of the same vulnerabilities as Argentina, as well as the disadvantage of being in a bad neighborhood" (2004, 69).

As noted in the introduction to this book, financial crises generate high levels of uncertainty that make it difficult for economic actors to determine the options that will best favor their interests. The Uruguayan government's IMF-financed rescue of the financial sector in August 2002 rose its external debt to what the IMF thought were unsustainable levels. This view was reflected in the advice of the Fund, first in August and the in December 2002, that Uruguay should restructure its debt and proceed to an orderly default that included a significant haircut (Steneri 2011, 85–7, 114). The Fund's advice was rejected both times by the Uruguayan authorities under the argument that the crisis was of liquidity rather than of solvency. Arguably, it was in the interest of the Uruguayan government to avoid default. But the line between liquidity and solvency is notoriously difficult to trace, as definitions of solvency need to take into account the willingness as well as the ability to pay. As Alejandro Atchugarry, the minister of economy in charge of the negotiations put it to me: "Uruguay refused to default [the debt] because its credibility is the only reason for the country being independent. Reputation is the only thing that separates Uruguay from being an Argentine province" (personal communication).

The voluntary debt exchange favored by the Uruguayan government raised questions about the exchange's enduring sustainability (Roubini and Setser 2004, 174). It also represented a heavy financial burden in interest payments for the succeeding government—and the FA was a favorite for the upcoming 2004 elections. This led the FA's leader, Tabaré Vázquez, to express serious concerns about the terms of the exchange at a time of great uncertainty about the party's interests. After an internal debate, he was persuaded to support the government's exchange proposal by the leader of the more moderate faction of the FA, his future economy minister Danilo Astori (Steneri 2011, 154–55). The voluntary exchange appeared to be in the best interest of both the government of the time and of the future FA government, and it legitimized the economic policies of the more moderate groups within the FA. Asked to reflect on the lessons of the crisis in its tenth anniversary, Vice President Astori said:

> It confirms that definitely is very important for a country like Uruguay ... to maintain the prestige that always results from honoring its commitments. This was the path chosen in 2002. I have no doubt that history and reality confirm that this was the right path. Today we are witnessing the results of that decision. (*El Observador* 13 July 2012)

In August 2002, only days after a US/IMF rescue package permitted the re-opening of the banks, Paul O' Neill visited Uruguay to show the US government's support for the government of Uruguay. President Batlle thanked his guest for the contribution of the Bush administration to the solving of the banking crisis during a joint press conference, acknowledged "the responsibility, common sense and sensibility" shown by the Uruguayan society when facing a "bad time," and affirmed his gratitude to "the judicial and political systems for their formidable and efficient activity." After remarking that no financial country in the world had ever been able to survive the almost 50 percent run on deposits, the president declared first in Spanish and then in English, "we are fantastic" (*Búsqueda* 8 August 2002b).[12] "We are fantastic" was as much an expression of relief for having avoided financial meltdown as it was a rather smug, self-congratulatory statement. In claiming that Uruguay was "fantastic" because of the way in which it dealt with the crisis, the president was not making a statement of fact. He was constructing hegemony by setting up the symbolic frontiers of what could be said and done in Uruguay: "we" all share the ideas and principles behind the successful strategy of crisis resolution and abide by them.

To borrow a term from Uruguay's dominant crisis narrative, *intangible elements*—that is, ideas, values, and the discourses that bring them to the public domain—lack the hard-core materiality of interests, structures, and institutions. It is also more difficult to establish their causal effect because they are often based on subjective perceptions. Partly because of this, it is easy to minimize their importance for political analysis by regarding them as just intervening variables in processes basically determined by underlying structural variables. Yet, while ideas and values do not float in a power vacuum or interact free from structural constraints, this view misses a lot of what is meaningful in political analysis. This chapter is a contribution to the retrieval of what is missing from the understanding of politics by taking into account the power of ideas, the importance of values, and the role of discourse in the study of politics.

Notes

1. For example, see: "On Debt Crisis South America Offers Some Lessons." *The Washington Post,* 3 November 2011.
2. In an attempt to boost confidence in the Argentine economy and generate a catalytic effect, the IMF and other multilaterals provided $20 billion in December 2000 (the so-called *blindaje*) and a further $8 billion in August 2001, of which $5 billion were actually disbursed.
3. For a detailed account of the policy initiatives during the period and their impact on economic and financial indicators, see Chapter 8 in Sturzenegger and Zettlemeyer (2006).
4. Text available at: http://www.fmmeducacion.com.ar/Historia/Cacerolazos/108ultimodiscursorua.htm [accessed 2 April 2013].
5. For a chronology of the events leading to De la Rúa's resignation, see Caucino (2011).

6. For a detailed account of the economic debate and the economic policies of the Duhalde administration, see Levy Yeyati and Valenzuela (2007).
7. For a more detailed discussion of the Kirchner's administration strengthening of the state, see Chapter 3, by Woodruff, in this volume.
8. The following quotes are representative of a comprehensive survey of the government's speeches, press conferences, statements, and interviews and a survey of the speeches and statements by the main opposition leaders taken from official Web sites, the two main newspapers (one close to the government and the other to the opposition), the main political weekly, and congressional transcripts between January and October 2002.
9. As a result of the crisis, the FA governments also made significant changes to the regulation and supervision of the financial sector and followed an active strategy of debt management that included the specification of the debt and the extension of its maturity.
10. Available at: http://www.uruguayxxi.gub.uy/bienvenido-a-uruguay/pais-confiable/ [accessed 25 September 2012].
11. In an editorial on Tuesday 6 August, the *New York Times* argued that the Department of the Treasury bridge loan to the Uruguayan government constituted a "welcome departure" from the administration's opposition to other rescues in the past (*Búsqueda* 8 August 2002a).
12. Originally, the remark was made in Spanish, "*somos unos fenómenos.*" After noting that there were English-speaking journalists in the room, President Batlle immediately repeated it in English.

References

Amadeo, Eduardo. 2003. *La salida del abismo: Memoria política de la negociación entre Duhalde y el FMI*. Buenos Aires: Planeta.
Auyero, Javier. 2007. *Routine Politics and Violence in Argentina: The Grey Zone of State Power*. Cambridge: Cambridge University Press.
Barros, Sebastián. 2006. "Ruptures and Continuities in Kirchner's Argentina." Paper presented at the Meeting of the Latin American Studies Association, San Juan, Puerto Rico, 15–18 March.
Batlle, Jorge. 2002a. "Conferencia de prensa del Pte. Dr. Jorge Batlle luego de la reunión con el Consejo de Ministros en el Edificio Plaza Independencia" [Press Conference of President Dr. Jorge Batlle from the Meeting with the Council of Ministers in the Plaza Independencia Building]. Real Audio, Montevideo, Uruguay. 1 March. http://archivo.presidencia.gub.uy/audionet/2002/03/03_2002.html.
Batlle, Jorge. 2002b. "Nota al Presidente Jorge Batlle" [Note to the President Jorge Batlle]. Real Audio, Montevideo, Uruguay, 7 January. http://archivo.presidencia.gub.uy/audionet/2002/03/03_2002.html.
Blustein, Paul. 2005. *And the Money Kept Rolling In (and Out): The World Bank, Wall Street, the IMF, and the Bankrupting of Argentina*. New York: Public Affairs.
Blyth, Mark. 2001. "The Transformation of the Swedish Model: Economic Ideas, Distributional Conflict and Institutional Change." *World Politics* 54: 1–26.
Bonasso, Miguel. 2002. *El palacio y la calle: Crónicas de insurgentes y conspiradores*. Buenos Aires: Planeta.
Bonvecchi, Alejandro. 2002. "Estrategia De Supervivencia y Tácticas De Disuasión: Los procesos políticos de la política económica después de las reformas estructurales." In *El derrumbe político en el ocaso de la convertibilidad*, edited by Marcos Novaro, 107–193. Buenos Aires: Norma.

Búsqueda. 2002a. "Acusan a la izquierda de desestabilizar; sus senadores dicen que sería 'muy fácil encender la pradera' pero tendría muchos riesgos." 4 July. 7.

Búsqueda. 2002b. "El secretario del Tesoro de EE.UU. prodigó elogios al Uruguay durante su estadía en Montevideo; Batlle recuperó su jovialidad." 8 August. 4.

Búsqueda. 2002c. "Ministro del Interior informó que los asaltos fueron planificados en ámbitos familiares con participación 'casi exclusiva' de mujeres." 8 August. 16.

Búsqueda. 2010. "Lo 'grave' de Batlle fue 'haber dicho' lo de los argentinos pero 'no haberlo pensado.'" 11 November. 120.

Caucino, Mariano A. 2011. *1980–2010. Una cronología política de la historia argentina reciente.* Buenos Aires: Ediciones Doble Hache.

Cherny, Nicolas. 2009. "Por qué cambia la política económica? El bobierno del cambio de política cambiaria en Argentina [1995–2003]." PhD diss., FLACSO, Argentina.

Damill, Mario, Roberto Frenkel and Mario Rapetti. 2005. "La deuda Argentina: Historia, default y restructuración." *Desarrollo Económico* 45: 187–233.

De la Rúa, Fernando. 1999. "Discurso De Fernando De La Rua. Texto completo del mensaje del presidente de la Nación, Fernando de la Rúa, tras jurar ayer ante la Asamblea Legislativa el día 10 de diciembre de 1999." http://www.buenastareas.com/ensayos/Discurso-De-Fernando-De-La-Rua/2791443.html.

El Observador. 2012. Los Protagonistas. *"La izquierda jugó un papel constructivo". Danilo Astori dice haber aprendido "muchísimo" con la crisis.* (Video interview). *http://www.elobservador.com.uy/especiales/crisis2002/los_protagonistas_danilo_astori.html* [accessed 2 April 2013]

El País. 2011. *"Mujica: ley de obras no esconde un sistema "tramposo de privatización."'* http://historico.elpais.com.uy/110315/pnacio-553435/nacional/mujica-ley-de-obras-no-esconde-un-sistema-tramposo-de-privatizacion-/ [accessed 2 April 2013]

Esteves, Ricardo. 2003. "Discurso político en la democracia Argentina reciente (1999–2003). La 'deuda' en los discursos de asunción de los presidentes, De la Rúa, Rodríguez Saá, Duhalde y Kirchner." Paper presented at the VI Congreso Nacional de Ciencia Política, Rosario, Argentina, November. http://www.saap.org.ar/esp/docs-congresos/congresos-saap/VI/areas/05/esteves.pdf [accessed 2 April 2013]

Grugel, Jean, and María Pía Riggirozzi. 2007. "The Return of the State in Argentina." *International Affairs,* 83: 87–107.

Haslam, Paul Alexander. 2010. "Foreign Investors over a Barrel: Nationalizations and Investment Policy." In *Latin America's Left Turns: Politics, Policies & Trajectories of Change,* edited by Maxwell A. Cameron and Eric Hershberg, 209–30. London: Lynne Rienner.

Hatchondo, Juan Carlos, and Leonardo Martínez. 2010. "The Politics of Sovereign Default." *Economic Quarterly,* 96: 291–317.

Hay, Colin. 2001. "The 'Crisis' of Keynesianism and the Rise of Neoliberalism in Britain: An Ideational Institutionalist Approach." In *The Rise of Neoliberalism and Institutional Analysis,* edited by John L. Campbell and Ove K. Pedersen, 193–218. Princeton: Princeton University Press.

Jessop, Bob. 2013. "Recovered Imaginaries, Imagined Recoveries: A Cultural Political Economy of Crisis Construals and Crisis-management in the North Atlantic Financial Crisis." In *Before and Beyond the Global Economic Crisis: Economics and Politics for a Post-Crisis Settlement,* edited by Mats Benner. Cheltenham: Edward Elgar.

Lanzaro, Jorge. 2010. "Uruguay: Persistence and Change in an Old Party Democracy." In *Political Parties and Democracy. Volume I. The Americas,* edited by Kate Lawson and Jorge Lanzaro, 195–216. Santa Barbara: Praeger.

La República. 2002a. "EN DOS SEMANAS LA IZQUIERDA PLANTEARÁ MEDIDAS; ENTRE ELLAS DESDOLARIZAR LA ECONOMÍA URUGUAYA." 22 January.

La República. 2002b. "'Un gobierno del FA hubiera actuado exactamente igual que Batlle' en la crisis de los bancos." 17 February.

La República. 2002c. "El nuevo 'ajuste patriótico' fue diseñado por el Ministro de Economía Alberto Bensión. Para el gobierno se abre la posibilidad de entablar un diálogo 'pragmático.'" 14 May.

Lavagna, Roberto. 2007. "Economy Minister of Argentina (2002–2005)." Video interview by Nicolás Cherny, Buenos Aires, 19 December.

Levy Yeyati, Eduardo, and Diego Valenzuela. 2007. *LA RESURRECCIÓN: HISTORIA DE LA POSCRISIS ARGENTINA*. Buenos Aires: Sudamericana.

Llach, Lucas. 2004. "A Depression in Perspective: The Economic and the Political Economy of Argentina's Crisis of the Millennium." In *The Argentine Crisis at the Turn of the Millennium*, edited by Flavia Fiourcci and Marcus Klein, 40–63. Amsterdam: Aksant.

Martínez, Juan, and Javier Santiso. 2003. "Financial Markets and Politics: The Confidence Game in Latin American Emerging Economies." *International Political Science Review*, 24: 363–395.

Novaro, Marcos. 2002. "PRESENTACIÓN: LO EVITABLE Y LO INEVITABLE DE LA CRISIS." In *El derrumbe político en el ocaso de la convertibilidad*, edited by Marcos Novaro, 9–30. Buenos Aires: Norma.

Pérez Antón, Romeo. 2008. "Parlamentarismo y Presidencialismo: Un Debate Inconcluso." In *Reforma Política en Uruguay: Debates y Alternativas*, edited by Federico Irazábal, Pablo Mieres, Romeo Pérez and Ignacio Zuasnabar, 15–66. Montevideo: Universidad Católica del Uruguay, Konrad Adenauer Stifund.

Peruzzotti, Enrique. 2005. "Demanding Accountable Government: Citizens, Politicians, and the Perils of Representative Democracy in Argentina." In *Argentina: The Politics of Institutional Weaknesses*, edited Steve Levitsky and Victoria Murillo, 229–49. Oxford: Oxford University Press.

Renes Lenicov, Jorge. 2008. "Minister of Economy of Argentina (January—March 2002)." Video interview by Nicolás Cherny, Buenos Aires, Argentina, 22 January.

Roubini, Nouriel, and Brad Setser. 2004. *Bailouts or Bail-ins? Responding to Financial Crises in Emerging Economies*, Washington, D.C.: Institute for International Economics.

Slipak, Daniela. n.d. "*Más allá y más acá de las fronteras políticas: apuestas de reconstrucción del vínculo representativo en el discurso kirchnerista*." http://webiigg.sociales.uba.ar/iigg/jovenes_investigadores/3JornadasJovenes/Templates/Eje%20representaciones/Slipak%20Discursos.pdf

Steneri, Carlos. 2011. *Al borde del abismo: Uruguay y la gran crisis del 2002–2003*. Montevideo: Banda Oriental.

Sturzenegger, Federico, and Jeromin Zettelmeyer. 2006. *Debt Defaults and Lessons from a Decade of Crises*. London: The MIT Press.

Suskind, Ron. 2004. *The Price of Loyalty: George W. Bush, the White House, and the Education of Paul O' Neill*. New York: Simon & Schuster.

Svampa, Maristella. 2005. *LA SOCIEDAD EXCLUYENTE: LA ARGENTINA BAJO EL SIGNO DEL NEOLIBERALISMO*. Buenos Aires: Taurus.

Taylor, John B. 2007a. *Global Financial Warriors: The Untold Story of International Finance in the Post-9/11 World*. London: W.W. Norton.

Taylor, John B. 2007b. "The 2002 Uruguayan Financial Crisis Five Years Later." Transcript of speech presented at the Conference on the 2002 Uruguayan Financial

Crisis and Its Aftermath, Montevideo, Uruguay, May 29). http://www.stanford. edu/~johntayl/Onlinepaperscombinedbyyear/2007/The_2002_Uruguay_Financial_ Crisis_Five_Years_Later.pdf [accessed 17 January 2013].

Torfing, Jakob. 1999. *New Theories of Discourse: Laclau, Mouffe and Žižek*. Oxford: Blackwell.

Whitehead, Laurence. 2006. "The Political Dynamics of Financial Crises in 'Emerging Market' Democracies." In *Statecrafting Monetary Authority, Democracy, and Financial Order in Brazil*, edited by Lourdes Sola and Laurence Whitehead, 13–36. Oxford: Centre for Brazilian Studies, Oxford University.

Wylde, Christopher. 2011. "State, Society and Markets in Argentina: The Political Economy of *Neodesarrollismo* under Néstir Kirchner, 2003–2007." *Bulletin of Latin American Research*, 30:436–52.

3 After Neoliberal Constitutionalism

Financial Crisis and State Resurgence in Russia and Argentina

David M. Woodruff, The London School of Economics

INTRODUCTION

In the 1990s, both Argentina and Russia were significant and closely watched exemplars of the international turn to neoliberal economic policy. The devastating financial crises they eventually suffered rocked international financial markets and appeared to portend further disasters ahead. However, what ensued was rather different: a substantial and surprising restoration of the power and discretion of the national state. Within a space of a very few years, national governments that had been widely derided as too weak to collect taxes and impose "necessary" reforms were able to become vastly·more assertive in their dealings with subnational governments, investors, international financial institutions, and foreign powers. After years of constant crisis, a sense that governments were teetering on the edge of an abyss, the long term had returned.

By the middle of the 2000s, both Argentina and Russia were led by highly popular presidents whose agendas faced no significant challenge from the legislature or political rivals, and who had both sought much more political distance from Washington than did their predecessors. Fiscal relations with subnational governments, previously a site of continual conflict and a subject of much neoliberal hand wringing, had been restructured to the decisive advantage of national authorities. Argentine and Russian leaders had implemented an aggressive bargaining stance with respect to international creditors with great success. While there was no wholesale revision of the results of the 1990s' privatizations, national officials in both states had come to take a much broader view of their economic role, including expanding state ownership of industry. There were differences between the two countries that should not be minimized. Trade unions and political parties had far more significant roles in Argentina than in Russia, and despite Kirchner's popularity, the space for political contestation was much wider in Argentina than in Russia.

Nevertheless, the parallel trends were striking. Indeed, is tempting to suggest that they amounted to the stirrings of a new paradigm, which one could perhaps christen *nationalist neostatism*. Indeed, some in Argentina have spoken of the emergence of a new developmentalism, or *neodesarrollismo* (Wylde

2011). Likewise, some Russian observers speak of an emergent "state capital-ism" (*goskapitalizm*). Russian discussions of "sovereign democracy" and the re-lated desire to foster nationally oriented business could be read as a manifesto for nationalist neostatism (Hanson 2007; Krastev 2008).

The emergence of nationalist neostatism can be explained on two levels. The first is the level of structural preconditions. How is it possible that so soon after a financial catastrophe national states widely perceived as feeble were able to regain capacity and autonomy? Whence the ability to bargain from a position of strength with investors and subnational governments? I will argue that the sud-den resurgence of state capacity reflected what was effectively an artificial weak-ness in the 1990s, which stemmed from an effort, inspired by neoliberal ideas, to "lock in" commitments to particular neoliberal policies. These policies were pursued to the point that they simply became institutionally unsustainable: their continuation undermined the two states' governance capacity.

The second level of explanation concerns ideological dynamics. Whence the emotional energy behind nationalist neostatism? Here, we will discover some interesting distinctions between Russia and Argentina.

THE CONSEQUENCES OF NEOLIBERAL CONSTITUTIONALISM

Stephen Gill's term *disciplinary neoliberalism* aptly summarizes the interna-tional intellectual atmosphere that decisively affected the 1990s reform efforts in Argentina and Russia (Gill 1995). Like liberalism before it, neoliberalism seeks to harness state power to the purpose of creating and sustaining a market econ-omy (Hayek 2007, 112–23; Friedman 2002, location 526–29, 558: Chapter 2, Chapter 3). To do so, it both prescribes and proscribes acts by the state. The state must enforce property rights, but must not itself expropriate property. A debtor's property must be seized to uphold a contract, but must not be taken to serve other ends of the state. The state must provide a monetary unit, but not issue it to inflationary excess.

To ensure that the state's prescribed market-sustaining powers are not turned to proscribed market-undermining purposes, liberals and neoliberals char-acteristically offer "constitutional" solutions that seek to put proscribed acts beyond the reach of politics (Friedman 2002, location 133–40: Introduction; Gill 1995, 412–13). Direct constitutional provisions forbidding the confiscation of property without fair compensation are only one example (Schneiderman 2008, 48–56). Others are institutional arrangements designed to ensure that participation in exercising market-sustaining powers is limited to those com-mitted to avoiding possible antiliberal applications, as in the case for inde-pendent central banks (Drazen 2002). While liberal advocates of markets have always faced a constitutional dilemma, a "new constitutionalism" seeking to insulate economic policy from democratic politics is a core aspect of the international influence of neoliberalism (Gill 1995, 2007; Schneiderman 2008, 1–17, 2000, 85–8).

Other arguments reinforce the neoliberals' commitment to constitutional strictures on the economic power of the state. Such strictures are held to increase the credibility of policy, which in turn is held to be vital for shaping the behavior of economic actors (Blackburn and Christensen 1989; North and Weingast 1989). Credibility arguments were an absolutely central element of the neoliberals' intellectual equipment (Grabel 2000). They even justified fixed exchange rates (rescuing a tenet of classical liberalism that for a time had fallen into disfavor), which were supposed to provide a credible signal of a government's intention to fight inflation by creating a situation in which devaluation would have disastrous consequences (Willett 1998; Tavlas 2000). Political considerations also promoted constitutional or quasi-constitutional commitments intended "lock in" promarket policies in the face of political hostility. This was necessary insofar as for neoliberals market reforms constitute a "public good," and in a world of free riders public goods have no friends except the heroically committed, or constitutionally constrained, liberals (Schamis 1999, 236).

Thus, neoliberal constitutionalism offers a number of rationales for insulating particular economic policies from political challenges. Arguments such as these formed an important part of the international and domestic intellectual atmosphere in which Russia and Argentina embarked on economic reforms in the 1990s. However, neoliberal constitutionalist arguments obscure a fact that the experience of the two countries powerfully reveals: properly political challenges may not be the only threat neoliberal policies face.

In fact, *neoliberalism in Argentina and Russia artificially dampened the apparent power of the national state by pushing it into policies that were not just highly controversial politically, but unsustainable institutionally.* To understand institutional unsustainability, it is necessary to take account of a fundamental aspect of capitalism. Capitalism involves state efforts to channel economic life through legally established institutions, the most important of which are money and property. The reliable functioning of these institutions, it should be recognized, depends not only on coercion but also on consent. A *general* reluctance to adhere to the rules of monetary institutions or to recognize property rights will swamp the enforcement capacities of any conceivable bureaucracies. A useful metaphor for such institutional unsustainability is legal prohibition of alcohol or drugs. Coercive enforcement never succeeds in entirely shutting down the markets for illicit goods. Relative to the task of eliminating these markets, therefore, the state appears "weak." While bureaucracies tasked with achieving the impossible will likely display incoherence and corruption, this is a consequence of their aim, not an explanation of their failure to achieve it.

In Russia and Argentina, stubborn pursuit of policies "locked in" based on neoliberal constitutionalist arguments did not merely prompt political discontent and, eventually, financial crisis. Instead, they created an institutionally unsustainable situation—one that undermined the functioning of the core capitalist institutions of money and property. Neoliberal policies also disorganized fiscal federalism in parallel fashion.

MONEY

Both Argentine and Russian authorities chose restrictive exchange rate regimes in an effort to broadcast a credible commitment to fighting inflation. In Argentina, the relevant decision was the 1991 introduction of convertibility, which fixed the peso–dollar ratio at one and provided for full backing of issued pesos with dollars or foreign currency (Palermo 1998, 44–7; Molano 2001; Panizza, Chapter 2, this volume).[1] Russia, for its part, implemented the so-called ruble corridor from mid-1995 (Woodruff 2005). This was a less restrictive policy than Argentina's, specifying a band within which the ruble's exchange rate could vary, periodically adjusted for inflation to avoid excessive real appreciation.

Inflexible exchange-rate regimes tie domestic monetary conditions very tightly to international capital flows and trade balances.[2] Inflows tend to produce easy monetary conditions and a boom in asset prices, while outflows have the opposite effects. Furthermore, if outflows threaten the sustainability of the exchange-rate regime, domestic monetary authorities may put up interest rates in order to encourage interest in domestic-currency assets. A commitment to an inflexible exchange-rate regime therefore requires, under a variety of plausible international shocks, a readiness to implement highly recessionary policies.

Both Argentina and Russia encountered such international shocks and sought to maintain their exchange rate commitments through implementing high interest rates and sanctioning recessionary conditions. The required measures were extraordinary. In Russia, capital inflows after Yeltsin's 1996 reelection as president allowed Russian real interest rates to drop from over 100 percent per annum to around 20 percent (still extremely high in comparative international terms) for most of 1997. However, a fall in oil prices and the outbreak of the Asian crisis in November 1997 required a hike in interest rates (Aleksashenko 1999, 118), including a desperate decision in May of 1998 that took the annual real interest rate to over 140 percent.[3] Argentina saw two episodes of recession caused by the changing tides of international monetary flows. The first, relatively short lived, was the "tequila crisis" of 1995, when the devaluation of the Mexican currency turned international investors against emerging markets. The second ensued from late 1998, as the international financial crisis hit capital inflows and then the devaluation of the Brazilian currency decreased Argentina's export receipts. Real interest rates surged, and while they fell to 10 percent in 2000, they averaged nearly 30 percent in 2001. Meanwhile, the country endured years of grinding deflation, with prices in 2001 nearly 5 percent below what they had been in 1995.[4]

These exceptionally restrictive policies had a remarkable result: the emergence, on a massive scale, of alternatives to official money that had, in effect, become too expensive to use in many transactions.[5] In Argentina, surrogate monies issued by the national and local governments amounted to around 26 percent of the peso money supply by the end of 2001 (de Torre, Schmukler and Levy Yeyati 2003, 75). Russia's surrogates were more varied in character and issuer, and harder to count, but in any event much more extensive. As early as 1996, around 40 percent of federal and 60 percent of provincial tax revenue was taking a nonmonetary form, and by 1998 some 50 percent of transactions in industry were being carried out through barter (Woodruff 1999, 169, 148).

The result was an institutionally unsustainable situation in the sense defined previously. The commitment to an international value of the ruble and peso remained strong, but state capacity to ensure exclusive use of the national money evaporated. Especially in Russia, where the spread of surrogates was more extensive, they became part of a self-undermining dynamic of exchange-rate policy. The tight monetary policies needed to maintain exchange-rate commitments pushed the spread of monetary surrogates, which created enormous fiscal difficulties; fiscal fears led investors to sell ruble-denominated government bonds and convert the proceeds, increasing pressure on the exchange rate. Procyclical fiscal and monetary policy in Argentina led to a parallel negative feedback loop there (Stiglitz 2002), though the extent to which monetary surrogates were relevant to Argentine tax-collection difficulties is hard to assess.

PROPERTY

A desire to build "constitutional" constraints also pushed policy beyond the limits of the institutionally feasible in the area of privatization. In Russia, privatization was carried out with extreme haste in hopes that this would make it irreversible.[6] That the policy was designed to constrain possible economic policies, and thus shared the logic of neoliberal constitutionalism, did not mean it was constitutional in form. In fact, the desire for speed prompted Russia's executive branch to institute a number of privatization measures via executive orders that were at times constitutionally dubious (Barnes 2001; Orenstein 1998). Although some of these measures directly contradicted parliamentary decisions, the privatization program as implemented nevertheless represented something of a compromise. Reformers wanted state-owned enterprises privatized as publicly traded companies with substantial outsider ownership, whereas many parliamentarians wished to ensure existing enterprise insiders a dominant role in newly privatized entities (McFaul 1995).

Privatization as carried out contained both of these elements. As a result, shares of stock in the new corporations were distributed with complete disregard to whether or not shareholders, and the managers nominally subject to their governance, had any reason to cooperate with each other. In point of fact they did not. Exercise of shareholder property rights entailed, for a long period, a zero-sum struggle between different groups of shareholders with no incentive to recognize one another's rights. The Russian state was formally committed to defending a structure of property rights, yet no feasible enforcement effort could have countered the almost universal efforts to evade or undermine its stipulations. This institutionally unsustainable situation spread corruption, cynicism, and confusion through the legal system (Woodruff 2004).

Argentina also privatized in the 1990s (although the much smaller scale of the program illustrates the magnitude of the distinction between a merely *étatiste* and a command economy). Privatization in Argentina focused on elements of infrastructure like electrical power, water supply, and roadways. Although the privatization program has been described as "populist" (Murillo 2002, 485–87), the bulk of the assets were sold to investors in a form that ensured they would be able to exploit monopoly power (Schamis 1999, 264–65). The neoliberal constitutionalist impulse here found expression in elaborate contractual arrangements designed to ensure a "credible commitment" regarding regulatory policy.[7] Power companies, for instance, were guaranteed that their prices would be indexed to the US's inflation rate. When Argentina began to suffer deflation due to tight monetary policy, these provisions meant that utilities' prices went up at the same time all other prices went down (Woodruff 2005, 25–6; Azpiazu and Schorr 2001). It is no surprise that the result of this was not only increasing but unavailing complaints by business that service prices were competitively unsustainable but also widespread failures of customers to pay their electricity bills (Woodruff 2005, 25–6). In short, the effort to combine Argentine privatization with a credible regulatory commitment pushed policy into an institutionally unsustainable realm.

FISCAL FEDERALISM

Another area where neoliberalism bred apparent institutional weakness was in fiscal federalism. Local authorities, more politically sensitive to the economic calamities of the decade and less bound by "constitutional" commitments, fought to protect their population. Not only did they promote the use of monetary surrogates, they also fought tooth and nail over revenues with the central government. Budget austerity and the chronic inability of national authorities to meet their commitments to finance provinces bred zero-sum struggles over tax revenues, with consequences for tax collection and control over local borrowing.[8] Again, the basic dynamic was one of maintenance of a policy that undermined consent to an institutional framework, in this instance, the one governing the division of revenue and responsibility between local and central authorities.

POSTCRISIS STRENGTHENING OF THE STATE

The financial crises that brought an end to the exchange-rate commitments of Russia and Argentina seemed, at the moment they happened, catastrophic.[9] However, despite some extremely painful consequences, especially in Argentina, devaluation and default on government debt (1998 in Russia, late 2001 to early 2002 in Argentina) launched a process whereby the state regained capacity, autonomy, and initiative.

A contributory factor was the ending of constant tension over the price of government bonds. With investors already so negatively inclined, Russian and

Argentine authorities had nothing to lose by taking an extremely hard line in negotiations over restructuring. Creditors, fearing they would be left with nothing, and expertly played off against one another by Russian and Argentine negotiators, agreed to extremely favorable terms (Sinyagina-Woodruff 2003, 539–41; Dhillon et al. 2006; Miller and Thomas 2007; Helleiner 2005).

More generally, however, the rapid comeback of the state in Argentina and Russia was possible because the state had never been as weak as it appeared in the 1990s. Put differently, once policy no longer aimed to achieve the impossible, a great deal became possible.

In monetary policy, both countries were able to run a much less restrictive policy than when they sought to maintain their exchange rate commitment. Real interest rates began dropping immediately after devaluation and in both countries were eventually negative for a number of years.[10] Bursts of inflation in each country resolved a number of nominal rigidity problems. In Russia, monetary surrogates quickly gave ground in favor of official money (Ivanenko and Mikheyev 2002, 407; Fleischman and Herz 2005), with positive consequences for fiscal receipts and system in taxation. In Argentina, provincial quasi-monies were retired by the national state in 2003. This required a 24 percent increase in the monetary base, which of course would have been impossible under the currency board regulations (Damill, Frenkel and Simpson 2011, 54). In sum, in both countries, national monetary sovereignty was quickly restored.

Fiscal capacity, another area in which both the Argentine and Russian states had seemed weak in the 1990s, also improved dramatically after the immediate disorganization of the financial crisis had passed. In Russia, general government revenue went from 33 percent of GDP in 1999 to 37 percent of GDP in 2002 (International Monetary Fund 2012). Equally important, the tax collection of monetary surrogates appears to have disappeared (Edwin, Owen and Robinson 2003). Argentina likewise saw huge gains in government revenue after its crisis, from 23 percent of GDP in 2002 to 29 percent of GDP in 2004 (IMF World Economic Outlook Database); as noted previously, it also eliminated monetary surrogates and thus their role in the tax system. Accounting for fiscal performance is complex, but the magnitude and suddenness of the gains, and the manifest precrisis role of recessionary conditions and use of monetary surrogates in depressing revenues, warrant ascribing a significant portion of this shift to the exit from an institutionally unsustainable policy.[11]

Finally, in fiscal federalism, devaluation had twin effects that strengthened the hand of the national government. First, it lowered the value of existing obligations to the provinces, making a simple continuation of prior policy very favorable to national authorities and thereby strengthening their bargaining position. Second, devaluation, and a concomitant run-up in commodity prices, generated massive new export receipts that accrued to national authorities. Their position thus improved; in both countries national authorities successfully asserted national power in fiscal relations.[12]

IDEOLOGICAL PROCESSES

These factors, essentially conjunctural in character, were the structural preconditions for the comeback of the national state. But they mandated steps toward
neither *étatisme* nor the nationalist sentiments that have accompanied them.
To explain these phenomena, we must return to the issue of privatization, a
sphere in which the legacy of neoliberalism has remained very relevant. And
we must canvass some important differences between Russia and Argentina.

In Argentina, as noted previously, public services were privatized to foreign
investors, who received extraordinary contractual guarantees of profits with
enforcement charged to international arbitration agencies. However, after devaluation, the Argentine government chose to redenominate utility prices in
pesos and effectively annulled the guarantees (Haselip 2005). Foreign investors
have sought to enforce the contract terms by pursuing their case with the relevant international arbitration agencies. CMS Gas, for instance, won a judgment
for over USD$132 million plus interest (Schneiderman 2008, 100).[13] However,
Argentina stalled repayment, in line with earlier government declarations that
it would find a way to shrug off adverse rulings (Kasenetz 2010, 746; Casey
2005). The initially modest expansion of state ownership seen in Argentina has
occurred in this context, as foreign investors have in some instances preferred
simply surrendering their assets to the state rather than continuing to fight
for their dead-letter contracts (Anonymous 2005a).[14] When the IMF tried to
intervene on the investors' behalf, the Argentine government paid off its IMF
loans (with money borrowed from Venezuela). This was an expensive measure,
but one that proved popular given the tremendous resentment of the foreign
investors, both for the unjustifiably high profits they reaped in the 1990s and
for the poor service some of them provided (Anonymous 2005b; Rohter 2006).
The external focus of this resentment is of great significance politically, for it
does not imply the delegitimation of domestic political forces.

In Russia, the expansion of state ownership was the latest in a long wave of
property redistributions following the unsustainable configuration of shareholder rights that had emerged with privatization (Barnes 2006). The chaotic
legal circumstances resulting for privatization meant that defense of property
rights against various forms of legal or quasi-legal challenge required great resources, and occasionally great ruthlessness. As a result, property passed into the
hands of those able to defend it, creating a small class of tycoons ("oligarchs")
(Pappe 2000; Woodruff 2000, 2004). The opacity of the emerging property rights
system, and the local knowledge required to operate successfully within it, meant
that foreign investors had only a secondary role among big business (Pappe
2000). By the 2000s, the oligarchs had effectively consolidated control over their
property and were ready to repackage it for sale to foreign investors (Boone and
Rodionov 2001). As stock-market capitalization rose, they acquired staggering
fortunes. However, these capitalization gains became the prize in a new struggle, in which state-owned companies now participated (Woodruff 2006). In the
process, the oligarchs and political forces they had backed became substantially
delegitimated, in part because state-owned companies and their political allies

suggested that foreign ownership in strategic industries was a threat to national interests (Kryshtanovskaya and White 2005, 1071).

Thus, to a much greater extent than in Argentina, dealing with the legacy of privatization implied political struggle among different domestic forces. It may be for this reason that nationalism, as a weapon in this struggle, took on a more suspicious character, with "fifth column" rhetoric never far from the surface (Mendelson and Gerber 2010, 132). This character was exacerbated by its cultural resonance, by Russia's dramatic loss of international status after the Cold War, the internal conflict around Chechnya, and the relentless application of double standards to Russia by the US.

CONCLUSION

Nationalist neostatism is still far from a consolidated model. Both in Russia and Argentina, economic policy is markedly more liberal than it was in the 1970s. Russia's expansion of state ownership has occurred largely, albeit not exclusively, through the offer of relatively attractive terms to private owners, on the basis of funding by international banks (Woodruff 2007). Nevertheless, there has been a decisive break with the neoliberalism of the 1990s and, in particular, with the idea that "constitutional" commitments to economic policies are a sine qua non for attracting investment.

In conclusion, it is worth considering the possibility that the failure of neoliberal constitution forestalled a more constructive version of constitutionalism. The purpose of constitutional and quasi-constitutional commitments under neoliberalism is paternalistic, seeking to constrain the state's behavior. But constitutions can also play a more productive role—in particular, in ensuring broad discussion about appropriate policy and encouraging engagement from a variety of social groups (Holmes 1988). Some of the most convincing current thought in development economics, which stresses the need for policies carefully crafted to correspond to local circumstances, all but requires constitutional democracy in this form (Rodrik 2007, 155). In both countries, however, the sudden resurgence of the national state appears to have contributed to the emergence of hyperpresidentialism that trumps other constitutional principles and narrows the scope of debate. The pathologies of neoliberal constitutionalism should not be allowed to discredit constitutionalism altogether.

Notes

1. Credibility, while an important motivation on the backdrop of recent hyperinflation, was not the only one. Argentine policy makers seem to have been well aware of the distributive possibilities a post-peg boom would offer, as Palermo (1998) and Molano (2001) emphasize.
2. For details and references, see Woodruff (2005).
3. Data from the Central Bank of Russia (www.cbr.ru) and the Russian Federal State Statistics Service, (www.gks.ru). Ex-post real rates using CPI deflator.

4. Data from the World Bank, see http://databank.worldbank.org. Deflation figure in text refers to GDP deflator; consumer prices were down 1.6 percent over the same period.
5. Monetary surrogates were used to pay obligations denominated in the national currency, but were less valuable than equivalent sums of national currency. Thus the formulation in the text that official money was "too expensive to use." Equivalently, money surrogates can be viewed as solutions to nominal rigidity problems. For details, see Woodruff (1999, 2005).
6. This was a point the reformers often made; see, for instance, remarks of privatization architect Anatolii Chubais, in Burke (1992).
7. For a sample, see Schneiderman (2008, 99–102). For an illustration of how the characteristic ideas of neoliberal constitutionalism were applied to utilities' privatization and privatization more generally, see Spiller (1993) and Schneiderman (2000).
8. For Argentina (though narrated through somewhat different lenses than employed here) see Benton (2009, 667–70) and Tommasi (2002, 34–43). For Russia, see Woodruff (1999, 130–42,169–73). Benton (2009, 669) notes the "zero-sum" character of the conflicts.
9. For an account of the origins of the crises, see Woodruff (2005).
10. World Bank data, see http://www.databank.org.
11. For the position that the key to fiscal recovery in Russia was that "the Putin administration saw through the transformation of a malignant tax regime," see Appel (2008, 319); a similar perspective is given in Chua (2003). However, neither piece takes systematic account of the effects of the remonetization of the economy on tax collection. For the enormous role of monetary surrogates in Russia's 1990s tax-collection difficulties, see Woodruff (1999, 168 n73).
12. For Argentina, see Benton (2009, 670–73). For Russia, see Solanko and Tekoniemi (2005, 14–19).
13. Argentina appealed, and the relevant committee concluded that the country's defense of its actions on grounds of necessity was legally convincing and the decision of the arbitration tribunal thus mistaken. Remarkably, under the pertinent rules this was insufficient ground for the award to be reversed (Kasenetz 2010, 729)!
14. State ownership has since expanded; for more recent developments, see "Argentina's Oil Industry: Feed Me, Seymour." *The Economist,* 16 April 2012. Available at: http://www.economist.com/node/21552927.

References

Aleksashenko, Sergei. 1999. *Bitva za rubl': Vzgliad uchastnika sobytii.* Moscow: Mater.
Anonymous. 2005a. "As Suez Packs Up, the Locals Dive." *Argentina's Economy.* 1 October.
———. 2005b. "Kirchner and Lula: Different Ways to Give the Fund the Kiss Off: Argentina, Brazil and the IMF." *The Economist,* 24 December.
Appel, Hilary. 2008. "Is it Putin or Is It Oil? Explaining Russia's Fiscal Recovery." *Post-Soviet Affairs* 24 (4): 301–23.
Azpiazu, Daniel, and Martin Schorr. 2001. "Desnaturalización de la regulación pública y ganacias extraordinarias." *Realidad Económica* 184, November-December.
Barnes, Andrew. 2001. "Property, Power, and the Presidency: Ownership Policy Reform and Russian Executive–Legislative Relations, 1990–1999." *Communist and Post-Communist Studies* 34 (1): 39–61.
Barnes, Andrew Scott. 2006. *Owning Russia.* Ithaca: Cornell University Press.
Benton, Allyson L. 2009. "What Makes Strong Federalism Seem Weak? Fiscal Resources and Presidential–Provincial Relations in Argentina." *Publius: The Journal of Federalism* 39 (4): 651–76.

Blackburn, Keith, and Michael Christensen. 1989. "Monetary Policy and Policy Credibility: Theories and Evidence. *Journal of Economic Literature* 27 (1): 1–45.

Boone, Peter, and Denis Rodionov. 2001. "Rent Seeking in Russia and the CIS." Paper presented at the EBRD 10th Anniversary Conference, London, December.

Burke, Justin. 1992. "Quiet Start for Russia's Privatization." *The Christian Science Monitor—CSMonitor.com.* 2 October. http://www.csmonitor.com/1992/1002/02061.html.

Casey, Michael. 2005. "Argentina Justice Min Seeks to Declaw World Bk Tribunal." *Dow Jones International News.* 12 April. http://global.factiva.com.

Chua, Dale. 2003. "Tax Reform in Russia." In *Russia Rebounds,* edited by David Edwin, Wynn Owen and David O. Robinson, 77–98. Washington, DC: International Monetary Fund.

Damill, Mario, Roberto Frenkel and Lucio Simpson. 2011. "Macroeconomía, regulaciones financieras y la reconstrucción del sistema bancario Argentino en los años 2000." Unpublished paper, CEDES [Centro de Estudios de Estado y Sociedad], Buenos Aires, April 2011. http://www.itf.org.ar/pdf/documentos/77-2011.pdf

de Torre, Augusto la, Sergio L. Schmukler and Eduardo Levy Yeyati. 2003. "Living and Dying with Hard Pegs: The Rise and Fall of Argentina's Currency Board. *Economía* 3 (2): 43–99.

Dhillon, Amrita, Javier Garcia-Fronti, Sayantan Ghosal, and Marcus Miller. 2006. "Debt Restructuring and Economic Recovery: Analysing the Argentine Swap." *The World Economy* 29 (4): 377–98.

Drazen, Allan. 2002. "Central Bank Independence, Democracy, and Dollarization." *Journal of Applied Economics* 5 (1): 1–17.

Edwin, David, Wynn Owen and David O. Robinson, eds. 2003. *Russia Rebounds.* Washington, DC: International Monetary Fund.

Fleischman, Gary, and Paul Herz. 2005. "An Empirical Investigation of Trends in Barter Activity in the Russian Federation." *The International Journal of Accounting* 40 (1): 39–63.

Friedman, Milton. 2002. *Capitalism and Freedom: Fortieth Anniversary Edition.* Chicago: University of Chicago Press. Kindle edition.

Gill, Stephen. 1995. "Globalisation, Market Civilisation, and Disciplinary Neoliberalism." *Millennium—Journal of International Studies* 24 (3): 399–423.

———. 2007. "European Governance and New Constitutionalism: Economic and Monetary Union and Alternatives to Disciplinary Neoliberalism in Europe." *New Political Economy* 3 (1): 5–26.

Grabel, Ilene. 2000. "The Political Economy of 'Policy Credibility': The New-Classical Macroeconomics and the Remaking of Emerging Economies." *Cambridge Journal of Economics* 24 (1): 1–19.

Hanson, Philip. 2007. "The Turn to Statism in Russian Economic Policy." *The International Spectator* 42 (1): 29–42.

Haselip, James. 2005. "Renegotiating Electricity Contracts after an Economic Crisis and Currency Devaluation: The Case of Argentina." *The Electricity Journal* 18 (3): 78–88.

Hayek, Friedrich A. von. 2007. *The Road to Serfdom: Text and Documents—The Definitive Edition.* Chicago: University of Chicago Press.

Helleiner, Eric. 2005. "The Strange Story of Bush and the Argentine Debt Crisis." *Third World Quarterly* 26 (6): 951–69.

Holmes, Stephen. 1988. "Precommitment and the Paradox of Democracy." In *Constitutionalism and Democracy,* edited by Jon Elster, 195–240. Cambridge: Cambridge University Press.

International Monetary Fund. 2012. International Monetary Fund World Economic Outlook Database, October 2012 Edition. http://www.imf.org/external/pubs/ft/weo/2012/02/weodata/index.aspx

Ivanenko, Vlad, and Dmitry Mikheyev. 2002. "The Role of Non-monetary Trade in Russian Transition." *Post-Communist Economies* 14 (4): 405–19.

Kasenetz, Eric David. 2010. "Desperate Times Call for Desperate Measures: The Aftermath of Argentina's State of Necessity and the Current Fight in the ICSID." *George Washington International Law Review* 41:709–47.

Krastev, Ivan. 2008. "Russia and the European Order: Sovereign Democracy Explained." *The American Interest* 4 (2): 16-24.

Kryshtanovskaya, Ol'ga, and Stephen White. 2005. "Inside the Putin Court: A Research Note." *Europe-Asia Studies* 57 (7): 1065–75.

McFaul, Michael. 1995. "State Power, Institutional Change, and the Politics of Privatization in Russia." *World Politics* 47 (2): 210–43.

Mendelson, Sarah E., and Theodore P. Gerber. 2010. "Us and Them: Anti-American Views of the Putin Generation." *Washington Quarterly* 31 (2): 131–50.

Miller, Marcus, and Dania Thomas. 2007. "Sovereign Debt Restructuring: The Judge, the Vultures and Creditor Rights." *The World Economy* 30 (10): 1491–509.

Molano, Walter T. 2001. "Argentina: The political Economy of Stabilization and Structural Reform." In *The Political Economy of International Financial Crisis: Interest Groups, Ideologies, and Institutions,* edited by Shale A. Horowitz and Uk Heo, 213–24. Lanham, MD: Rowman & Littlefield.

Murillo, M. Victoria. 2002. "Political Bias in Policy Convergence: Privatization Choices in Latin America. *World Politics* 54 (04): 462–93.

North, Douglass C., and Barry R. Weingast. 1989. "Constitutions and Commitment: The Evolution of Institutions Governing Public Choice in Seventeenth-Century England." *The Journal of Economic History* 49 (4): 803–32.

Orenstein, Mitchell. 1998. "Lawlessness from Above and Below: Economic Radicalism and Political Institutions. *SAIS Review* 18 (1): 35–50.

Palermo, Vicente. 1998. "Moderate Populism: A Political Approach to Argentina's 1991 Convertibility Plan." Trans. by John Collins. *Latin American Perspectives* 25 (4): 36–62.

Pappe, Ia Sh. 2000. *Oligarkhi': Ekonomicheskaia khronika, 1992–2000.* Moskva: Vysshaia shkola ekonomiki.

Rodrik, Dani. 2007. *One Economics, Many Recipes: Globalization, Institutions, and Economic Growth.* Princeton: Princeton University Press.

Rohter, Larry. 2006. "As Argentina's Debt Dwindles, President's Power Steadily Grows. *New York Times,* 3 January.

Schamis, Hector E. 1999. "Distributional Coalitions and the Politics of Economic Reform in Latin America." *World Politics* 51 (2): 236–68.

Schneiderman, David. 2000. "Constitutional Approaches to Privatization: An Inquiry into the Magnitude of Neo-liberal Constitutionalism." *Law and Contemporary Problems* 63 (4): 83–109.

———. 2008. *Constitutionalizing Economic Globalization: Investment Rules and Democracy's Promise.* New York: Cambridge University Press.

Sinyagina-Woodruff, Yulia. 2003. "Russia, Sovereign Default, Reputation and Access to Capital Markets." *Europe-Asia Studies* 55 (4): 521–51.

Solanko, Laura, and Merja Tekoniemi. 2005. "To Recentralise or Decentralise—Some Recent Trends in Russian Fiscal Federalism." *BOFIT Online Publications* 5. http://

www.suomenpankki.fi/bofit_en/tutkimus/tutkimusjulkaisut/online/pages/bon0505.aspx

Spiller, Pablo T. 1993. "Institutions and Regulatory Commitment in Utilities' Privatization." *Industrial and Corporate Change* 2 (1): 387–450.

Stiglitz, Joseph E. 2002. "Argentina, Shortchanged: Why the Nation That Followed the Rules Fell to Pieces." *Washington Post*, 12 May.

Tavlas, George S. 2000. "On the Exchange Rate as a Nominal Anchor: The Rise and Fall of the Credibility Hypothesis." *Economic Record* 76 (233): 183–201.

Tommasi, Mariano. 2002. *Federalism in Argentina and the Reforms of the 1990s*. Working Paper, Universidad de San Andres, Departamento de Economia. Victoria, Argentina.

Willett, T. D. 1998. "Credibility and Discipline Effects of Exchange Rates as Nominal Anchors: The Need to Distinguish Temporary from Permanent Pegs." *World Economy* 21 (6): 803–26.

Woodruff, David M. 1999. *Money Unmade: Barter and the Fate of Russian Capitalism*. Ithaca, NY: Cornell University Press.

———. 2000. "Rules for Followers: Institutional Theory and the New Politics of Economic Backwardness in Russia." *Politics & Society* 28 (4): 437–82.

———. 2004. "Property Rights in Context: Privatization's Legacy for Corporate Legality in Poland and Russia." *Studies in Comparative International Development* 38 (4): 82–108.

———. 2005. "Boom, Gloom, Doom: Balance Sheets, Monetary Fragmentation, and Politics of Financial Crisis in Russia and Argentina." *Politics & Society* 33 (1): 1–44.

———. 2006. "Nestabilnost' chastnoi sobstvennosti v rossii: Ekonomicheskie i politicheskie prichiny." In *Russkie Chteniia*, 206–19. Moscow: Gruppa Ekspert.

———. 2007. "The Expansion of State Ownership in Russia: Cause for Concern? *Development & Transition*, 7: 11–13.

Wylde, Christopher. 2011. "State, Society and Markets in Argentina: The Political Economy of Neodesarrollismo under Néstor Kirchner, 2003–2007." *Bulletin of Latin American Research* 30 (4): 436–52.

4 The Neoliberalization of South Korea after the 1997 Economic Crisis

A Cultural Political Economy of Crisis Discourse and Management[1]

Joo-Hyoung Ji, Kyungnam University (South Korea)

INTRODUCTION

This chapter conducts a cultural political economy (CPE) analysis of crisis, crisis discourse, and crisis management with reference to the 1997 economic crisis in South Korea (hereafter, Korea). It aims to illuminate the close but little-examined connection between crisis, crisis discourse, and crisis management in capitalism. Capitalist crisis produces various crisis discourses, that is, interpretations on the nature and causes of the crisis. However, in contrast to crisis discourse as such, the causes and effects of these discourses attract less attention. The causes and effects of crisis management, as well as the relation between crisis discourses and crisis management, attract even less attention. Such little interest in the nature of crisis discourse and management may well mislead and distort our understanding of crises. In other words, it is not possible to understand crises without adequately understanding crisis discourse and management. Crises are not independent from crisis discourse and management. Their nature is defined and shaped by their discursive mediation and practical management. Crisis discourse and management must thus be analyzed as an indispensable part of crisis analysis.

For this purpose, this chapter adopts a CPE approach (Jessop 2004; Campbell 1969). This approach pays particular attention to how cultural, symbolic, and discursive semiosis cause, constitute, and transform political and economic actions, strategies, and institutions. Still, it does not reduce the reality to discourse since it recognizes that discourse does not automatically turn into reality and hence needs to be realized and consolidated through material practices. The approach thus conceptualizes political economic transformations in four analytically distinct stages: variation, selection, retention, and reinforcement of strategic actors and their strategic discourses and practices. A complex reality does not permit immediate access and thus needs discursive mediations that can reduce its complexity into various narratives: hence, discursive variation. However, certain discourses and practices are more advantageous than others in their realization because semiotic and strategic selectivity operates in and through social and political struggle—hence, selection. Selected discourses and practices are in turn materialized, institutionalized, and consolidated to create a new political economic order—hence, retention and reinforcement.

Here it should be noted that discursive semiosis plays a larger part in earlier stages and material and strategic selectivity plays a larger part in later stages.

The Korean case can offer an excellent illustration of the cultural political economy of crisis, crisis discourse, crisis management, and political economic transformation on the whole. The 1997 crisis had a very complex nature, provoked debates on the nature of the crisis as well as on East Asian capitalism, and resulted in Korea's neoliberalization with a great shift in discourses and practices. This chapter will proceed as follows. First, it will show the complexity of the Korean economic crisis. Second, it will examine major social actors' politically bounded discursive variation (i.e., how they reduced the complexity of crisis differently in accordance to their interests). Third, it will look into international and intranational struggle that differentiated actual crisis management from crisis discourse. Fourth, it will show how this process contributed to the selection and retention of certain strategic actors and practices by privileging certain aspects of the crisis over others at the critical juncture of path shaping. Finally, it will discuss how this process had lasting effects on Korea's political development through neoliberalization.

THE COMPLEXITY OF THE KOREAN ECONOMIC CRISIS IN 1997

Korea suffered from an economic crisis of an unprecedented scale in 1997. The origins of the crisis go back to the late 1980s and early 1990s. The Korean economy began to face trouble in the early 1990s due to the aggressive US foreign-trade policy, increased international competition, cost pressures such as wage increases and high interest rates, and the lack of rational investment coordination. This resulted from a change in the national and international environment: the end of the Cold War, the expansion of the Japanese-led regional production network called "flying geese" in East Asia, and Korea's democratization in the late 1980s. The Korean government actively pursued globalization and neoliberal reforms to secure international competitiveness and cut financial and labor costs. However, financial globalization greatly increased the short-term foreign debt in the private sector, and the government failed to push corporate, labor, and financial reform forward. The *chaebol* (Korean business conglomerates), trade unions, and the imminent presidential election created a catastrophic balance of forces that undermined the authority of the state to the extent that it could not implement any meaningful reform until 1997.

The year 1996 saw a record-high deficit in the international balance of payments, partly as a result of the decline in the price of semiconductors in the context of fierce international competition. From early 1997, highly indebted *chaebols*, such as Hanbo, Kia, and Jinro, went bankrupt. The massive amount of accumulated nonperforming loans had devastating effects on the balance sheets of major commercial banks. Meanwhile, the "Asian flu" (which spread from Southeast Asia beginning in 1997) affected the Korean financial markets and foreign lenders. Investors refused to rollover matured short-term loans and began to withdraw cash from Korea.[2] This, in turn, collapsed the Korea stock market and sharply depreciated the national currency, thereby rapidly exhausting the country's foreign reserves. On the brink of bankruptcy, the Korean government asked the International Monetary Fund (IMF) for a bailout in December 1997 and subsequently had to comply with IMF conditionalities, such as austerity measures. This further aggravated the economic situation by crunching credits and liquidities, escalating corporate bankruptcies, and skyrocketing unemployment.

The Korean economic crisis was thus not a simple crisis. It was indeed a complex set of multiple, overlapping, and interacting crises and crisis tendencies: (a) *a crisis of the developmental model* after democratization and liberalization (i.e., wage rises, increasing business–politics collusion and state-controlled distortion of finance, the lack of rational investment coordination, and increased rent-seeking); (b) *an international balance of payment crisis* due to the regional overproduction/capacity as a result of globalization and international competition in the post–Cold War and post–Bretton Woods contexts; (c) *a corporate and industrial crisis* due to the *chaebol's* overinvestment and excessive diversification based on high financial leverage or foreign debts (a foreign debt crisis due to the dependence on foreign capital as well as imprudent financial liberalization—which itself constitutes an economic policy crisis); (d) *a financial crisis* due to the risky financial arbitrage that borrowed short term and lent long term (especially to the *chaebol* and abroad); (e) *a foreign exchange crisis* due to the contagion of the "Asian flu" as well as speculative attacks and financial panics in the region; (f) *a political crisis* due to the imminent presidential election as well as the catastrophic balance of social forces—which, in turn, led to the economic reform failure and the crisis of corporate and financial crisis management; (g) the overkill of the so-called IMF crisis—which subjected the Korean economy to harsh macroeconomic conditionalities; and finally, (h) *a crisis of labor and livelihoods* as a result of mass bankruptcies and unemployment.

The complexity of a crisis such as Korea's invites a variety of interpretations and responses from different social actors, for such complexity can easily be reduced into different narratives that selectively highlight certain aspects of the crisis. However, not all of these interpretations and responses are equally influential, and only some discourses and practices are privileged and selected through political struggle. Thus, the discursive reduction of complexity as a primary basis of action is not merely epistemologically bounded but also—and what is more important—politically bounded.

THE POLITICS OF CRISIS DISCOURSE: NEOLIBERALISM AND ITS DISCONTENTS

In response to the Korean crisis, contrasting interpretations were proposed by different social actors: the IMF, the Korean government, the *chaebol*, and labor.[3] Such discursive variation from late 1997 to early or mid-1998 can be explained by the dialectic of path dependency and path shaping (see Grarrouste and Ioannides 2001). First, these interpretations were an attempt not only to defend the actors' positions and interests but also to understand the situation under conditions of limited time and information. Second, the interpretations depended largely on their previous strategic and discursive paths. Third (and most important), they were not only the basis of crisis management but also a means of social struggle aimed to lessen their burdens and burden other social actors by indicating who was to blame for the crisis (e.g. debtors or creditors, capital or labor). In short, through crisis interpretations and discourses, social actors tried to take advantage of the crisis as an opportunity to create and disseminate a path that was favorable to them. In this sense, the struggle over the meaning of the crisis constituted a critical and indispensable moment for subsequent development ('t Hart 1993; Hay 1996).

Political Struggles over the Meaning of the Crisis

The IMF's View: "Crony Capitalism"

The IMF's view of the Korean economic crisis was congruent with the infamous "crony capitalism" thesis, which argues that business–politics collusion results in "moral hazard"—that is risky investments for higher returns based on the belief that the government will pick the tab for investment losses for big businesses that are too big to fail. In particular, it suggested that the Korean financial system was undermined by: excessive government interference in the economy; close linkage between banks, conglomerates and the state, which distorted resource allocation; and inadequate sequencing of capital account liberalization, lacking prudential regulations that should accompany liberalization.[4] The IMF view thus pinpointed the longstanding lack of market discipline and efficiency in the economic system as the most fundamental cause of the crisis (IMF 1998; Fischer 1998).

The IMF called for full liberalization and deregulation of the financial system as well as the closure of insolvent banks and corporations. However, the IMF's prescription was not heavily based on its crisis interpretation. Indeed, much of it represented the ready-made IMF policy package or neoliberal Washington Consensus *and* Wall Street–led global financial capital's interests in profitable investment opportunities. Thus, the IMF prescribed the conventional IMF medicine for financial crisis—that is austerity policy (including high interest rates and fiscal surplus) and the full opening of Korean financial and capital markets and labor market flexibility to promote foreign takeover of Korean businesses.[5]

The Korean Government's View: The Lack of Democracy

The presidential election in December 1997 peacefully transferred power to the opposition party for the first time in Korean history. Though more sophisticated, the new Kim Dae Jung (DJ) government's view was basically the same as the IMF's. It suggested state-controlled finance and business–politics collusion as the cause of the crisis. However, in contrast to the IMF view, the DJ government's view did not limit itself to the technical analysis of the economic model. It politically criticized the previous authoritarian governments, alleging that the lack of democracy resulted in the longstanding problem of business–politics collusion that distorted resource allocation. As a consequence, commercial banks' lending decisions were made in favor of the *chaebol*, and, in turn, this led to the *chaebol*'s high debts, overinvestment, and excessive diversification (Ministry of Finance and Economy and Korean Development Institute 1999). In addition, the DJ government tried to scapegoat its civilian predecessor, the Kim Young Sam (YS)'s government, by putting the former finance minister and a presidential aide on trial.[6] This interpretation reflected not only the political rhetoric of Kim Dae Jung and his political party but also the discourses of the promarket and anti-*chaebol* intellectuals and the financially and globally oriented neoliberal faction within the economic bureaucracy, which had become significant social forces inside and outside the state since the 1987 democratization.

In line with this interpretation, the DJ government suggested the parallel development of "democracy and market economy" as an alternative. In particular, it called for the reform of the *chaebol*'s financial, business, and corporate governance structures to weaken their economic power and promote market competition: debt-to-equity ratio reduction, business specialization, the prohibition of cross-guarantees, shareholders increased participation, and so forth. In addition, it faithfully embraced the IMF's neoliberal prescription for financial liberalization and deregulation in order to liberate banking and finance from state control and attract foreign capital. Finally, in order to overcome the crisis, the DJ government called for equal "pain sharing" between the government, management, and labor, including *chaebol* reform and labor market flexibilization (Lee et al. 1999).

The Chaebol's View: The Failure of State-Controlled Economy and the IMF Conspiracy

The *chaebol*'s and their advocates' view was a sharp contrast to the IMF and DJ government's neoliberal view. First, the *chaebol* blamed the government regulation and interference rather than business–politics collusion: regulating long-term foreign borrowing led to excessive short-term borrowings; exchange rate manipulation led to the overvaluation of the national currency; politicians' and bureaucrats' interference in bank management led to risky lending behavior and, hence, mounting bad loans in the banking sector. Second, the *chaebol* criticized the IMF for inadequately dealing with the crisis. Though they welcomed the IMF's neoliberal demand for deregulation, liberalization, and labor market flexibilization, they criticized *chaebol* reform measures on corporate governance, debt-to-equity ratio, and so forth. The *chaebol* leaders even suspected that behind the IMF intervention was a conspiracy of highly developed countries to break up the *chaebol* and sell off their assets to foreigners at fire-sale prices. They also complained over the tight fiscal and monetary policy because it was killing many viable companies. Finally, the *chaebol* blamed domestic financial capital's refusal to extend credits during the crisis, and even audaciously claimed that people's "overconsumption" raised labor costs (Sohn 2000; Kim 1997; Choi et al. 1998; Kirk 2000).

In contrast, the *chaebol* did not particularly highlight the corporate industrial sector as a cause of the crisis and played down the scale of corporate bankruptcies in 1997. Although the *chaebol* admitted that their overoptimism about high growth and concentration on productive capacity expansion was a cause of the crisis, it was treated rather as one element of the entire "bubble economy" (Sohn 2000, 60-61). In this way, the *chaebol* blamed the IMF, the government, the financial sector, workers, and the people while obscuring their responsibility for the crisis. Indeed, since they believed that the corporate sector was not responsible for the crisis and remained healthy, many of the *chaebol* interpreted the crisis as intrinsically short term. For example, Kim Woo Choong, the chairman of Daewoo group and the Federation of Korean Industries, interpreted the crisis as a short-term phenomenon and, instead of downsizing his businesses, purchased Ssangyong Motors at the height of the financial crisis on 8 December 1997 (Kirk 2000, 28). Samsung and LG electronics also became more aggressive in research and development in the initial period of the crisis, again seeing it as short term (Lee 2002, 209).

Thus, some *chaebol* leaders suggested "old wisdom" under the "exportist" developmental state[7] as a solution to the crisis and tried to resist *chaebol* reforms. In the initial period, they even urged the government to freeze or postpone the corporate debt repayment to banks for a considerable length of time through an emergency presidential decree and to temporarily reintroduce a trade credit system to support exports, as the Korean developmental state once did for them in the 1970s (Sohn 2000, 118–19). Kim Woo Choong also claimed that exporting was the best strategy to recover from the crisis which he regarded merely as a short-term problem resulting from the shortage of foreign exchange (Kirk 2000, 50). However, this is inconsistent with their position that criticized the government intervention in general.

Korean Confederation of Trade Union's View: Employment Security and Wage Stabilization[8]

The Korean Confederation of Trade Unions (KCTU)'s interpretation of the crisis was the most comprehensive but lacked a distinctive alternative. The earlier response of the KCTU was to blame the *chaebol*, the government, and their collusion that distorted resource allocation and industrial structure (Kwon 1997). It reflected the KCTU's preexisting position on the *chaebol* problem but was not distinct from the IMF's and DJ government's views. However, it became more sophisticated after the IMF intervened with its bailout package. The KCTU located the causes of the crisis not only in domestic factors, such as the *chaebol*'s successive bankruptcies (due to the family-dominated governance, excessive diversification, high debt-to-equity ratio, excessive financial expenses, and low profitability), the banking sector (which concentrated loans to the *chaebol* and took excessive overseas borrowings in the short term), and political elites and bureaucrats who had developed a systematic relationship of collusion (corruption and bribery) with big business. It also clearly identified the exodus of international "hot money" and the IMF's intervention that caused a sharp decline in investor confidence with its structural reform plan and austerity policy as sharing responsibility for the crisis (Yoon 1997).

In this way, the KCTU offered a more sophisticated view on the crisis than the IMF and DJ government. It was also more consistent than the *chaebol*, which criticized and demanded government intervention simultaneously, and than the IMF, which introduced a ready-made policy and Wall Street agenda into the program without serious analysis. However, there was no causal focus in the KCTU's eclectic analysis. The government, the *chaebol*, the IMF, and "hot money" were blamed more or less equally. This is because its real strategic focus was "employment security and wage stabilization" (KCTU 1997). Accordingly, the KCTU did not develop its own distinctive program of structural reform. The KCTU's interpretation worked as a defensive argument that labor was not guilty and should not be sacrificed. It has never become a discursive basis for the overall structural reform of the Korean political economy.

The Politics of Discursive Variation

Politically Bounded Reduction of Complexity in Crisis Discourse

Table 4.1 summarizes discursive variation on the Korean economic crisis. Each discourse emphasizes different points and dynamics of the crisis (see Jessop 2004 on the discursive mediation of crisis). The bold characters signify alleged causes of the crisis, and the underlined words points to actors allegedly responsible for the crisis in each actor's interpretation.

Herbert A. Simon's notion of "bounded rationality" and Niklas Luhmann's notion of 'the reduction of complexity" suggest that starting from a certain entry point or systematizing the complex world in accordance with certain codes or criteria is not only an efficient and effective basis but also an inevitable feature of any attempts to deal with complex problems, such as the Korean economic crisis.[9] However, it does not mean that such boundedness or reduction is a purely cognitive matter, as can be seen in the Korean case. First, it can be said that these discourses understood the nature of the crisis differently by highlighting different aspects of the crisis in their discursive reduction of complexity ("Nature" column). Second, politically bounded, each interpretation concealed the pertinent actor's faults and exposed other social actors' deficiencies ("Causes and Villains" column). Third, each solution thus tried to turn the crisis into an opportunity to benefit the pertinent actor and impute the cost of crisis management to other actors ("Solution" column). For example, the IMF and DJ government focused on the crisis of the developmental model and the

Table 4.1 Politics of Discursive Variation on the Korean Economic Crisis

	Nature	Causes and Villains	Solutions
IMF (US and Wall Street)	System/Model crisis	Policy weakness: **State-controlled finance;** **State-bank-conglomerate collusion**	*"Washington Consensus"*: - Financial deregulation & liberalization; - Austerity policy; - Market opening
DJ Gov't	System/Model crisis	**Authoritarian politics:** **State-controlled finance;** **State-business collusion**	*"Democracy and Market Economy"*: - Financial deregulation & liberalization;
	Corporate/Industrial crisis	*Chaebol's* domination	- *Chaebol* reform - Market economy - Pain sharing (including labor market flexibilization)
Cf. YS Gov't	Foreign exchange crisis	Financial speculators' panic	
	Political crisis	Failure of economic reform: Opposition Party	
Chaebol	System/Model crisis	**State regulation** **State-controlled finance**	National protectionism & mercantilism: - Trade credits; - Export supports
	IMF crisis	**IMF's macroeconomic and labor policies** Reluctant banks; People's overconsumption and workers' high wage	- Debt reliefs
KCTU (no clear focus)	System/Model crisis	**State: politics-bank-chaebol collusion;**	- *Chaebol* reform
	Corporate/Industrial crisis	*Chaebol's* domination	
	Foreign exchange crisis	Financial speculators' panic	- Employment security and wage stabilization
	IMF crisis Livelihood crisis	**IMF's macroeconomic and labor policies**	

industrial/corporate sector and blamed authoritarian and/or corrupted governments and the *chaebol*. However, they were basically silent on the role of the financial panic and capital flight and the effects of the IMF's austerity policy. In contrast, the *chaebol* and KCTU criticized the IMF's neoliberal policy, but the *chaebol* were silent on their high debts and overinvestment. In turn, the IMF and DJ government demanded the sacrifice of the *chaebol* and, to a lesser extent, labor, but the *chaebol* demanded the government to support their business and exports, and the KCTU demanded job security. Here it is clear that the reduction of complexity in crisis discourse formation was not neutral but was politically bounded as a part of social and political struggle.

CRISIS DISCOURSE VERSUS CRISIS MANAGEMENT

In retrospect, it was the IMF's and the DJ government's interpretations that became dominant and widely accepted in Korean society in the initial period of the crisis and during crisis management. Indeed, the view is that the IMF program was more or less thoroughly implemented in Korea (in contrast to Indonesia, where its implementation was rather difficult) and that the DJ government strongly pushed forward structural reforms on the corporate, financial, labor, and public sectors. However, this process of structural adjustment, or better, crisis management, was not of the unilateral kind and did not fully reflect the dominant discourses that the IMF and DJ government originally put forward. In other words, the politics of discourse or discursive variation does not fully determine the politics of crisis management, including strategic selection and retention. The reasons are as follows. First, social actors are pressured to pretend to know everything clearly in their discourses, even though they do not—and cannot—fully understand the nature of the crisis in order to secure a better position in social struggles. Second, because crisis refers to a situation in which old prescriptions and solutions do not work, it is not surprising that such discourses significantly deviate from reality. Third, in their implementation, discourses need to be adjusted to structural and material realities, and these processes are, again, socially and politically mediated: hence, some gaps between ideological discourses and actual practices. Therefore, we need to examine the politics of actual crisis management beyond the politics of crisis discourse in order to understand the nature of strategic selection and retention.

THE POLITICS OF CRISIS MANAGEMENT: NEOLIBERALIZATION

Korea's economic restructuring under the IMF program was intrinsically political in two ways. First, it was an outcome of open and covert political struggles. Second, their outcomes (i.e. the economic restructuring processes) distributed the effects and burdens of the economic crisis unevenly among different social forces both internationally and nationally.[10] These processes, in turn, made the politics of crisis management distinct from politics of crisis discourses. They also had a critical effect on the process of strategic selection and retention and therefore on the subsequent developmental path of Korean capitalism.

Political Struggles over Crisis Management

International Struggle

Internationally, the US government became aware of the possibility of financial crisis early on but did not give a hint to the Korean government.[11] It also blocked the Japanese attempt to build the Asian Monetary Fund, which could have rescued Korea, in order to remain an economic hegemon in the region.[12] Finally, the US pressed the Korean government hard to seek a bailout from the IMF in which it had a commanding influence. The IMF program included harsh conditionalities that clearly represented the interests of US-backed, Wall Street–led global financial capitals that should duly have paid for their decisions on lending to *chaebols*, banks, and financial institutions. It thus unevenly distributed financial burdens and responsibilities between international creditors and domestic debtors. The IMF's standard assistance package included a policy of macroeconomic austerity designed to secure foreign debt repayment. In particular, it aimed to attract foreign capital with extremely high interest rates. In addition, it also stipulated financial liberalization and deregulation while regulating on Bank for International Settlement (BIS) capital adequacy ratio of banks and financial institutions. The IMF austerity policy and the banks' unwillingness to extend credits caused liquidity and credit crunches, the bankruptcy of many profitable businesses, and mass unemployment. In contrast, global financial capital secured the repayment of their loans with relatively high interest rates, with the Korean government's guarantee under the meditation of the IMF. It also obtained profitable investment opportunities with a further opening of Korean capital markets—indeed, 1997 was one of the best years in the history of Wall Street (Ji 2006, 214–15).

Nonetheless, the victory of the IMF (and the US Treasury) did not mean that the actual process of crisis management exactly followed their neoliberal interpretation of the crisis interpretation and its solution. In order to prevent the collapse of the Korean economy, the US Treasury had to "persuade" Wall Street to rollover Korea's short-term debts, and the IMF had to instruct G-7 countries to press their banks to rollover Korean debts on a daily basis for a while (i.e. politics–business collusion). In addition, the IMF organized a meeting for rescheduling Korea's foreign debts in which international banks demanded the Korean government guarantees for private debts (i.e. moral hazard). The emergency as well as hypocrisy played a great part in this international process of crisis management (Blustein 2001; Blustein and Chandler 1998).

Intranational Struggle

While the austerity and financial liberalization policy as such did not reflect the specific character of the Korean economic crisis, the IMF program also included structural reform plans suggested by the Korean economic bureaucrats during the negotiations. Thus, it shifted the domestic balance of forces and became an alibi for the neoliberal faction of the economic bureaucracy to pursue their reform agenda again: *chaebol* reform, financial liberalization, central-bank independence, labor market flexibilization, and so forth.[13] In addition, with the need to comply with the IMF conditionality, the election of a new government, and the urgent need to address economic emergency, by early 1998 the Korean state dramatically recovered the authority it lost in the previous year.

However, the Korean state's crisis management also significantly deviated from its official crisis discourse, as social and political struggles between the DJ's government, *chaebols*, banks, and labor unevenly distributed the burden of the crisis at the domestic level. First, despite the government's emphasis on equal pain sharing, it was labor and small- and medium-sized enterprises (SMEs) that paid the highest price for the crisis with mass bankruptcies and redundancies. Established in early 1998, the Tripartite Commission was originally expected to discuss the equal sharing of burden between labor, capital, and the government. However, the main issue on the table was labor market flexibilization. Korean neoliberals had sneaked this into the IMF program (Blustein 2001, 190–98) and claimed that it would be essential for raising international investors' confidence and attracting foreign capital. Indeed, inward foreign investment had become an absolutely necessary strategy of crisis management. In a speech on January 1998, Kim Dae Jung, then the president-elect, even argued: "It is not possible to live without foreign investment in a globalized economy . . . We have to welcome foreign investment . . . Redundancies are necessary for attracting foreign investors. In particular, they will make a very significant contribution to the rollover of short-term foreign debts" (cited in Park 1998, 281). Organized labor was defeated in this struggle and *de facto* forced to accept the revision of labor law to legalize mass redundancies and layoffs as well as manpower lease systems in large corporations. Thus, redundancy was legitimized, and management could then more easily persuade labor to accept wage freeze/cuts or earlier retirement programs. Furthermore, liquidity and credit crunches created by the IMF's austerity policy drove many of the SMEs and smaller *chaebols* into bankruptcies in the initial period of crisis. As a result, unemployment and unorganized, casual and contingent forms of employment sharply increased. In face of such threats, the labor movement has weakened with the decline of the already low unionization rate from 12.2 percent in 1997 to 10.1 percent in 2011.[14]

Second, despite the DJ government's hardline rhetoric, the largest *chaebols* avoided or resisted major reform and consolidated their domination of the Korean economy. This was because they had a strategic importance as an engine of growth and exports as well as the capacity to procure financial resources on their own. Except for the largely symbolic gesture on "The Big Deal," the government did not really press the top five *chaebols* (i.e. Hyundai, Samsung, LG, Daewoo, and SK) to reform on the ground that they had the capacity to restructure themselves.[15] Thus, the top five *chaebols* were in principle exempted from the government-guided and bank-led rationalization program called "workout." In addition, they did not suffer greatly from liquidity shortages because they were considered "too big to fail" in corporate bonds and papers markets. On the whole, corporate reform enhanced the top *chaebol*'s financial structure, and the rise of the exchange rate strengthened their international competitiveness. Most of top *chaebol* leaders retained their control over their business empire, and they returned this favor with the success in export markets. In particular, Samsung, LG, and Hyundai Motors emerged as top players in the global market by the early 2000s after they streamlined their business lines through "The Big Deal."[16]

Third, despite the rhetoric of promoting self-regulating markets, the DJ government, under the IMF regime, was never neutral and remained heavily engaged in *dirigist* activities. However, the point of state intervention was not industrial development or expansion, as it had been in the past. The crisis offered a splendid chance for Korea's neoliberal bureaucrats to resume financial liberalization that they had attempted but failed many times before. Thus, the DJ government was significantly biased towards finance and financial logic and prioritized the financial recovery of both the banking and corporate sectors, even at the loss of industrial capacity. Though many banks and financial institutions were closed down, the surviving banks were temporarily nationalized and rapidly recapitalized with massive public funds. The banks were then encouraged to expand their size and international competitiveness by attracting foreign capital and transforming into holding companies. In turn, as a proxy for the market mechanism, the creditor banks were expected to supervise the *chaebol*'s corporate restructuring from their own standpoint, independent of the *chaebol*. This resulted in the overall prioritization of debt repayment and interest payment in favor of financial capital. As a result of this financially oriented corporate restructuring, the traditionally cooperative and industry-friendly relationship between banks and corporations was reversed. No matter how promising their future prospects, unprofitable and insolvent businesses and industries with large debts had to be removed immediately. Sixteen out of the thirty largest business groups (as designated by the Fair Trade Commission in 1997) disappeared by 2003. Furthermore, despite special ties with the DJ government,[17] Daewoo, then the second largest *chaebol*, and part of Hyundai group (the largest *chaebol*), were dismantled in 1999 and 2000–2001, respectively, for they had exceptionally continued to practice their old but financially risky ways of doing business—that is aggressive investment based on high leverage, which was not permitted by the "IMF regime."

The Politics of Strategic Selection and Retention

The actual process of crisis management was defined by the complex political struggle between the IMF, the Korean government, the *chaebol*, and labor. It was distinct from the politics of crisis discourses because the struggle created some political and economic differentiation among the actors as well as significant gaps between dominant discourses and practices. Table 4.2 illustrates this point. The underlined characters indicate newly added or elaborated elements during the actual process of crisis management.

Politically Bounded Reduction of Complexity in Crisis Management

The political struggle differentiated the reduction of complexity in actual crisis management significantly from that in the dominant crisis discourse that the IMF and the Korean government originally put forward. Despite its discursive emphasis on the structural aspect of the crisis, that is Korea's longstanding problems such as business-politics collusion, state-controlled finance, and the resultant rent seeking of the *chaebol*, the Korean state initially focused on short-term solutions to quickly overcome the foreign exchange, foreign debt, international balance of payment, and financial crises. It thus promoted inward foreign investment and exports in various ways (including labor market flexibilization) to increase foreign-exchange reserves, repay foreign debts, and reduce current account deficits. In addition, it prioritized the recovery of the financial sector and put emphasis on the financial health of industrial corporations.

As a result, the discourse of equal "pain sharing" turned into labor market flexibilization, *chaebol* reform into *chaebol* dominance, and "the market economy" into the primacy of financial recovery in actual crisis management. In this sense, Korea's crisis management strategies became even more neoliberal than what the IMF and DJ government originally suggested. Behind this neoliberalization was the complex political struggle among social actors that frustrated some agenda but succeeded in promoting others: financial liberalization and market opening (the US and Korean neoliberals), international competitiveness and export (the *chaebol*), and quick recovery from crisis (the DJ government).

Strategic Selection and Retention in Crisis Management

This process, in turn, distributed the impact and burden of crisis management unevenly among social actors. It empowered and benefitted transnational capital, Korean neoliberal bureaucrats, banks and financial institutions, and some of the largest *chaebols*, at the expense of smaller *chaebols*, SMEs, workers, and organized labor. As a result, neoliberal strategies and practices were selected, retained, and reinforced.

First, this process involved the weakening, penalizing, or even removal of the social forces that continued old practices from the period of the developmental state. Thus, many *chaebols* went bankrupt and disappeared, and labor movement weakened significantly. With the extinction of the bearers of old strategies, old strategic practices also diminished. For example, as a result of labor market flexibilization, organized labor's more politically oriented militancy subsided. In addition, with the breakup of Daewoo and part of Hyundai groups, the *chaebol*'s traditional business strategy (i.e., high leverage, aggressive

Table 4.2 Politics of Crisis Management

	Discourse				Practice		
	Villains	Nature of Crisis	Solutions	Actual Solutions	Focus of Crisis Management	Winners & Losers	Strategic Selection & Retention
IMF (US and Wall Street) & DJ Gov't	Authoritarian government and corrupt politicians; Banks;	System/Model crisis	- "Washington Consensus" and "Democracy and Market Economy"; - Financial deregulation & liberalization;	- Financial deregulation & liberalization	System/Model crisis	Winners: Wall Street and global financial capital; Korean banks and Financial institutions; Some top *chaebols* (Samsung, LG, Hyundai Motors); Korean neoliberal bureaucrats, etc.	Selected/Retained practices Corporations: - Low leverage; - Cash flow and profits - Exportism; - Labor market flexibility
			- Austerity policy; - Market opening	- Austerity policy - Market opening & active foreign capital inducement	Foreign exchange crisis		Finance: - Enhanced prudence - Financialization & securitization; - Globalization;
	Chaebol	Corporate/ Industrial crisis	- *Chaebol reform*; - Market economy - Pain sharing (including labor market flexibilization)	- Exportism - *Chaebol reform*: Self-restructuring vs. "workout" - Primacy of financial recovery - Primacy of labor market flexibilization in pain sharing	International balance of payment crisis Corporate/ industrial crisis/ Financial crisis	Losers: Other top chaebols (Daewoo, part of Hyundai group); Smaller *chaebols*; SMEs; Organized labor; Workers, etc.	- Increase in household lending Labor: - Cooperative economism Extinct/declined practices: Corporations - High leverage; - Market share; - |Aggressive industrial investment/expansion; Finance - Corporate lending Labour - Labor militancy

investment, excessive diversification, and emphasis on market share) also largely came to an end.

Second, in contrast, this process greatly rewarded and reinforced social actors and forces that adopted or adapted to neoliberal strategies, such as foreign capital inducement, financial recovery, and labor market flexibilization. For example, many banks and financial institutions cleaned up their troubled assets and increased their size through public funding and foreign capital. In addition, as stated previously, the surviving top *chaebols*, such as Samsung, Hyundai Motors, and LG, grew even further through their success in export markets. Finally, the neoliberals' influence within the government had become strong enough to pursue neoliberal projects: to create a global financial center and a nexus of free-trade agreements in Korea.

Third, as a result of such experiences, neoliberal practices were diffused and reinforced. For example, through privatization and foreign shareholders' involvement, bank management became independent from the government and industries. As a result, banking strategies shifted from corporate loans towards household loans and securities investment in order to reduce risk exposure and increase financial health (as calculated by BIS capital adequacy ratio). Similarly, surviving *chaebols* reduced their debts (even below 100 percent), slowed down industrial investment, and focused on cash flow, profits, asset value, risk management, shareholder value, and so forth. In consequence, they increasingly financialized their business lines as well as attracted foreign capital, expanded exports, and made their workforce flexible. Finally, organized labor moved towards defensive and cooperative economics.

In sum, Korea's crisis management strategies such as export growth, foreign capital inducement, rapid financial recovery, and labor market flexibilization have critically conditioned and constrained the subsequent path of political economic development in Korea in a neoliberal manner. This is not only because the strategies were neoliberal but also, and more importantly, because the dominance of these strategies meant the neglect and marginalization of alternative strategies at the critical juncture of path-shaping. In other words, the complexity of the crisis was understood, managed, and reduced in a neoliberal manner, and as a result, Korean capitalism was quickly neoliberalized.

Neoliberalization as a Biased Solution to the Crisis

Because it reduced the complexity in a particular way, Korea's neoliberalization had its own price to pay. As discussed previously, the Korean economic crisis of 1997 was a complex set of multiple crises and crisis tendencies: the "crisis of the developmental model," "an international balance of payment crisis," "an industrial and corporate crisis," "a foreign debt crisis," "a financial crisis," "a foreign exchange crisis," "a political crisis," "an IMF crisis," and "a crisis of labor and people's livelihood." However, these were neither equally highlighted discursively nor equally addressed practically. Even when they were addressed, they were not adequately dealt with in practice. That is, Korea's neoliberal

Table 4.3   *Consequences of Neoliberal Crisis Management*

Crisis Type	Crisis Response	Consequences
System/Model Crisis	Discursively strong; practically weak	New forms of business–politics collusion (e.g. "Samsung Republic"); The continuation of rent seeking
Industrial/ Corporate Crisis		Limited chaebol reform; Economic and political dominance of top *chaebols*; Greater gap between big business and SMEs
Int'l Balance of Payment and Foreign Debt Crisis	Discursively strong; practically strong	Exportism and success in export markets; Excessive dependence on export markets; Stagnated domestic economy
Financial Crisis		Financial health; Financial profits; Decreased corporate loans and increased household loans/debts; Decline of corporate investment growth and "growth without employment"
Foreign Exchange Crisis		Growth of inward foreign investments; Foreign domination of the banking sector and stock markets; Increased financial instability
Political Crisis	Discursively weak; practically weak	Social disintegration; Intensified sociopolitical conflicts
IMF Crisis		Weakening of growth potential
Livelihood Crisis		Casualization of work; Increasing poverty; Socioeconomic polarization

crisis management highlighted or addressed certain crises while marginalizing or neglecting other ones. This means that, no matter how successful it might look, Korea's neoliberalization only offered a biased solution that could not adequately deal with other problems. Let me explain this further (see Table 4.3).

First, the IMF and DJ government neither highlighted nor adequately addressed "the IMF crisis," "the political crisis," or "the labor and people's livelihood crisis." The IMF denied the inadequacy of its monetary policy and was not concerned about how it would damage the economy and its growth potential. Despite its rhetoric of "pain sharing," the DJ government failed to secure social integration and the people's livelihood because it passed the cost of crisis management onto labor through labor market flexibilization, and its effort to minimize unemployment was largely limited. As a result, casual work, poverty, and socioeconomic polarization increased, and sociopolitical conflicts intensified.

Second, although the IMF and the DJ government's discourses highlighted "the crisis of the developmental model" and "the industrial and corporate crisis" as the fundamental causes of the crisis, the IMF and the DJ government could not address these issues adequately. IMF conditionality prohibited government subsidies to business corporations and state intervention in bank management. In addition, the DJ government promised to end business–politics collusion and state-controlled finance, and pushed forward *chaebol* reform. However, the DJ government had difficulties disciplining and reforming the largest *chaebols*. As a result, *chaebol* reform was limited, *chaebol*'s rent seeking continued, and the gap between big business and SMEs became even greater. Furthermore, top *chaebols*' political power became so great that even a new form of business–politics collusion, called the "Samsung Republic," emerged later in the Roh Moo Hyun government.

Finally, in a significant deviation from their original crisis discourse, the IMF and the DJ government focused on the "international balance of payment," "foreign debt," "foreign exchange," and "financial crises" in actual crisis management. Inward foreign direct investment, exports and financial recovery were prioritized over employment security, *chaebol* reform, and industrial development. This was done through financial liberalization, capital market opening, labor market flexibilization, exchange-rate stabilization, and the injection of public funds. Accordingly, the crisis was labeled (and also defined in practice as) "a financial crisis," or as "a foreign-exchange crisis." As a result, Korea's exports, the financial health of the banking and corporate sector, and inward foreign investment dramatically increased. Korea's postcrisis recovery was indeed remarkable in terms of capital accumulation. For example, ordinary profits (operating profits minus financial costs) relative to sales increased from -0.21 percent in 1997 to 7.03 percent in 2004, and 6.21 percent in 2005 (Bank of Korea Economic Statistics System n.d.).

However, neoliberalization had its own price to pay—new crisis tendencies from new strategies. "Exportism" has resulted in Korea's excessive dependence on export markets. According to *Joongang Daily* (8 January 2013), Korea's export relative to gross domestic product (GDP) was 57.3 percent in 2012. This means that Korea's economic performance heavily depends on the variation of external conditions. Besides, financial liberalization and the increase in inward foreign investments not only destabilized financial markets but also resulted in the foreign domination of stock markets and the banking sector. Foreigners' stock market investments have accounted for around 30 percent of the aggregate market value since the early 2000s (e.g. 37.5 percent in 2005, 27.2 percent in 2008, and 32.5 in 2012).[18] The massive inflow and outflow of foreign investments can have destabilizing effects on exchange rates as well as stock prices as in the Korean financial markets during the 2008 subprime mortgage crisis and the 2011 downgrading of the US sovereign ratings. In addition, foreigners came to hold about half of the shares in major commercial banks such as Kookmin, Shinhan, and Hana since the late 1990s. Furthermore, as a result of the shift in corporate and banking strategy, the proportion of household loans increased (from 32.6 percent in 1997 to 56.3 percent in 2005) and that of corporate loans decreased (from 64.6 percent in 1997 to 42.1 percent in 2005) in commercial banks' lending (Financial Supervisory Service, n.d.). In consequence, the growth of corporate investment tended to decline and economic growth no longer created as many jobs as before the crisis.[19] In addition, household debts relative to disposable income reached 153 percent in 2009, which was even higher than that in the United States at the time of the subprime crisis (138 percent) (Bank of Korea 2010). Finally, the "growth without employment" and mounting household debts, as well as the casualization of work and socioeconomic polarization, contributed to the contraction of domestic demand and to the relative stagnation of the domestic economy.

In short, despite the complexity of the crisis, only certain aspects of the crisis were highlighted and addressed adequately in the actual process of crisis management: hence the necessarily troubled neoliberalization of Korean capitalism.

CONCLUSION

In sum, the Korean economic crisis of 1997 provides a paradigmatic case for the study of the cultural political economy of crisis, crisis discourse, and crisis management. In particular, it shows how political struggles matter in the reduction of the complexity of capitalist crisis in its interpretation and management. The Korean crisis was of a particularly complex nature, and thus increased the scope of discursive variation and the reduction of complexity. The variation of crisis discourses reflected social forces' struggle to turn the crisis into an opportunity to advance their interests and transfer burdens to others. Initially, the IMF's and DJ government's neoliberal discourses became dominant, and they defined the postcrisis reform in the direction of financial deregulation and liberalization. However, these discourses were not implemented as originally formulated. This is because the process of crisis management involves dynamic political struggles that create some gaps between the initial discourse and putting them into practice.[20] Kim Dae Jung's attitude towards foreign investments, Korean neoliberal's own inputs, organized labor's defeat, and the *chaebol*'s resistance contributed to the even further neoliberalization of Korea by more or less ignoring the original discourses on equal pain sharing, *chaebol* reform, and self-regulating markets but instead pushing forward foreign capital inducements, financialization, labor market flexibilization, and governmental support for international competitiveness in export markets, which had not been particularly emphasized initially. The dominance of these practices in the process of crisis management resulted in the uneven distribution of the burdens of crisis and crisis management among social actors. As a result, at this critical juncture of political economic transformation, old strategies and their bearers vanished while neoliberal strategies and their containers were selected, retained, and reinforced. It thus created a neoliberal path of development in Korea. However, as neoliberalization addressed only part of the complexity rather than the totality of the crisis, it failed to address other aspects of the crisis adequately and created new crisis tendencies of its own.

NOTES

1. A version of this article is published in *Korean Political Science Review*, 47 (3). Unless otherwise stated, historical and factual data used in this article draw on Ji (2006, 2011).
2. The "Asian flu" refers to the financial crisis that affected the Asian region in 1997. The crisis was highly contagious due to the herd behaviour of investors who withdrew credits from the affected countries. The affected countries include Thailand, Indonesia, Malaysia, Hong Kong, and Korea.
3. However, this chapter does not deal with commercial banks' view on the crisis. They did not express their position clearly because they had no organization representing financial capital's interests that was comparable to the *chaebol*'s business association as well as no independent management from the government at the time of the crisis.
4. The Korean government imprudently liberalized short-term foreign debts while regulating long-term debts in the mid-1990s. As a result, short-term foreign debts increased sharply by 1997.
5. See Korea's Letter of Intent to the IMF on 3 and 24 December 1997 (Korea 1997a, 1997b).
6. In contrast, bureaucrats and politicians from the YS government (in courts, public hearings and their memoirs) denied their responsibility. They claimed that the crisis was mainly caused by irresistible external forces, that is the panic in global financial markets and the abrupt flight of capital. Also YS himself blamed DJ that his opposition party blocked economic reforms.
7. For the notion of "exportism" as a strategy specific to the postwar East Asian growth regime, see Sum (1998, 41–77).
8. This paper focuses on the Korean Confederation of Trade Unions (KCTU), the more progressive wing of the labor movement, rather than organized labor as a whole.
9. Simon's notion of "bounded rationality" indicates that because the limit to the amount of information the human brain can process and calculate, individuals and organizations consider only a small number of alternatives. Similarly, Luhmann argues that self-referential systems need to select, reduce, and organize the complexity with their own operational codes and programs in order to adapt to their complex environment. See Simon (1972) and Luhmann (1995).
10. David Easton defines politics as the authoritative allocation of social values. Similarly, the politics of crisis management can also be understood as the authoritative allocation of crisis effects and burdens. See Easton (1953).
11. Recently declassified US government documents show that, well before the outbreak of the crisis in October 1997, the Central Intelligence Agency (CIA) was aware of the possibility of a financial crisis in Korea. The CIA reported that "Korea's short-term debt to reserves ratio is the highest of any EMC [emerging market country]" (CIA 1997a, 2) and that "South Korea—with large amounts of short-term debt relative to reserves—may face a liquidity crunch if foreign banks cut credit lines" (CIA 1997b, 3).
12. In a recently declassified US government document, then US Treasury Secretary Robert Rubin reports to then US President Bill Clinton that "We were . . . successful in achieving our objective that the IMF remain at the center of the international monetary system and any international response to financial crises. The Japanese originally put forth a proposal for a large Asian Monetary Fund, . . . [but] in the

end, we were able to take [back] this proposal—which would have undercut both the IMF and the need for the Asian economies to adopt strong policy reforms—and frame it in a way that strengthening the international financial system" (Department of the Treasury 1997, 1).

13. In response to a question asked in a workshop held by a private economic research institute, John Dodsworth, the senior representative of the IMF in Korea, answered, "[You] asked me to distinguish which policies were made by the IMF, IBRD and the [Korean] government, but it is difficult to distinguish because we negotiated many times. As you know, the Koreans are very good at negotiation. . . . There were inputs from many people. From the IMF's viewpoint, the so-called 'Big Deal' reform isn't found in the IMF programme; neither is 200 percent cap on debt-to-equity ratio" Korea Economic Research Institute (1999, 84).

14. "Unionization Rate," the Korean Government, E-nara Index, http://index.go.kr/egams/stts/jsp/potal/stts/PO_STTS_IdxMain.jsp?idx_cd=1511&bbs=INDX_001 [accessed 24 January 2013].

15. "The Big Deal" refers to the state-mediated business swaps and mergers between top *chaebols* to streamline their business portfolio and reduce overcapacity in 1998.

16. In consequence, Samsung got rid of the troubled Samsung Motors, and LG Electronics got rid of its semiconductor division.

17. The Daewoo chairman was said to have supported DJ's election campaign, and Hyundai was involved with politically important businesses with North Korea and was a de facto agent of the government in the North.

18. See Korean Government, E-nara Index "Foreigners' Stock Investments," http://index.go.kr/egams/stts/jsp/potal/stts/PO_STTS_IdxMain.jsp?idx_cd=1086&bbs=INDX_001 [accessed 24 January 2013].

19. For example, the growth of equipment investment fell from 11.4 percent (1991–1996 average) to 4.7 percent (1998–2006 average). See Cho (2007, 32).

20. In this sense, crisis management is not fully driven by preexisting discourses or interests. Rather, the latter are continually modified and redefined through actual practices that involve learning. For more detailed argument, see Chapter 9 in Ji (2006).

References

't Hart, Paul. 1993. "Symbols, Rituals and Power: The Lost Dimensions of Crisis Management." *Journal of Contingencies and Crisis Management* 1: 36–50.

Bank of Korea. 2010. *Monetary Policy Report (September 2010)*. Seoul: Bank of Korea (in Korean).

Bank of Korea Economic Statistics System. n.d. *Financial Statement Analysis*. http://ecos.bok.or.kr [accessed 24 January 2013].

Blustein, Paul. 2001. *The Chastening: Inside the Crisis That Rocked the Global Financial System and Humbled the IMF*. New York: Public Affairs.

Blustein, Paul, and Clay Chandler. 1998. "Behind the S. Korean Bailout: Speed, Stealth, Consensus." *The Washington Post*. 28 December.

Campbell, Donald T. 1969. "Variation and Selective Retention in Socio-Cultural Evolution." *General Systems* XIV: 69–85.

Central Intelligence Agency. 1997a. *Intelligence Report—Emerging Market Financial Vulnerabilities Review*. 5 August. Office of Transnational Issues. Washington, DC: Central Intelligence Agency.

———. 1997b. *National Intelligence Daily*. 4 September. Director of Intelligence. Washington, DC: Central Intelligence Agency.

Cho, Young-Cheol. 2007. *Financial Globalization and the Direction of the Korean Economy*. Seoul: Humanitas (in Korean).

Choi, Jong Hyun et al. 1999. "A Letter to the IMF Director Mr. Camdessus on the National Economic Situation and Policy (February 9, 1998)." In *Command Economy? No More!*, edited by Jwa Sung-Hee, 272–76. Seoul: Nanam Publishing House (in Korean).

Department of the Treasury. 1997. *Background for APEC on Recent Developments in Asia.* 19 November. Washington, DC: Department of the Treasury.

Easton, David. 1953. *Political System.* New York: Knopf.

Financial Supervisory Service. n.d. *Bank Management Statistics.* Seoul: Financial Supervisory Service (in Korean).

Fischer, Stanley. 1998. "The Asian Crisis: A View from the IMF." *Journal of International Financial Management and Accounting* 9: 167–76.

Grarrouste, Pierre, and Stavros Ioannides, eds. 2001. *Evolution and Path Dependence in Economic Ideas.* Cheltenham: Elgar.

Hay, Colin. 1996. *Re-stating Social and Political Change.* Buckingham: Open University Press.

International Monetary Fund. 1998. *Annual Report of the Executive Board for the Financial Year Ended April 30, 1998.* 30 April. Washington, DC: International Monetary Fund.

Jessop, Bob. 2004. "Critical Semiotic Analysis and Cultural Political Economy." *Critical Discourse Studies* 1: 159–174.

Ji, Joo-Hyoung. 2006. "Learning from Crisis: Political Economy, Spatio-Temporality, and Crisis Management in South Korea, 1961–2002." PhD diss., Lancaster University.
———. 2011. *The Origins and Formation of Korean Neoliberalism.* Seoul: Chaeksesang (in Korean).

Kim, Jung Ho. 1997. "The Diagnosis and Prescription for the Foreign Exchange Crisis." 24 November. Seoul: Centre for Free Enterprise (in Korean).

Kirk, Donald. 2000. *Korean Crisis: Unraveling of the Miracle in the IMF Era.* Basingstoke: Macmillan.

Korea Economic Research Institute. 1999. *One and a Half Years after the IMF Economic Crisis: Assessment and Agenda.* Seoul: Korea Economic Research Institute (in Korean).

Korea, Republic of. 1997a. *The Letter of Intent to the IMF (and Korea—Memorandum on the Economic Program).* 3 December. Washington, DC: The International Monetary Fund.

Korea, Republic of. 1997b. *The Letter of Intent to the IMF.* 24 December. Washington, DC: The International Monetary Fund.

Korean Confederation of Trade Unions. 1997. "The KCTU Proposal for an Agreement to Overcome the Economic Crisis." 15 December. Seoul: Korean Confederation of Trade Unions.

Korean Government E-nara Index. n.d. "Labour Unionization Rate." http://index.go.kr/egams/stts/jsp/potal/stts/PO_STTS_IdxMain.jsp?idx_cd=1511&bbs=INDX_001 [accessed 24 January 2013].

Korean Government E-nara Index. n.d. "Foreigners' Stock Investments." http://index.go.kr/egams/stts/jsp/potal/stts/PO_STTS_IdxMain.jsp?idx_cd=1086&bbs = INDX_001 [accessed 24 January 2013].

Kwon, Young-Kil. 1997. "Korea at Cross-Roads: Crisis, Choices and Challenges: The Response of the Trade Union Movement." Paper presented at the European Union Korea Association, Seoul, Korea, 29 October.

Lee, Jong-Ho. 2002. *Corporate Learning and Radical Change: The Case of Korean Chaebol.* PhD diss., University of Durham.

Lee, Sun, Kyunghwi Min, Hyun-Joon Jang and Seyol Chong. 1999. *Democracy and the Market Economy: Theoretical and Economic Historical Examinations of DJnomics.* Seoul: Korean Institute for Industrial Economics and Trade (in Korean).

Luhmann, Niklas. 1995. *Social Systems.* Trans. by John Beduarz and D. Baeker. Stanford, CA: Stanford University Press.

Ministry of Finance and Economy. 1999. "The Road to Recovery in 1999: Korea's Ongoing Economic Reform," February.

Ministry of Finance and Economy and Korea Development Institute. 1999. *DJnomics: A New Foundation for the Korean Economy.* Seoul: Korea Development Institute.

Park, Jeong-Tae. 1998. *The Asian Economic Crisis 1997–1998.* Seoul: Bookie (in Korean).

Simon, Herbert A. 1972. "Theories of Bounded Rationality." In *Decision and Organization: A Volume in Honor of Jacob Marschak*, edited by Charles Bartlett McGuire and Roy Radne, 161–76. Amsterdam: North-Holland.

Sohn, Byung-Doo. 2000. *The Survival Strategies for the New Millennium: Beyond the Waves of the IMF.* Seoul: FKI Media (in Korean).

Sum, Ngai-Ling. 1998. "Theorizing Export-Oriented Economic Development in East Asian Newly-Industrializing Countries: A Regulationist Perspective." In *Dynamic Asia,* edited by I.G. Cook, M.A. Doel, R.Y.E. Li and Y. Wang, 41–77. Aldershot: Ashgate.

Yoon, Jin-Ho. 1997. "IMF Bailout and Employment Crisis: The Labor Response." 11 December. Seoul: KCTU Taskforce on the IMF.

5 The United States

Institutional Continuities, Reform, and "Critical Junctures"

Edward Ashbee, Copenhagen Business School

INTRODUCTION

"American exceptionalism" is an overused phrase. Nonetheless, there are significant differences between the forms of economic policy making pursued in the wake of the financial crisis in the US and those adopted in other Western countries. The crisis also affected the American political landscape in distinct ways.

In overall terms, the US policy response to the crisis can be characterized, to use Jonas Pontusson and Damian Raess' term, as "liberal Keynesian." Pontusson and Raess draw a distinction between liberal Keynesianism and the social Keynesianism that was adopted in earlier crisis periods.[1] Social Keynesianism, which informed the policies pursued in Sweden during the 1970s, and to a lesser extent, Germany, France, and (at least during 1974–1975) the US, was structured around the use of government expenditure increases in periods of recession. Tax concessions and other revenue reductions were for the most part on a lesser scale.[2] These increases in government spending were largely directed towards lower-income groupings. They created additional employment or saved existing jobs and expanded the scope of social provision through, for example, the extension of unemployment benefits (Pontusson and Raess 2012, 22–3). Such measures swelled overall demand levels and had long-run redistributive effects.[3]

In contrast, policy responses to the Great Recession have been largely characterized by liberal Keynesianism. Although there were significant government expenditure increases as the depth of the recession became fully evident, tax concessions constituted a large proportion of the overall stimulus packages that governments adopted. As Pontusson and Raess note:

> Whereas social Keynesianism emphasizes public spending and redistributive measures to sustain long-term prosperity, liberal Keynesianism focuses on demand stimulation during economic downturns and favors tax cuts over spending increases. (2012, 31)

Liberal Keynesianism has other defining characteristics. It seeks to alleviate the toll taken by recession rather than engage in long-run economic and social restructuring. In many countries, liberal Keynesianism turned towards fiscal retrenchment at an early stage and, once austerity became the principal economic policy-making goal, sought government expenditure reductions rather than revenue rises.

Nonetheless, although US policy responses lie, if taken collectively, towards the liberal end of the Keynesian continuum, they incorporate significantly more social elements than the recovery strategies adopted in Europe.[4] First, once the American Recovery and Reinvestment Act (ARRA) was signed in February 2009, the overall stimulus (if the measures adopted in both 2008 and 2009 are added together) was not only larger than the one adopted in other nations but also rested on expenditure programs to a greater extent than tax concessions. In March 2009, the Organization for Economic Co-operation and Development (OECD) published estimates of the relative size of the discretionary fiscal measures adopted in different countries. The US federal government had, at that point, committed itself to discretionary measures equivalent to 5.6 percent of 2008 Gross Domestic Product (GDP). In contrast, German measures amounted to 3 percent, those adopted in France totaled 0.6 percent, and the United Kingdom figure was 1.4 percent (adapted from *OECD Economic Outlook* 2009, 110). Third, although much of ARRA was structured around short-term measures that would sustain or create employment and ease the revenue crisis facing state and local governments, it also incorporated elements that aimed at longer-term forms of economic restructuring, including, for example, assistance for renewable energy projects. Fourth, although some other nations provided financial aid to their car industries, and government assistance was time limited, the "bailout" of Chrysler and General Motors recalled the forms of industrial policy pursued across some countries in earlier decades insofar as it sought to use government leverage and resources to restructure particular firms and sectors (Bermeo and Pontusson 2012, 13).[5] Fifth, whereas other nations turned away from stimulus policies and towards the retrenchment of government expenditure programs at a relatively early stage, the US had the capacity to delay the imposition of retrenchment measures. As other nations turned towards austerity, US policy makers forged compromise arrangements, such as those concluded in December 2010 that postponed tax rises and extended federal benefits. Sixth, the financial crisis set the stage for electoral victories by the left and opened the way for a substantive political reform process that drew, at least to a degree, upon the left's long-held agenda. In contrast, in many other countries, the right made electoral gains, and postcrisis retrenchment was tied to a sustained reduction in the size and capacity of the state. In the United Kingdom, it took a very pronounced form as Conservative Party strategists talked of constructing a "big society."

Nonetheless, despite these differences, the degree of economic and political change that followed in the wake of the financial crisis should not be overstated. This chapter considers the crisis as a "critical juncture," the hopes and aspirations of those who sought reform, the constrained character of the reforms that were pursued and enacted, and the reasons why the crisis did not lead to more far-reaching forms of change.[6] The chapter concludes by reflecting on the character of critical junctures and their relationship with processes of change.

REFORM PLANS AND PROCESSES OF CHANGE

The crisis period at the end of 2008 and beginning of 2009 appeared to constitute a "critical juncture." Established ideational certainties had seemingly been shaken up as the Bush administration had embraced the politics of the "bailout" and amidst talk of an electoral realignment that had established the Democrats as the hegemonic party. There was a sense of institutional fluidity and perceptions that actors could shape outcomes in ways that had not been attainable in noncrisis periods. The words of incoming White House Chief of Staff Rahm Emanuel have been widely cited: "Never let a serious crisis go to waste. What I mean by that is it's an opportunity to do things you couldn't do before" (quoted in *The Wall Street Journal* 2009, paragraph 1).

Those who sought reform or hoped to utilize the openings presented in a moment of crisis drew upon the policy critique of the neoliberal order put forward by commentators (including figures such as Robert Reich, Robert Kuttner, and Joseph Stiglitz) who might, in this context, be dubbed policy or, perhaps, "norm entrepreneurs," and through the reports and studies published by movement think tanks, including the Economic Policy Institute. They brought together policy ideas that were in part derived from "paths not taken" at an earlier point and, just as importantly, particular representations of "paths taken" in earlier decades and in other countries. The reform critique drew on particular understandings of European social provision and industrial policy in the "coordinated market economies" while at the same time building on economic policy themes that invoked representations of the New Deal and were more specifically American in character. It put forward an indictment of the American economy, incorporated and built upon a set of background assumptions derived from notions of justice and equity long associated with the left, and sought to counter widely held claims that growth and national competiveness were a function of market freedom.

The critique had six principal components. First, it drew attention to the long-run stagnation in real median incomes and growing income inequality. Inequality was not only a matter of social justice but, from this perspective, held back demand levels and thereby fuelled the credit explosion that paved the way for the financial crisis. Second, although they distanced themselves from earlier *dirigiste* versions and instead branded it as a "competitiveness" strategy, commentators drew upon earlier notions of industrial policy, whereby government would invest, or harness, private-sector investment in industries and sectors that would have importance in terms of comparative advantage and long-run economic growth. The suggestions of industrial policy were, however, updated so as to emphasize the new technology sector and the strategic significance of, for example, broadband expansion to the country's economic future. Third, there had to be a much greater level of state investment in human capital, particularly in education and health. Robert Kuttner (a cofounder of the Economic Policy Institute) pointed to the European countries, particularly those in the Nordic region, as examples of economies that offered extensive social provision but were at the same time economically successful. Kuttner focused on the Danish model of *"flexicurity,"* which appeared to combine labor-market flexibility with an assured income (Kuttner 2008, 154–59). Fourth, there was an echo of John Kenneth Galbraith's celebrated 1958 indictment of "private affluence" and "public squalor." From this, Democratic Party reformers argued for the resurrection of public services and the country's decaying physical infrastructure. Fifth, the reform critique conveyed representations of countervailing power. Labor, it was said, had been so profoundly weakened that political and economic elites were largely unchallenged. This absence of restraint had allowed neoliberalism to pursue a policy of marginal tax reductions and deregulation. It had imposed a culture of hypercompetitive short-termism, based upon low wages and labor market insecurity while at the same time hobbling the long-run prospects for the US economy. Last, capital itself had become increasingly unbalanced and lopsided as Wall Street and the financial sector displaced manufacturing processes. To a degree, earlier populist critiques, which had portrayed financiers and "rentier" capitalism as inherently parasitic, fused with contemporary representations of Wall Street and the ways in which the housing bubble that preceded the financial crisis had distorted more "natural" forms of economic activity.

Despite the forcefulness with which this critique was sometimes advanced, most of those who sought reform did not think of displacing established institutional structures but instead accepted the need to seek less direct forms of change. For the most part, they were very conscious of the array of institutional and structural obstacles that they confronted. Some, either consciously or unconsciously, thought in terms of what scholars of institutional change have termed "conversion," "layering," and "drift." *Conversion* refers to changes in the interpretation of institutional rules and the ways in which they are applied (Mahoney and Thelen 2010, 17). *Layering* describes the imposition of new arrangements on top of established structures or alongside older arrangements. *Drift* refers to the ways in which institutional arrangements fail to keep pace (often because of deliberate political intent rather than inertia) with broad contextual shifts, thereby changing the character of their impact (Streeck and Thelen 2005, 18–27). These are incongruent or subversive forms of change insofar as, although their intent may be obscured, they contribute to the erosion and undermining of the existing institutional architecture and the construction of new arrangements. Former speaker of the House of Representatives, Newt Gingrich, was exceptionally candid in talking of the ways in which the seeking of private-sector arrangements would undermine Medicare. In remarks to a 1995 conference, he reportedly said: "Now, we don't get rid of it in round one because we don't think that that's politically smart, and we don't think that's the right way to go through a transition. But we believe it's going to wither on the vine because we think people are voluntarily going to leave it—voluntarily" (quoted in *The New York Times* 1996, paragraph 5).

As the financial crisis unfolded, there were suggestions that incongruent change was indeed taking place. It seemed that the dramatic collapse of the private sector in 2008–2009, taken together with the automatic processes governing fiscal policy, would, by adding to government expenditure in a period of recession, enlarge the role of government in ways that would be difficult or impossible to roll back at a later stage. According to *The International Herald Tribune*: "We are seeing a paradigm shift towards a more European, a more social state" (quoted in Steinmo 2010, 3). A February 2009 edition of *Newsweek* proclaimed: "We Are All Socialists Now: The Perils and Promise of the New Era of Big Government." It went on to assert that "in the absence of a robust private sector, the government will fill in the gap" (quoted in Benoit 2009). According to one of the magazine's contributors: "Whether we like it or not—or even whether many people have thought much about it or not—the numbers clearly suggest that we are headed in a more European direction." (Meacham 2009, paragraph 6). He tied this to the expansion of government during both the Bush and Obama presidencies and the long-term growth of spending on Social Security and Medicare: "As entitlement spending rises over the next decade, we will become even more French" (Meacham 2009, paragraph 6).

There were also hopes that discretionary policy changes would add to the effects of these processes. John Judis, veteran contributor to *The New Republic*, suggested that the ARRA, the large-scale fiscal stimulus adopted in February 2009, when taken together with the Fiscal Year 2010 federal budget had, whatever Obama's initial thinking about the role of government, begun a process of radical transformation with its own logic and dynamic:

> There is the sheer size of Obama's intervention . . . as has happened before, the extent of government intervention is likely to remain permanent. At the least, the Obama budgets will shift even more dramatically the balance of economic power away from the private and toward the public sector. The American relationship of state to economy will begin to look more like that of France and Sweden. (Judis 2009, paragraphs 9-10)

CONGRUENT INSTITUTIONAL CHANGE

During its first two years, the Obama administration and congressional Democrats secured three major policy changes: the ARRA (the $833 billion fiscal stimulus), the Patient Protection and Affordable Care Act (ACA), and the Dodd-Frank Wall Street Reform and Consumer Protection Act. Despite the large-scale character of these reforms, they should be set in perspective. Although their provisions led to further partisan polarization, they in many ways represented significant retreats when set against the earlier hopes of Democratic reformers. The forms of *incongruent* change that some had had talked of during 2008–2009, when they spoke of a shift towards the European model, were not realized. If the size of the American state is considered through government expenditure as a proportion of GDP, it fell back after 2009, and White

House projections envisaged, on the basis of assumptions about economic growth rates, a further rolling back. Whereas federal government outlays had constituted 25.2 percent of GDP in 2009, the figure was to be reduced to 22.2 percent by 2017 (The White House 2012).

Furthermore, the major reforms enacted by the 111th Congress and the Obama administration were limited insofar as they were constructed on top of, or alongside, existing institutional structures. In other words, as Theda Skocpol and Lawrence Jacobs have noted, they provided "revised frameworks for already pervasive federal regulations, benefits, and taxes—but not first-time interventions" (Skocpol and Jacobs 2011, 35). Whereas the New Deal led, despite the limitations noted below, to the creation of myriad new government agencies, and the growing might of the executive branch redefined its relationship with Congress, the Obama reforms were much more modest. They can for the most part be regarded, if the concepts associated with institutional change are employed, as *congruent* forms of conversion, layering and drift insofar as, in a bow to the processes of path dependency, they did not seek to subvert or erode established institutional frameworks but instead extended the level of provision, the intensity of application, and the extent of their coverage.

Although the ARRA temporarily changed the balance between fiscal and monetary policy, and created some new forms of employment, the primary purpose of the act was to save existing employment and services primarily within the public sector. Although some commentators have subsequently stressed the place of industrial policy within the Act (a process that critics charge rests upon picking "winners" and "losers"), it was limited.[7]

While the Dodd-Frank Act created some new structures and institutions (most notably, the Financial Stability Oversight Council, the Office of Financial Research, and the Bureau of Consumer Financial Protection), its overall effects are still uncertain. The details of the implementation process were largely left to regulatory bodies leaving those details open to a prolonged period of contestation. A banker cited by *The Economist* forecasted a "decade of grind, with constant disputes in courts and legislatures, finally producing a regime riddled with exceptions and nuances" (*The Economist* 2012, paragraph 6). In broad terms, the Act sought to add to the existing regulatory process rather than supplant the overall regulatory architecture. Although there were elements of conversion, much of the Act can be understood as congruent layering. The Financial Stability Oversight Council seemed to add to the functions of the twelve Federal Reserve Banks that were created in 1913 to curb market panics:

> In Washington, when a bureaucracy fails to accomplish its assigned goal politicians typically don't do away with the agency, they create another agency with the same goal. That's how we got the FSOC. (McKinley and Fitton 2012, paragraph 10)

Furthermore, the Act left some sectors, most notably Fannie Mae and Freddie Mac, largely untouched (*The Economist* 2012). Arguably, it was too heavily shaped by the risks exposed in 2007–2008, thereby failing to address other forms of risk. It may also have maintained the notion that the biggest "systemically significant" banks are simply "too big to fail," or as one commentator put it, "too interconnected to fail" (Hensarling 2012).

Broadly similar conclusions can be drawn if health-care reform is considered. In place of "socialized medicine" or the single-payer arrangements that define health provision in Europe, the ACA built on the existing framework of health-care provision. As has been said, "it was like adding a new wing to a dilapidated house" (quoted in Luce 2012, 35).[8]

The ACA did not challenge the structural character of existing institutional arrangements. Instead, it sought to build on the existing institutional architecture by providing clusters of incentives, disincentives, and mandates to different actors. Insurers were, for example, required to provide cover for most applicants with preexisting conditions but were "rewarded" with the individual mandate (requiring that individuals take out insurance coverage) that promised to bring in swathes of new purchasers, many of whom would be relatively young and in comparatively good health.

Measures within the legislation that could have provided a form of *incongruent* layering were scaled back. In particular, although included in the version of the bill passed by the US House of Representatives, the "public option" within health-care reform was abandoned. Proposals for a "public option" took different forms. However, in most of these forms, government insurance would lead to the progressive "crowding out" of the private insurance companies. Many on the right saw the danger. In an October 2009 article, Iowa Republican Senator Chuck Grassley asserted: "The government is not a fair competitor. . . . It's a predator" (quoted in Benen 2009, paragraph 2). There was opposition among some Democrats as well as Republicans. Senator Blanche Lincoln stated that: "One of our biggest concerns is that it doesn't need to be a government plan that usurps that ability to compete in the marketplace, which I'm concerned that a totally government-run option would do" (quoted in Beckel 2009). These concerns, taken together with the many veto points facing legislation in the US Congress, led to the abandonment of the "public option." A *Washington Post* blog noted:

> By summer 2009, liberals were adamant that the public option was central to health care reform, to the point that some wound up opposing health reform when the voters weren't there to include it. And now? It's apparently been forgotten. (Bernstein 2012, paragraph 2)

REPRESENTATIONS OF THE ECONOMIC CRISIS

Why did the crisis and, alongside it, the promise held out by the 2008 presidential election, give rise to only limited and constrained reforms that, taken in aggregate, constituted *congruent* change—or institutional extension—rather than displacement? Put another way, why did a "critical juncture," which by definition would seemingly offer opportunities for radical change, largely reproduce rather than restructure precrisis institutional arrangements?

The answer is to some degree ideational. Exogenous shocks and the critical junctures that arise in their wake have to be represented, interpreted, and understood. The different understandings that take shape, and in some circumstances solidify, give rise to different forms of politics and to different types of coalitional bloc.

In the transition period between the presidential election and his inauguration, and during the early months of his presidency, the Obama team defined the crisis and the demand deficiency arising from the bursting of a financial bubble that as a consequence of market excesses. Against this background, many of those around Obama who had occupied key positions in the Clinton administration and embraced many of the defining tenets of neoliberal economics now endorsed a large-scale fiscal stimulus and other forms of government interventionism; the overall crisis was understood as a "special case" within the market order. Such a special case required dramatic measures from which more orthodox market adherents would shrink. Figures such as Lawrence Summers and Peter Orszag (who was to become director of the Office of Management and Budget) had been schooled by financial crises in countries such as South Korea and Mexico during the 1990s and believed in the use of overwhelming force by governments and central banks. The phrase "overwhelming force" was, Noam Scheiber suggests, uttered "like a ritual incantation" (Scheiber 2011 30). Correspondingly, in a crisis period defined by uncertainty and anxiety, fiscal measures had to be large enough to sway the economic decisions of both firms and households.

Such representations laid the basis for ARRA and other measures. Their thinking was, however, constrained by an internalized recognition of the ways in which institutionalized veto points put limits on their capacity for action, despite the unambiguous character of the November 2008 election results.[9] Thus, as discussions continued within the transition team during December 2008, Obama's advisers reduced the scale of the proposed stimulus. A memo that Lawrence Summers (President Clinton's treasury secretary, who was to become director of the National Economic Council in the Obama administration) submitted to the president-elect excluded the option of a $1.2 trillion figure that Christina Romer (incoming chair of the Council of Economic Advisers) had included as a compromise in place of her belief that the US economy required an $1.8 trillion stimulus if recovery was to be assured. Only the $600 billion and $800 billion options were included. The incoming White House chief of staff, Rahm Emanuel, reportedly insisted that "one point two trillion dollars is nonplanetary" (quoted in Scheiber 2011, 41). At the same time, the economic goals underpinning the fiscal stimulus were modified. As output levels fell dramatically, it was becoming evident that the crisis would be deeper, and as a consequence more prolonged, than some had initially anticipated. Within such a context there were limits to the capacity of government. Despite the hopes of some, the December 2008 memo that Summers submitted to the president-elect represented the stimulus as an "insurance package against catastrophic failure" rather than a means of securing economic recovery (quoted in Scheiber 2011, 41).

At about the same time, there was an increasingly solidified conviction within the administration that the markets would react negatively to what they saw as excessive levels of government spending and borrowing. There were perceptions that a stimulus much above the amount that was decided upon would require borrowing that would crowd out the private sector and thereby place employment and growth in jeopardy. While the US had much more long-run and short-run leeway than other nations because of the role of the dollar as a reserve currency and fears about the fate of other countries, the memo used language associated with Peter Orszag to point out that a very large stimulus would cause anxiety among government bondholders who feared the consequences of higher budget deficits (Scheiber 2011, 40). Summers also reportedly resisted the inclusion of large-scale infrastructural projects within the stimulus package (Skocpol and Jacobs 2011, 17).

Ideational factors should be considered at mass as well as elite level. As Colin Hay notes, policy making may remain within a preexisting paradigm even if there are policy failures. Indeed, without:

> [W]ide-scale public debate about such policy failures and fiascoes that manages to link policy contradictions to a more generic sense of crisis . . . the narration and definition of the problem is likely to remain internal to the state apparatus itself. Under such circumstances the likely consequence is iterative (as opposed to fundamental) policy modifications within the parameters defined by the existing policy paradigm. (2001, 200)

Thus, paradigmatic shifts depend upon a sense of "crisis" among substantial sections of the population and the embrace of ideas tied to a new paradigm. Without this, policy making continues within existing frameworks.

There was indeed a wide-scale sense of crisis as the events of 2008 and 2009 evolved. By early October 2008, 59 percent of respondents asked in a CNN/ Opinion Research Corporation poll believed that it was "somewhat" or "very" likely that the US was entering a depression comparable with that of the 1930s (PollingReport.com 2008). However, a sense of crisis is necessary, but not sufficient. Paradigmatic shifts also require a sense of political efficacy and a degree of faith in counterhegemonic crisis narratives. During much of the crisis, and even, it seems, at its most intense, there was considerable fatalism that was tied to skepticism about the capacities and usefulness of government. At the end of February 2009, an NBC News/*Wall Street Journal* poll asked about ARRA and the extent to which respondents felt that it would assist the US economy. Just 8 percent said "a great deal." More than half (51 percent) said "only a little" (PollingReport.com 2009.)

INSTITUTIONAL CLUTTERING

Ideas, perceptions, and understandings, whether at elite or mass level, only secure traction in particular institutional circumstances (Hansen and King

2001). In other words, they require particular institutional and ideational contexts within which they can secure political credibility, and which will bring forth ideational entrepreneurs who are willing and able to bring policy ideas forward and the ability to employ "appropriate framing resources" (Béland 2009, 702). Indeed, there is a process of interaction between ideas, the discretionary choices made by actors, institutions, and, as noted below, underlying structural variables. Actors adjust and reframe ideas within the parameters of their perceived credibility. That credibility is shaped in significant part by the institutional paths that have formed over time.

There is a danger, if the part played by those institutional paths or structural variables is not acknowledged and integrated within accounts of junctures and change, of inflating agency and the degree of discretion given to actors. Although, as Stephen Bell argues, the impact of institutions and the ways in which paths affect actors "are substantially constituted by agents themselves through ideational processes and choices and there are times when actors come to the fore ... more ordinarily, institutions confront agents in the here and now as embedded, already structured terrains" (Bell 2011, 890). Choices are, in practice, constrained, although the precise character and location of those constraints is subject to a continual process of contestation and shift. Thus, although path dependency does not impose the rigid set of policy constraints depicted in some caricatures, it does influence outcomes in periods of both crisis and noncrisis. As Bell notes:

> Institutional or structural environments can exert real (though always interpreted) effects by imposing costs or benefits on agents, by shaping actor interpretations and preferences, the scope of "bounded discretion" of agents in institutional life, and the resources and opportunities that are available to actors. (2011, 892)

In part, the choices facing policy makers in the Great Recession were shaped by the formal institutional variables stressed by the old institutionalism. As has been widely noted, the checks and balances that define the US system of constitutional government (taken together with institutionalized rules, such as the requirement for supermajority in the US Senate) and the degree of partisan polarization imposed countless de jure and de facto veto points on the legislative process.[10] Despite Obama's declared commitment to "postpartisanship," ARRA secured just three Republican votes. The fate of the ACA hung in the balance and was only passed in the Senate in its final form through the use of the reconciliation process, which requires only a simple majority.

However, "old" or formal institutionalism can only provide part of the answer. As Theda Skocpol and Lawrence Jacobs note, the broader institutional landscape, much of which lay beyond the Washington DC beltway, should also be considered. It was highly "cluttered." Indeed, there is a much higher level of cluttering than in the 1930s. That cluttering stems from the expansion of government and the extended character of institutional arrangements that have created large clusters of constituencies that, when change seems likely, define themselves, however inchoately, as "winners" or "losers." Skocpol and Jacobs have noted the ways in which all of this created formidable political obstacles for the Obama administration:

> He is not starting from scratch like FDR was. He is redirecting resources—and at the same time necessarily asking some citizens and interests already enjoying regulatory advantages, governmental subsidies or benefits, and tax breaks to accept less. (Skocpol and Jacobs 2011, 35–6)[11]

Cluttering has particular significance in creating obstacles to reform because the American state has an exceptionally pliable and porous character. Desmond King and Lawrence Jacobs refer to "the administrative state's generally porous, easily penetrated boundaries" (Jacobs and King 2010, 798). Studies such as these emphasize the absence of independent expertise and authority in the upper echelons of the state apparatus; the state's size and sprawling character; the structural jostling between Congress and the executive branch; the extent of dependence upon external sources of policy formulation; the degree to which commercial and financial interests penetrate the state through the character of those appointed to senior positions in the administration and the federal bureaucracy (many of whom are drawn from, e.g. Wall Street); the "revolving door" between public service and corporations; the degree of access that influential lobbies have to members of Congress and administration members (a process arguably facilitated by campaign contributions); the extent of "producer capture" within particular departments, agencies, and bureaus; the close associations between regulatory commissions and those that are the subject of regulation; and the extent to which decision-making processes (particularly the making of the annual budget) are subject to prolonged periods of uncertainty, instability, and doubt. Within this context, different and in some cases relatively small constituencies can exert significant influence, particularly in preventing the passage of legislation or the imposition of regulatory measures.

The effects of institutional cluttering have been compounded by a further factor. In the US, the growth of government provision took a more piecemeal, partial, and incremental form than in many of the western European countries where reform, whether driven by social democracy or conservatism, often had a broader character. Furthermore, when the American state expanded, as, for example, in the Progressive era, it was often in tandem with different blocs and coalitions (King and Stears 2011, 507).

As a consequence, social and economic reform led to the formation of, or bolstered, constituencies, and at the same time laid a basis for particularistic and often competing notions of self-interest. Often it deepened the cleavages between constituencies and at the same time limited the circumstances in which coalitional interest blocs (whereby a cluster of constituencies come to perceive a shared commonality of interest) might take shape. Reform efforts had therefore to negotiate amidst and between these representations of self-interest. The challenges this imposed are evident, if Medicare is considered.

Polling data suggest that many Medicare recipients, and those who would become eligible for Medicare within a relatively short period, constituted what E. E. Schattschneider, in his celebrated account of reform, termed "fighting legions."[12] There were anxieties that the extension of health-care coverage to others would "dilute" the provision they themselves received. As a consequence, there was significantly greater opposition to the ACA among senior citizens (Kaiser Family Foundation 2010). Similarly, business organizations feared the cost implications once firms became subject to financial penalties under the provisions of the Act if they failed to offer "affordable care." As the US Chamber of Commerce argued: "It imposes mandates and penalties on businesses that will slow economic growth and job creation at a time we can ill afford it" (United States Chamber of Commerce 2012, paragraph 3).

UNDERLYING STRUCTURAL VARIABLES

The logics imposed by certain underlying structural economic variables, and representations of them, were also in play. They shape the relative "stickiness," or pliability, of a particular institutional path. As Jonas Pontusson noted in a study of the car industry: "Corporate choices regarding technology and works organization can, in large measure, be seen as responses to the structure of constraints and opportunities set by product markets, labor markets, and capital markets" (Pontusson 1995, 126). Structural variables such as these, Pontusson suggests, interact with institutional structures. They "influence political or economic actors through institutional arrangements, and it is both pointless and impossible to assign separate explanatory weight to these variables" (Pontusson 1995, 144). Moving beyond particular industrial sectors, structural variables include the extent of the output gap in periods of recession; factor endowments in particular countries; the distribution of income and wealth; the extent to which the economy is open (measured through the contribution of exports and imports to GDP); the occupational structure; the sectoral composition of industry; productivity rates; the structure and character of the government budget; and the defining characteristics of many capital, exchange, commodity, and labor markets. Arguably, the US has comparative institutional advantages in the provision of financial services, thereby leading policy makers towards deregulatory policies (Iversen and Soskice 2012, 35). Furthermore, the weight of interest payments and the growth of "entitlement" spending have alone imposed substantial constraints on contemporary policy makers. As Paul Pierson notes, politicians have, since about 1980, been "bill collectors for previous promises" (Pierson 2007, 37).

This is not to suggest that the linkages between the economy and institutional structures have an unproblematic or straightforward character. Within particular countries, the relationship between variables and institutional paths may be mediated through, for example, the modes of coordination between firms, the distribution of political power, and the differential abilities of constituencies to mobilize politically. Furthermore, as noted previously, there are processes of interaction between structures, institutions, and ideas. Thus, the impact of underlying economic variables should not been seen through the prism that Frank Dobbin calls "economic realism," which suggests that "economic reality is singular, and conforms everywhere to the same external laws" and thereby asserts that "functional requisites appear to determine policy choices" (Dobbin 1994, 7). As Mark Blyth stresses, the economic logic of the Great Depression during the 1930s provoked a diversity of political responses, including the New Deal, Swedish social democracy, the French emphasis on the franc's exchange rate, and fascism (Blyth 2007, 763–764). Indeed, there is no necessary, inherent, or functional "pull" towards economic efficiency or the most economically optimal outcomes.

Nonetheless, although there are different economic realities, and economically suboptimal arrangements persist through processes of path dependence, some constructions have primacy over others. While there are counterhegemonic discourses structured around populist hostility to the larger firms and the banking sector, firms, and business, organizations have generally been pivotal in defining economic realities. Such "realities" impose parameters on the pursuit of particular paths and at the same time shape the relative stickiness of those parameters. Although the peak business organizations, such as the US Chamber of Commerce, gave cautious backing to the passage of ARRA, they opposed Dodd-Frank and the ACA. Indeed, relations between the Obama White House and business deteriorated badly during 2009 and 2010 as business interests criticized the costs of regulation and the uncertainty that, they asserted, Democratic policy making had created.

The role that business interests play in defining what is or is not economically feasible stems in part from structural power but also from the porosity and permeability of the federal government apparatus. In such a context, those with extensive and largely concentrated resources hold institutional sway within the policy networks that form between legislators, executive branch officials, and outside interests. This has ideational consequences. The formation and character of such networks narrow "the range of ideas likely to receive a hearing as it establishes authoritative voices and modes of discourse" (Weir 1992, 210).

THE CRISIS AND CRITICAL JUNCTURES

Others have also noted the limited character of institutional change in the US during 2009 and 2010, and the extent to which the period was characterized by institutional extension rather than displacement: "Rather than restructure the American political economy, the financial crisis highlighted its dominant features" (McCarty 2012, 226).

This raises broader questions about the character of crises and critical junctures, and the extent to which they offer opportunities for path-departing measures. As noted above, crises have customarily been represented in much of the literature as relatively short moments of flux, triggered by exogenous shocks, in which institutional constraints are radically loosened and, as a consequence, contingency and agency become paramount. In such moments, as Stephen Bell puts it in a critique of such approaches, "only ideas appear to matter in informing agents about their interests and strategies in shaping institutional change" (Bell 2011, 888). Furthermore, during critical junctures, there is a "substantially heightened probability" that the policy choices made by actors will affect and shape political outcomes (Capoccia and Kelemen 2007, 348). Once a juncture has passed, decisions that were made will have set off "sticky" path-dependent processes that will solidify over a relatively long time period.[13] It is, in at least its classical form, a "punctuated equilibrium" model.

However, the concept of a critical juncture raises some difficulties.[14] It is often tied, in some cases by definition, to the embrace of path-departing change. However, the circumstances and conditions in which crises or critical junctures *do not* displace existing institutional arrangements or create new and different paths need to be considered more fully. As Capoccia and Kelemen argue:

> Contingency implies that wide-ranging change is possible and even likely but also that re-equilibration is not excluded. If an institution enters a critical juncture, in which several options are possible, the outcome may involve the restoration of the pre-critical juncture status quo. (2007, 352)

There is, however, a case for going beyond this conclusion. The policy responses to the Great Recession illustrate the extent to which choices (and the part played by contingency) are, as noted above, limited by institutional constraints and underlying economic variables. Thus, the distinction that is either implicitly or explicitly drawn in many accounts between "crisis" and "noncrisis" periods (the former being characterized by contingency while the latter is defined by constraint) is, at the least, an overstatement.

This has implications. If there is less of a distinction than some accounts imply between crisis and noncrisis periods, this strengthens the claims made in recent historical institutionalist accounts that have stressed long-run, incremental forms of change (Mahoney and Thelen 2010). There may be further reasons for questioning the part that crises play in bringing about institutional change. As noted above, there must not only be a widely shared sense of crisis but there also must be substantial faith in an as-yet untested alternative policy paradigm. More often than not, even in moments of perceived crisis, familiar and established ideas appear to provide certainty, even if some of these ideas no longer fit some perceptions of economic reality. Furthermore, when change occurs, it may be confined to just one or a small number of policy domains.[15] This is because such domains have different institutional characteristics, and there will therefore be different choices and dynamics within each.

If the responses to the Wall Street Crash and the Great Depression of the 1930s are considered, path-departing policy change was drawn out, partial, and uneven. Despite mass unemployment, policy makers clung to the gold standard for almost four years after the Wall Street Crash. Although the Roosevelt administration expanded the scope of government through cartelization and the later "second" New Deal reforms, it continued to adhere to the principles of "sound finance" and the deflationary steps that were taken so as to curb the federal budget deficit contributed to a further recession in 1937 (Temin 2010, 121). There were also significant differences between policy domains. Arguably, Keynesianism was only institutionalized and legitimized as the basis of economic policy making (and then only partially) during the 1940s and 1950s. It took a succession of profound shocks, as well as the long accumulation of tensions between different policy domains, before Keynesianism took an embedded form.

Despite all of this, the New Deal secured an important place in the iconography of the left. However, although Obama will undoubtedly be hailed as a pivotal figure, few will seek to describe his presidency as transformative.

Notes

1. The US had, of course, followed a very different course during the recession at the beginning of the 1980s, when monetary targets were set and supply-side goals pursued.
2. Nonetheless, revenue increases were used in upturns so as to reduce budget deficits.
3. Social Keynesianism was at times allied with other policy responses. Some countries pursued industrial policy to aid and restructure economic sectors deemed economically significant through subsidies or the provision of long-term credit to firms. Other nations adopted antidumping measures, imposed nontariff barriers to trade, or devalued their currencies in the hope of boosting their export industries.
4. Although social provision is more limited than in much of Europe, unemployment assistance was substantially increased in June 2008 as the recession took hold and then extended as the severity of the crisis became evident. Between 2009 and 2011, individuals could claim unemployment insurance provision in states with unemployment rates of 8.5 percent or above for a total of up to 99 weeks (Stone 2012).
5. In the "auto bailout," the Obama administration added more comprehensive assistance to the temporary rescue package provided by the Bush White House. The "bailout" was, however, tied to a large-scale restructuring of the industry so as to ensure greater competiveness (Amberg 2011). Although the companies were saved, the costs were high and an estimated 365,000 jobs were lost (Caldwell 2012).
6. "Critical junctures" are subject to different definitions. John W. Hogan suggests that such junctures have three stages: crisis, ideational change, and "radical change" (Hogan and Doyle 2007, 884). John Campbell also ties junctures to change. They are "major shocks and crises that disrupt the status quo and trigger fundamental institutional changes" (Campbell 2004, 68). Others treat them as broadly synonymous with crises, thereby accepting that a juncture may offer the promise of change but may not necessarily lead to it. For Giovanni Capoccia and R. Daniel Kelemen, critical junctures are "brief phases of institutional flux ... during which dramatic change is possible" (Capoccia and Kelemen 2007, 341).
7. Writing in *Foreign Policy*, Michael Grunwald argues that ARRA "created dozens of competitive, results-oriented races to the top for everything from lead-paint removal to the smart grid to innovative transportation projects" (Grunwald 2012, 6). Significantly, however, the Congressional Budget Office did not include the prospects for developments of this type in its commentaries on the Act's long-run effects (Congressional Budget Office 2012, 8–9).
8. US health-care provision is structured around employer-sponsored insurance schemes, Medicare, Medicaid, and personal insurance schemes. In total, as of 2010, 169.3 million people (55.3 percent) were covered by employment-based health

insurance; 95 million were covered by government health insurance (31 percent) while 48.6 million people (15.9 percent) were covered by Medicaid (United States Census Bureau n.d.).

9. Arguably, Obama's capacity for path-departing action was also constrained by his de facto co-option into the outgoing Bush administration's "save-Wall-Street-first approach" (Skocpol and Jacobs 2011, 15).

10. Republican partisanship was bolstered by the emergence and growth of the Tea Party movement. The movement owed much to the weakness of Republican Party structures at precinct level and the gap between conservatives and the Republican "establishment." However, the Tea Party narrative was also fuelled by the increasing size of government and the growing number of mandates on which the processes of institutional extension during Obama's first two years rested. Writing in another context, Steven Teles has pointed to the ways in which the structural or ideational character of government programs can create opportunities for a countermobilization (Teles 2007, 169).

11. The extent, scale, and character of institutional cluttering differ between policy domains. Within each, there are different arrays of constituencies and veto opportunities. Some constituencies are more entrenched than others and command more resources than others. They are well placed to exploit veto opportunities. Reform in certain policy domains therefore may not only be difficult but face intractable problems. Fiona Ross has noted the way in which the Republicans retreated from President George W Bush's 2005 plan to partially privatize Social Security, despite their majorities in both chambers of Congress. The constituencies opposing reform in that particular domain were too firmly entrenched (Ross 2007).

12. Although written more than half a century earlier, the words of E. E. Schattschneider are instructive. In his 1935 study of US tariff policy, he spelled out how, to use his celebrated formulation, "new policies create a new politics" (Schattschneider 1963, 288). Protectionist trade policies, he asserted, have unintended consequences. They lay the basis for the growth of economic interests (under the "shelter" of tariffs) that will then seek to maintain those tariffs and other restrictions on trade. These industries "form the fighting legions behind the policy." They gain further traction and influence because, at the same time, "the losers adapt themselves to the new conditions imposed upon them, find themselves without the means to continue the struggle, or become discouraged and go out of business" (Schattschneider 1963, 288).

13. "Path dependency" can also be understood in different ways. It has been represented as inertia, increasing returns that solidify and strengthen a particular path, and as a sequence based upon a "chain-reaction of developments and events that are determined by developments and events in the preceding stage (Mahoney 2000, 508–509).

14. Some of the difficulties associated with the concept of critical junctures have been surveyed by John W. Hogan (2006).

15. Nonetheless, long-run tensions and clashes between domains may create an important impetus for change in others.

References

Amberg, Stephen. 2011. *The Obama Administration and the Long Crisis of the American Automobile Industry*. Unpublished paper presented at the Conference on the Power and the History of Capitalism. The New School. April 15–16. New York.

Beckel, Michael. 2009. "Fence-sitting Senators Say the Darnedest Things about Health Care Reform." *OpenSecrets* (blog). 9 July. http://www.opensecrets.org/news/2009 07/ fencesitting-senators-say-the.html.

Béland, Daniel. 2009. "Ideas, Institutions, and Policy Change." *Journal of European Public Policy* 16 (5): 701–18.

Bell, Stephen. 2011. "Do We Really Need a New 'Constructivist Institutionalism' to Explain Institutional Change?" *British Journal of Political Science* 41: 883–906.

Benen, Steve. 2009. "Grassley Demands Perfection". *Washington Monthly*. 25 August. http://www.washingtonmonthly.com/archives/individual/2009_08/019634.php

Benoit, Gary. 2009. "Newsweek: 'We Are All Socialists Now.'" *The New American*. 11 February. http://www.thenewamerican.com/economy/economics/item/4417-news week-"we-are-all-socialists-now".

Bermeo, Nancy, and Jonas Pontusson. 2012. "Coping with Crisis: An Introduction." In *Coping with Crisis: Government Reactions to the Great Recession*, edited by Nancy Bermeo and Jonas Pontusson, 1–31. New York: Russell Sage Foundation.

Bernstein, Jonathan. 2012. "Liberal Activists and the Disappearing Public Option." *The Washington Post—WP Opinions* (blog). 15 June. l. http://www.washingtonpost. com/blogs/post-partisan/post/liberal-activists-and-the-disappearing-public-op-tion/2012/06/15/gJQAUAfXfV_blog.html

Blyth, Mark. 2007. "Powering, Puzzling, or Persuading: The Mechanisms of Building Institutional Orders." *International Studies Quarterly* 51: 761–77.

Caldwell, Leigh Anne. 2012. "New Romney Ad Blames Auto Bailout for Job Losses." *CBS News*. 1 August. http://www.cbsnews.com/8301-503544_162-57484452-503544/ new-romney-ad-blames-auto-bailout-for-job-loss/.

Capoccia, Giovanni, and R. Daniel Kelemen. 2007. "The Study of Critical Junctures: Theory, Narrative, and Counterfactuals in Historical Institutionalism." *World Politics* 59 (April): 341–69.

Congressional Budget Office. 2012. *Estimated Impact of the American Recovery and Reinvestment Act on Employment and Economic Output from January 2012 through March 2012*. http://www.cbo.gov/sites/default/files/cbofiles/attachments/05-25-Im-pact_of_ARRA.pdf.

Dobbin, Frank. 1994. *Forging Industrial Policy: The United States, Britain, and France in the Railway Age*. Cambridge: Cambridge University Press.

The Economist. 2012. "Too Big not to Fail." *The Economist*. February 18. http://www. economist.com/node/21547784.

Grunwald, Michael. 2012. "Think Again: Obama's New Deal." *Foreign Policy*. September–October. http://www.foreignpolicy.com/articles/2012/08/13/think_again_ obamas_new_deal

Hansen, Randall, and Desmond S. King. 2001. "Eugenic Ideas, Political Interests, and Policy Variance: Immigration and Sterilization Policy in Britain and the U.S." *World Politics* 53 (January): 237–63.

Hay, Colin. 2001. "The 'Crisis' of Keynesianism and the Rise of Neoliberalism in Britain." In *The Rise of Neoliberalism and Institutional Analysis*, edited by John L. Campbell and Ove Kaj, 193–218. Princeton: Princeton University Press.

Hensarling, Jeb. 2012. "Jeb Hensarling: Dodd-Frank's Unhappy Anniversary." *The Wall Street Journal*. 25 July. http://online.wsj.com/article/SB10000872396390443437504 57 754 73203 18621132.html.

Hogan, J.W. 2006. "Remoulding the Critical Junctures Approach." *Canadian Journal of Political Science*, 39 (3): 657–79.

Hogan, J.W., and David Doyle. 2007. "The Importance of Ideas: An A Priori Critical Juncture Framework." *Canadian Journal of Political Science* 40 (4): 883–910.

Iversen, Torben, and David Soskice. 2012. "Modern Capitalism and the Advanced Nation State: Understanding the Causes of the Crisis." In *Coping with Crisis: Government*

Reactions to the Great Recession, edited by Nancy Bermeo and Jonas Pontusson, 35–64. New York: Russell Sage Foundation.

Judis, John. 2009. "Fundamentally Different." *The New Republic*. 23 April. http://www. carnegieendowment.org/2009/04/27/fundamentally-different/4xbf.

Kaiser Family Foundation. 2010. *Seniors and Health Reform*. 29 July. http://www.kff. org/pullingittogether/072710_altman.cfm.

Jacobs, Lawrence, and Desmond S. King. 2010. "Varieties of Obamaism: Structure, Agency, and the Obama Presidency." *Perspectives on Politics* 8 (3): 793–802.

King, Desmond S., and Marc Stears. 2011. "How the U.S. State Works: A Theory of Standardization." *Perspectives on Politics* 9 (September): 505–18.

Kuttner, Robert. 2008. *Obama's Challenge: America's Economic Crisis and the Power of a Transformative Presidency*. White River Junction, Vermont: Chelsea Green.

Luce, Edward. 2012. *Time to Start Thinking: America and the Spectre of Decline*. London: Little, Brown.

Mahoney, James. 2000. "Path Dependence in Historical Sociology." *Theory and Society* 29 (4): 507–48.

Mahoney, James, and Kathleen Thelen. 2010. "A Theory of Gradual Institutional Change." In *Explaining Institutional Change: Ambiguity, Agency and Power*, edited by James Mahoney and Kathleen Thelen, 1–37. Cambridge: Cambridge University Press.

McCarty, Nolan. 2012. "The Politics of the Pop: The US Response to the Financial Crisis and the Great Recession." In *Coping with Crisis: Government Reactions to the Great Recession*, edited by Nancy Bermeo and Jonas Pontusson, 201–32. New York: Russell Sage Foundation.

McKinley, Vern, and Tom Fitton. 2012. "The Financial Stability Oversight Council: Late To Crises Every Time." *Forbes*. 25 July. http://www.forbes.com/sites/realspin/ 2012/ 07/25/the-financial-stability-oversight-council-late-to-crises-every-time/.

Meacham, Jon. 2009. "We Are All Socialists Now." *Newsweek*. 6 February. http://www. thedailybeast.com/newsweek/2009/02/06/we-are-all-socialists-now.html.

The New York Times. 1996. "Politics: Gingrich on Medicare". *The New York Times*. 20 July. http://www.nytimes.com/1996/07/20/us/politics-gingrich-on-medicare.html.

OECD Economic Outlook. 2009. "Chapter 3—The Effectiveness and Scope of Economic Stimulus." *OECD Economic Outlook*. 24 March. http://www.oecd.org/data oecd/3/62/42421337.pdf.

Pierson, Paul. 2007. "The Rise and Reconfiguration of Activist Government." In *The Transformation of American Politics: Activist Government and the Rise of Conservatism*, edited by Paul Pierson and Theda Skocpol, 19–38. Princeton: Princeton University Press.

PollingReport.com. 2008. *Economic Outlook* (p. 3). http://www.pollingreport.com/con sumer3.htm.

PollingReport.com. 2009. *Budget, Taxes, Economic Policy* (p. 9). http://www.pollingre port.com/budget9.htm.

Pontusson, Jonas. 1995. "From Comparative Public Policy to Political Economy: Putting Political Institutions in their Place and Taking Interests Seriously." *Comparative Political Studies* 28: 117–47.

Pontusson, Jonas, and Damian Raess. 2012. "How (and Why) Is This Time Different? The Politics of Economic Crisis in Western Europe and the United States." *Annual Review of Political Science* 15: 13–33.

Ross, Fiona. 2007. "Policy Histories and Partisan Leadership in Presidential Studies: The Case of Social Security." In *The Polarized Presidency of George W. Bush*, edited by George C. Edwards III and Desmond King, 419–46. Oxford: Oxford University Press.

Schattschneider, E. E. 1963. *Politics, Pressures and the Tariff: A Study of Free Private Enterprise in Pressure Politics, as Shown in the 1929–1930 Revision of the Tariff*. North Haven: Archon Books.

Scheiber, Noam. 2011. *The Escape Artists: How Obama's Team Fumbled the Recovery*. New York: Simon & Schuster.

Skocpol, Theda, and Lawrence R. Jacobs. 2011. "Reaching for a New Deal: Ambitious Governance, Economic Meltdown, and Polarized Politics." In *Reaching for a New Deal: Ambitious Governance, Economic Meltdown, and Polarized Politics in Obama's First Two Years*, edited by Theda Skocpol and Lawrence R. Jacobs, 1–49. New York: Russell Sage Foundation.

Steinmo, Sven. 2010. *The Evolution of Modern States: Sweden, Japan, and the United States*. Cambridge: Cambridge University Press.

Stone, Chad. 2010. "Congress Can't Let Emergency Unemployment Expire" *US News & World Report*. 6 September. http://www.usnews.com/opinion/blogs/economic-intelligence /2012/09/06/congress-cant-let-emergency-unemployment-expire.

Streeck, Wolfgang, and Kathleen Thelen. 2005. "Introduction: Institutional Change in Advanced Political Economies." In *Beyond Continuity: Institutional Change in Advanced Political Economies*, edited by Wolfgang Streeck and Kathleen Thelen, 1–39. Oxford: Oxford University Press.

Teles. Steven M. 2007. "Conservative Mobilization against Entrenched Liberalism." In *The Transformation of American Politics: Activist Government and the Rise of Conservatism*, edited by Paul Pierson and Theda Skocpol, 60–188. Princeton: Princeton University Press.

Temin, Peter. 2010. "The Great Recession and the Great Depression." *Daedalus* (Fall): 115–24.

United States Census Bureau. n.d. *Health Insurance—Highlights: 2010*. http://www.census.gov/hhes/www/hlthins/data/incpovhlth/2010/highlights.html.

United States Chamber of Commerce. 2012. *U.S. Chamber Statement on the Two-Year Anniversary of the Health Care Law*. 23 March. http://www.uschamber.com/node/30806/%252Fmarch.

Weir, Margaret. 1992. "Ideas and the Politics of Bounded Innovation." In *Structuring Politics: Historical Institutionalism in Comparative Analysis*, edited by Sven Steinmo, Kathleen Thelen and Frank Longstreth, 188–216. Cambridge: Cambridge University Press.

The Wall Street Journal. 2009. "A 40-Year Wish List: You won't believe what's in that stimulus bill." 29 January. http://online.wsj.com/article/SB123310466514522309.html.

The White House. 2012. *Historical Tables—Table 1.2—Summary of Receipts, Outlays, and Surpluses or Deficits (−) as Percentages of GDP: 1930–2017*. http://www.whitehouse. gov/omb/budget/Historicals.

6 Financialization, Financial Crisis, and Deficit Hysteria
Neoliberalism Redux

Bob Jessop, Lancaster University

INTRODUCTION

This contribution offers an account of different forms of neoliberalism and focuses on the neoliberal regime shift that occurred under successive Conservative, Labour, and Conservative-Liberal Democratic coalition governments in the United Kingdom (UK) from the 1970s until late 2012. In this context, it relates neoliberalism to financialization and the expansion of a finance-dominated accumulation regime that superseded the flawed Fordism that developed in the UK in the first 30 years following the Second World War. Financialization is especially prominent in the UK because of the distinctive role of the City of London as the leading international financial center for international financial transactions. This has long given a hegemonic position to financial capital in the British power bloc and is reflected in the dominance of neoliberal policy paradigms at different sites in the state apparatus and political regime. While there was a brief period when the North Atlantic Financial Crisis was interpreted as a crisis *of* neoliberalism, massive state intervention has since created conditions for a return to neoliberal "business as usual" in the societies where neoliberal regime shifts occurred. This illustrates the relevance of Karl Deutsch's dictum that power is the ability not to have to learn from one's mistakes (Deutsch 1963, 110), and shows how the financial interests at the heart of neoliberalism have regained hegemony and/or dominance over the definition and resolution of the financial crisis in the UK.

NEOLIBERALISM

Neoliberalism is a heterogeneous phenomenon that cannot easily be encapsulated in a single definition. This section distinguishes four forms of neoliberalism and also identifies the successive phases of the form found in Anglo-Saxon liberal market economies. The four forms are: (1) postsocialist neoliberal system transformation; (2) neoliberal regime shifts based on principled rejection of the postwar institutionalized class compromise typical of Atlantic

Fordism and pioneered in the Reagan and Thatcher regimes but anticipated, in quite different circumstances, under Chile's military dictatorship from 1973; (3) neoliberal policy adjustments based on pragmatic modifications in economic policy in regimes that retain a basic commitment to their inherited modes of growth, for example the Scandinavian social democracies or Rhenish coordinated market economies, but where these adjustments can cumulate steadily, ratchet-like, to produce more substantial, unintended, and unanticipated changes (especially when these economies are integrated into a world market organized in the shadow of neoliberalism and exposed to its "race-to-the-bottom" logic), producing what Mudge terms "neoliberalism without neoliberals" (2011, 365); and (4) the top-down imposition of neoliberal policies and economic restructuring in line with the Washington Consensus as part of a quid pro quo for financial and other assistance, to crisis-ridden economies in parts of Africa, Asia, Eastern and Central Europe, East Asia, and Latin America.[1] These differences help to explain why some commentators and critics argue that one should refer to neoliberalisms in the plural or to diverse patterns of (an always incomplete) neoliberalization rather than treat it as having an unchanging, context-free essence (Peck 2010).

The high point of neoliberalization was in the 1990s. This decade saw a largely contingent mix of neoliberal system transformation, a stepwise shift from "roll-back" to "roll-forward" policies in neoliberal regimes, a temporary ascendance of cyclical neoliberal policy adjustments elsewhere, and continuing efforts to impose neoliberal structural adjustment in many crisis-prone countries. Yet, signs soon emerged that neoliberalism was failing in key respects on all fronts. Neoliberal system transformation failed as a "grand project." Neoliberal regime shifts required flanking and supplementing by "Third Way" policies, networks, and public–private partnerships to ensure that market failures did not undermine the market economy and threaten the cohesion of market society; neoliberal policy adjustments were contested in the name of alternative economic, political, and social projects; and the quack cure of neoliberal structural adjustment often aggravated the disease, leading, in Latin America (and, more recently, in Europe), to the revival of populist politics and demands that governments distance themselves from neoliberal excesses.

Of the four forms, the most relevant here is, obviously, the neoliberal regime shift. This does not occur in a sudden, once-and-for-all rupture but evolves through trial-and-error experimentation oriented to advancing a specific accumulation strategy, associated state project, and hegemonic vision in the face of the changing balance of forces, reactions to unanticipated effects of neoliberal experimentation, and broader developments in the world market. The neoliberal project was intended to modify the balance of forces in favor of capital, and it largely succeeded, as reflected in welfare cuts, increasing personal debt to invest in housing, pensions, education, health, or simply to maintain living standards, and a growing share of income and wealth in the hands of the top decile (especially the top percentile) of their respective populations. In addition to Thatcherism and Reaganism, similar shifts occurred in Australia, Canada, New Zealand, Ireland, and Iceland under center-left as well as right-wing parties.

Other examples occurred in Latin American economies, where, with a little help from northern friends and/or military dictatorships, similar shifts occurred from the 1970s through to the 1990s in response to inflationary and debt crises in the previously dominant import-substitution growth model.

Peck and Theodore (2012) suggest that the complex, unevenly developing spatialities of actually existing neoliberalism are quintessential rather than contingent aspects of the neoliberal project. They reject one-sided emphasis on the essential structural coherence of actually existing *neoliberalism* or, conversely, on the necessary heterogeneity of its many instantiations. They prefer cross-case analyses of the multiple, sometimes intersecting, sometimes divergent, paths of *neoliberalization* as a multiscalar, multipolar historical process. In other words, it does not evolve in pure form but interacts with the broader contexts in which neoliberal projects and resistance thereto are embedded and entangled. Thus, even if neoliberalization is the goal of regime shifts in the leading Anglo-Saxon economies and is also the dominant force in the present world market, its effects even in the neoliberal heartlands cannot be assigned to neoliberalization alone—its contexts are always coconstitutive. This is quite clear in both the US and UK cases.

Building on this argument a crude distinction (probably too crude for Peck and Theodore) can be drawn between four phases of neoliberal regime shifts to date—with further phases likely. There was an initial stage where the institutional framework and compromises associated with the postwar settlements were rolled back; a consolidation phase where the neoliberal policy approach was rolled forward; a third phase of "blowback," when unexpected negative economic, social, or political externalities began to accumulate and/or resistance mounts to the roll-forward phase—leading to modifications under the rubric of the Third Way, which provides flanking and supporting measures to maintain the neoliberal momentum; and, fourth (but not necessarily last), as a result of cumulating pathologies, the crisis *of* finance-dominated accumulation and an associated crisis *in* neoliberalism that, together, represent both a threat and an opportunity to the neoliberal project. In the UK as well as the US case, this conjuncture has prompted a *rassemblement* of forces to defend neoliberalism and roll it forward again. It is in this context that one can speak of neoliberalism redux.

This narrative periodization of neoliberal regime shifts frames my analysis of the recent and continuing North Atlantic Financial Crisis (NAFC) and the successful renewal of the neoliberal project following the initial shocks to the legitimacy of the neoliberal project and the disorientation of the neoliberal power bloc when the model on which its economic and political strategy was based was shown to be profoundly deficient. The NAFC has finance-dominated, neoliberal accumulation at its core. It was made in the US and first broke out there, spreading via a mix of contagion and endogenous crisis-tendencies to other parts of the world market, even when these had not undergone neoliberal regime shifts or even when they took defensive measures against such contagion. But the UK was also a crucial co-producer of the conditions for the crisis and its actualization thanks to the parallel advance of neoliberal regime shifts in both countries, the greater significance of finance-dominated accumulation in the UK economy, and the strong financial interdependence between the US and UK economies. Before turning to the British case, however, I offer some further theoretical preliminaries.

To establish why neoliberalisms and neoliberalization have been and, despite their crisis tendencies, remain so influential on a world scale, we must look beyond the political sphere and relate these tendencies to the logic of capital. Here I draw on, and develop, Marx's distinction between the use-value and exchange-value aspects of the commodity. In the first instance, the commodity is both a use-value and an exchange-value: without use-value, it would not be purchased; without exchange-value, it would not be produced. Analogous properties can be identified in other dimensions of the capital relation. The worker is both a concrete individual with specific skills, knowledge, and creativity *and* an abstract unit of labor power substitutable by other such units (or, indeed, other factors of production); the wage is both a source of demand *and* a cost of production; money functions both as a "national" currency circulating within a monetary bloc and subject to state control *and* as an international money exchangeable against other monies in currency markets; productive capital is a more or less concrete stock of time and place specific assets undergoing valorization *and* abstract value in motion (notably as realized profits available for reinvestment); land is a gift of nature *and* a monopolistic claim on revenues; knowledge circulates as part of the intellectual commons *and* can also become the object of intellectual property rights; and so forth. In each case, as we shall see below, neoliberalism privileges exchange-value over use-value. This one-sided treatment can only disguise, but not suppress, the significance of the use-value aspect of these relations. Eventually, its importance to the reproduction of capitalism (and social life, more generally) is reasserted and, in the absence of appropriate ways to handle the contradictions between use- and exchange-value, crises emerge that effect a forcible reimposition of the unity of the capital relation.[2]

The typical neoliberal policy set comprises: (1) liberalization to promote free market competition, or at least greater market competition to the detriment of monopoly or state monopoly competition where the latter two forms are noncontestable; (2) deregulation, based on a belief in the efficient market hypothesis and the prudential, self-preserving instincts of companies and financial institutions; (3) privatization to roll back the frontiers of the polity in favor of the profit-oriented, market-mediated economy and the efficient allocation of resources and dynamic innovative potential that markets are expected to deliver; (4) the introduction of market proxies in the residual state sector to favor efficient, effective, and economical delivery of public services, thereby reducing the scope for nonmarket logics in the public sector, especially when combined with cuts in state budgets; (5) reductions in direct taxation on corporate income, personal wealth, and personal income—especially on (allegedly) entrepreneurial income—in order to boost incentives for economic agents to earn, save, invest, innovate, create, and accumulate individual and corporate wealth rather than to allow the state to determine the level and content of the national output; and (6) the promotion of internationalization to boost the free flow of goods and services, profit-producing investment and technology transfer, and the mobility of interest-bearing capital, all with a view to completing the world market.

Neoliberalism tends to judge all economic activities in terms of profitability and all social activities in terms of their contribution to capital accumulation. Separately and together, these neoliberal measures privilege value in motion, the treatment of workers as disposable and substitutable factors of production, the wage as a cost of (international) production, money as international currency (especially due to the increased importance of derivatives), nature as a commodity, and knowledge as intellectual property. It emphasizes cost reduction and cost recovery and subjects all economic activities to the treadmill of matching or exceeding the prevailing world market average rate of profit. World market integration also enhances capital's capacity to defer and/or displace the effects of its internal contradictions by increasing the global scope of its operations, reinforcing its capacities to disembed certain of its operations from local material, social, and spatio-temporal constraints, enabling it to deepen the spatial and scalar divisions of labor, creating more opportunities for moving up, down, and across scales, commodifying and securitizing the future, and rearticulating time horizons. In short, it is capital in its exchange-value aspect that is most easily disembedded from broader socio-spatial-temporal contexts and thereby freed to "flow" relatively smoothly through space-time. This intensifies the influence of the logic of capital on a global scale as the global operation of the law of value commensurate local conditions at the same time as it promotes the treadmill search for super-profits. Compared to the largely intermediary and risk-management role of finance in Fordism or a more productivist, post-Fordist knowledge-based economy, neoliberalism promotes a finance-dominated accumulation regime based on speculation and risk taking. This increases the significance of the financial sector relative to the nonfinancial sector.

NEOLIBERALISM AND FINANCE-DOMINATED ACCUMULATION

Neoliberalism and finance-dominated accumulation are connected in two ways in neoliberal regime shifts. Structurally, the connection is rooted in the neoliberal privileging of exchange-value over use-value and the fact that interest-bearing capital is the most abstract and general expression of exchange-value, not only in the capitalist mode of production but also in capitalist formations. Strategically, the connection is rooted in the organization of the transatlantic neoliberal power bloc, its privileged position in the American and British states, the dominance of the US in most global economic governance regimes, and the interests of global financial capital in exploiting the possibilities of regulatory arbitrage that exist between financial centers in the US and in the UK. I develop the first, structural point here and consider the second, strategic point in the next section.

I begin with some general comments on financialization as a principle of economic organization and, what is more important, as a principle of societal organization. Money, credit, and debt are long-established social relations; capitalist credit money is one of the basic forms of the capital relation and is essential to its continued reproduction. Beyond these commonplaces, interest-bearing capital and fictitious capital are also major features of the capitalist mode of production and have become increasingly critical in the dynamics of a world market organized in the shadow of neoliberalism. Indeed, in economies where they have secured significant autonomy from the circuits of profit-producing (conventionally, but misleadingly, described as "industrial") capital, they have also come to play major roles in modern social formations more generally. Indeed, using Habermasian language, one could say that interest-bearing capital and fictitious capital are major vectors of the colonization of the lifeworld (Habermas 2004). Financialization matters because it modifies the functioning of capitalist economies from the micro to macro levels. Specifically, it increases the significance of the financial sector relative to the non-financial sector. It is associated with the autonomization of financial capital; the growing importance of fee-producing activities relative to traditional intermediation; the increased role of securitization, leverage, and shadow banking; and changes in nonfinancial firms' strategic orientations and performance as shareholder value orientation increases and financial speculation becomes more significant in differential accumulation (Nölke 2009). This creates the conditions for differential accumulation in favor of the financial sector based on financial innovation and speculation. Especially relevant to the NAFC and its repercussions is how financialization makes the economy more prone to recession and the debt-deflation-default trap that produces an epic recession (Rasmus 2010). More generally, we see the financialization of everyday life as household debt levels rise and the welfare functions (or the social wage) have been recommodified (housing, pensions, higher education, health care); and it increases inequalities of income and wealth, limiting the impact of the wage as a source of demand (Dore 2008; Krippner 2005; Lapavitsas 2011).

In contrast with the structured coherence of the Atlantic Fordist regime when it was *en régulation* (relatively stable thanks to institutional complementarities and a largely positive-sum economic and political compromise among the main class forces), the spread of financialization tends to undermine the structured coherence of accumulation regimes and their regulation and, through its impact on the distribution of income and wealth, to undermine inherited institutionalized class compromises. This can be seen in the impact of financialization not only in Atlantic Fordism but also in the export-oriented economies of East Asian and the viability of import-substitution industrialization strategies in Latin America and Africa. This destructive impact is reinforced through the neoliberal approach to accumulation through dispossession (especially the politically licensed plundering of public assets and of the intellectual commons) and the dynamic of uneven development (enabling financial capital to move on when the disastrous effects of financialization weaken those productive capitals that have to be valorized in particular times

Table 6.1   Finance-Dominated Accumulation en Régulation?

Basic Form	Primary Aspect	Secondary Aspect	Institutional Fixes	Spatio-Temporal Fixes
Money / Capital	Fast, hyper-mobile money (+ derivatives) as general form	Valorization of capital as fixed asset in global division of labor	Deregulation of financial markets; state targets price stability, not jobs	Disembed flows from national or regional state controls; grab future values
(Social) Wage	Private wage plus household credit (promote private Keynesianism)	Cut back on residual social wage as (global) cost of production	Numerical + time flexibility; new credit forms for households	War for talents + race to bottom for most workers and "squeezed middle"
State	Neoliberal policies with Ordoliberal constitution	Flanking plus soft + hard disciplinary measures to secure neoliberalism	Free market plus authoritarian "strong state"	Intensifies uneven development at many sites + scales as market outcome
Global Regime	Create open space of flows for all forms of capital	Dampen uneven growth; adapt to rising economies	Washington consensus regimes	Core periphery tied to US power, its allies, and relays

Key:

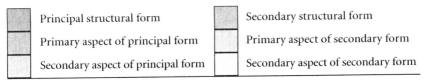

	Principal structural form		Secondary structural form
	Primary aspect of principal form		Primary aspect of secondary form
	Secondary aspect of principal form		Secondary aspect of secondary form

and places). It is also supported by the growing markets opened for the "symbionts and parasites" of the dominant capital fractions in their heartlands.

Table 6.1 presents a thought experiment on the institutional and spatiotemporal fixes of finance-dominated accumulation that would be required for this regime to be *en régulation*. It is not a description of an actually existing regime but is intended to provide insights into the instabilities of finance-dominated accumulation. Drawing on the analytical distinctions of the French regulation approach (Boyer and Saillard 2002; Jessop 2013a), it depicts the relation between its different structural forms. The *principal* (or dominant) structural forms are money (as capital) and the (social) wage relation; the two other forms are subordinated to these in potentially destabilizing ways. This is amply demonstrated in the genesis and repercussions of the NAFC. The primary aspect of money (as capital) in this regime is (world) money as the most abstract expression of capital and its disembedding in a space of flows (in contrast to the more territorial logic of Atlantic Fordism or a productivist knowledge-based economy). The primary aspect of the wage form is its recommodification based on labor market flexibility and precariousness.

The secondary aspect of money (real assets) is secured through the neoliberal policy boost to aftertax profits. In practice, however, this was not always reflected in productive investment in financialized neoliberal regimes. Indeed, the neoliberal bias towards deregulation creates "unusual deals with political authority," predatory capitalism, and reckless speculation—all of which helped to fuel the global financial crisis. An Ordoliberal framework would provide an appropriate institutional and spatio-temporal fix, including the embedding of neoliberalism internationally in a new, disciplinary constitutionalism and new ethicalism (Gill 1995; Sum 2010). Needless to say, Ordoliberalism is absent in the UK and US cases. The secondary aspect of the (social) wage relation was handled via private consumer credit (sometimes called privatized Keynesianism) and the lean welfare state.

In the short term, financial accumulation depends on pseudovalidation of highly leveraged debt (or fictitious capital), but finance capital (let alone capital in general) cannot escape its long-term material dependence on the need for surplus value to be produced before it is realized and distributed. Neither can it escape its material dependence on the performance of other institutional orders (e.g., protection of property rights and contracts, basic education, effective legislation, scientific discoveries). And, of course, it always remains prisoner of its own crisis tendencies.

This is not the space for a detailed analysis of the genesis, aetiology, and path of the NAFC. But we should note it is more than financial. It is a complex nexus of crises with interconnected technological, economic, financial, political, geopolitical, social, and environmental aspects. This said, it can be summarized as a crisis triggered by growing problems rooted in a hypertrophied, finance-dominated economy in which fictitious money, fictitious credit, fictitious capital[3] (and, increasingly, fictitious profits derived from control fraud) played an increasingly autonomous role in economic dynamics. The overaccumulation of interest-bearing capital, enabled by its dissociation from, and indifference to, other moments of the capital relation, was a crucial factor in the eventual bursting of financial bubbles around the world. Such bubbles have occurred before, of course, but the present crisis has a more specific, intense form due to the *hyperfinancialization* of advanced neoliberal economies and, notably, to practices of deregulated, opaque, and sometimes fraudulent financial institutions that benefit from a corrupt relation with political authority. This was facilitated by the effects of four decades of neoliberalism that had depoliticized monetary policy, interest-rate policy, and regulatory policy by promoting the independence of central banks from direct government control and extending neoliberal policies that contributed to the depoliticization of economic policy. This created, as eventually it was bound to do, the implosion of the financial bubble, creating the conditions for debt-default-deflation dynamics.

In contrast to the thought experiment presented in Table 6.1, Table 6.2 presents the actually existing features of finance-dominated accumulation in crisis. It can be seen that this crisis inverts many features of the ideal-typical institutional and spatio-temporal fixes that might have provided some partial,

Table 6.2   Finance-Dominated Accumulation in Crisis

Basic Form	Primary Aspect	Secondary Aspect	Institutional Fixes	Spatio-Temporal Fixes
Money/ Capital	Rising antagonism between "Main Street" and "Wall Street" (City, etc.)	Epic recession based on debt-default-deflation dynamics (D4)	Deregulation→ crisis of TBTF predatory finance + contagion effects	Protectionism in core economies, growing resistance to free trade from periphery
(Social) wage	Credit crunch puts private Keynesianism into reverse	Austerity reinforces D4, leads to double-dip recessions	Growing reserve army of surplus, precarious labor	Global crisis and internal devaluation; Reproduction crisis
State	Political capitalism undermines Ordoliberalism	Austerity policies meet resistance, harsher discipline	Crises in political markets reinforce "postdemocracy"	Cannot halt uneven development at many sites + scales
Global Regime	Unregulated space of flows intensifies "triple crisis"	Multilateral, multiscalar imbalances and race to bottom	Crisis + rejection of (post) Washington Consensus	Crisis of US hegemony; BRICS in crisis and disarray

provisional, and temporary stability for this regime. The neglect of investment in fixed assets and the emphasis on cost reduction to increase shareholder value produced a rising antagonism between interest-bearing capital (Wall Street, the City of London) and profit-producing capital (conventionally identified with industrial capital, but more extensive than this). This is reflected in the US and UK's increasingly urgent demands for infrastructural investment to support manufacturing (especially as current interest rates are effectively negative in real terms). Second, thanks to the credit crunch and rising unemployment or precarious employment, private Keynesianism is thrown into reverse, further contributing to the crisis through the effects of private financial deleveraging. When coupled with neoliberal and neoconservative calls for welfare retrenchment and other austerity measures, this has reinforced the debt-default-deflation dynamic because it leads to recession, increasing the public debt to GDP ratio rather than reducing it. Indeed, recent econometric work by the IMF shows that the multiplier effect of government austerity is far greater than previously assumed and can prove counterproductive (Blanchard and Leight 2013). This reinforces uneven development and is also likely to increase popular resistance, prompting harsher financial discipline and police action. This is associated with the trend to "postdemocracy" (Crouch 2004; Jessop 2013c).

Despite the neoliberal commitment to free trade and world market integration, the actually existing crisis of finance-dominated accumulation has promoted growing calls for protectionism in the US, reflecting the pathological codependence of the US and Chinese economies, and for renegotiation of the UK's relationship with the EU (especially in the field of postcrisis financial regulation, which reflects a threat to the position of the City as the leading and remarkably deregulated international financial center for international financial transactions). The crisis has also increased the reserve army of labor and created conditions for stagnant or falling wages and downward pressures on the social wage, which reinforces the debt-default-deflation dynamic in the absence of compensating public expenditure—a measure regarded as taboo by the neoliberal power bloc. The measures needed to manage the economic state of emergency have produced a further centralization of political power in the executive branch of government and in independent financial institutions (national, European, and international), reinforced the tendency towards "unusual deals with political authority" in the bailouts of too big to fail, too interconnected to fail, and politically too well-connected financial institutions. This leads to loss of political legitimacy (reflected in the 99 percent mantra of the Occupy movement and declining support for mainstream parties) and to the growth of "postdemocracy" or authoritarian statism. Finally, I note en passant that the crisis has also produced problems in the legitimacy of the (post-)Washington Consensus, the search for postneoliberal strategies in Latin America and elsewhere, and attempts to move to a more multilateral global order, based in part on increasing economic, trade, and financial cooperation among the BRICS (Brazil, Russia, India, China, South Africa) economies

THATCHERISM, NEW LABOUR, NEOLIBERALISM, AND FINANCIALIZATION

Given the City's historical dominance, did the neoliberal regime shift promoted under Mrs. Thatcher and consolidated under all subsequent governments also involve a reorganization of the power bloc? This category is as much structural as political in nature. It denotes:

A stable, structurally determined, and organized bloc of dominant classes (or class fractions) and dominant social and political categories (for example, top bureaucrats, military elites, intellectuals). This bloc is typically organized around a specific accumulation strategy, state strategy and hegemonic project. Its stability derives not only from the organic character of these projects but also from ... structural constraints ... in the society and economy that privilege the pursuit of these interests and their associated objectives over those of groups outside the power bloc. In this sense, a power bloc should not be confused with temporary alliances for specific goals, or purely defensive rassemblements, etc. For the stability ... of a power bloc depends on its relations to a specific state form, the leading sectors of the economy, and a shared ideological outlook. Nor, then, should it be reduced to organizations or alliances in the political sphere: party politics, tripartism, and other political groups may often be mediated reflections of the power bloc (or of its crisis), but the political sphere has its own irreducible properties and dynamics. (Jessop et al. 1988, 162–63)

What is crucial in examining a power bloc is finding the basis for complementary strategic interests rather than searching for common sociocultural bonds. At best the latter provide one means of organizing a power bloc—but they could just as easily obstruct the formulation of new strategies. Conversely, a power bloc can prove durable even when common sociocultural bonds are absent. The key to this is rational, organic strategies, the organizational capacities to advance them, and the capacity to secure structural dominance in the leading economic and political institutional orders.

Using the concept of power bloc within an Amsterdam regulationist perspective, Henk Overbeek suggested that a new power bloc was emerging in the 1980s (Overbeek 1989). It was organized around a neoliberal "concept of control." This reflected, he argued, a shift in dominance towards money capital at the expense of productive capital. One indicator of this was shifts in the primary source of contributions to the Conservative Party; another was the uneven development and profitability of different sectors of capital. Financial capital benefitted and, to the extent that it survived, industrial capital was monetized. These are typical features of finance-dominated accumulation. Overbeek explains that Thatcherism was brought to power by a fractional compromise in 1979 when capital's continued survival was at stake (205–7). The broad support that capital gave to Thatcherism in the late 1970s seems to have been more of a defensive *rassemblement*, however, than the first steps in the organization of a new power bloc. Thus the Thatcher regime could not reconstruct British industry because the new power bloc lacked a well-considered industrial strategy and a coherent alternative view of the state (213, 218). This might not prevent continued accumulation for the leading sections of the British power bloc, whose ties with British economic space and the British working class are limited; but it did pose political problems for any consolidation of Thatcherism in the face of continued economic decline (215–16).

There is real merit in Overbeek's argument as far as it applies to the crisis of Britain's flawed Fordism, which intensified during the 1970s, especially given the broader crisis of Atlantic Fordism and the resulting rallying of all fractions of capital around the Thatcher project. But it is misleading on two counts: first, financial capital (in the form of money-dealing capital, stock-dealing capital, and interest-bearing capital) has long been dominant in the British power bloc (see Ingham 1984); and, second, the dominance of a power bloc does not depend on its integration of all fractions of capital but on its capacity to develop an accumulation strategy, state project, and hegemonic vision that advances the interests of the leading fraction(s) without radical challenge from other fractions—which could be due to their fragmentation, lack of organizational capacities, or dependence for survival on minor economic-corporate concessions from the power bloc and the state. This seems to have been the case in the UK, where traditional heavy industry, retail capital, and small and medium enterprises lacked the capacity to challenge the hegemony of financial capital. In addition, after Overbeek published his analysis, financial capital has changed considerably, thanks to the increasing weight of interest-bearing capital, its new-found capacities for leverage, and its massive internationalization, so that the City of London has become a key operating center for national, regional, and international financial capital from around the world.

I described Thatcherism above as a leading exemplar of a liberal regime shift. This needs qualifying in two respects. First, before the point of no return that prepared the ground for Mrs. Thatcher's electoral victory in 1979, there were a series of pragmatic neoliberal policy adjustments in the preceding Labour government. Second, although Mrs. Thatcher eventually resigned as prime minister, her legacy was maintained by her successor, John Major, in a form that I have described elsewhere as Thatcherism with a grey face, and, later, under New Labour, led first by Tony Blair and then Gordon Brown, marking a new phase in neoliberalism, which can be described as neoliberalism with a Christian Socialist face (Hay 1999; Jessop 2007). The defeat of New Labour in the wake of the NAFC restored the Conservatives to power, and they are now pursuing neoliberal austerity politics and using the crisis as an opportunity to make further inroads into what remains of the institutions that embodied the postwar settlement. In this respect, they are implicitly following the advice of Rahm Emanuel, Obama's chief of staff, who, in November 2008 argued that one should not let "a serious crisis go to waste." Emanuel's wish list of changes was US-specific,[4] whereas the Cameron-Clegg government is pursuing policies adapted to the British context.

The initial approach to neoliberal restructuring pursued by the Thatcher government had monetarism as a key plank. Some have claimed that this is the expression of money as the elemental form of "capital in general" and not as the specific form assumed by money capital in particular (Clarke 1988, 92). We can certainly note that the emergence of Thatcherism received "general support from the City, mixed blessings from industry, and divided opposition from organized labor" (Jessop et al. 1988, 92). Whether the neoliberal policies being pursued would really advance the long-term interests of financial capital (interest-bearing capital) was less certain. This question was being posed at the point where the case for a Thatcherite power bloc would seem to be strongest: the City of London. Thus, a 1989 report in the Bank of England's *Quarterly Bulletin* raised doubts about the benefits of London's role as an international financial center. It noted:

> There may of course be disadvantages in hosting a major financial centre. Salaries and wages may be forced up, thus driving up rents and house prices, with undesirable social consequences. Regional disparities may be exacerbated and the congestion of local transport systems may be aggravated. The economy may face risks due to over-dependence on a single

sector. The operation of monetary policy may become complicated by the need to nurture the financial sector. Regulation may need to be more complex than otherwise. Finally, it has sometimes been argued that the financial sector merely preys on the rest of the economy, adding to costs and distorting other markets—by, for instance, attracting able individuals who might be more socially productive in other areas such as manufacturing. (Davis and Latter 1989, 516).

Having conjured up this specter, however, the Bank's authors sought to exorcise it with various counterarguments.[5] They concluded that "on balance, the financial sector may be judged to offer substantial net benefits to the economy" (516). With hindsight, it seems that these worries were well founded; indeed, the tendencies that Davis and Latter identified have intensified in the intervening decades. The problems that these cumulating asymmetries create have made it increasingly hard to reverse the dependence of the UK economy on international finance and have intensified uneven development to the benefit of London and the rest of the south-east and the detriment of other regions. In short, the problems that become evident in the financial crisis in 2007–2008 did not emerge out of the blue—they are rooted in changes that occurred over more than 30 years and were anticipated more than 25 years ago.

I now discuss six ways in which Thatcherism helped skew, if not deform, the mode of growth in Britain. But this is not just a story of Thatcherism: these trends continued under New Labour and survive today. First, in pursuing banking deregulation and (at least initially) a monetarist counterinflation strategy, Thatcherism created conditions discouraging investment in the "real" economy. Banking profits come from making loans, and financial institutions compete to invent new financial instruments. Deregulating and liberalizing banking capital promotes this and helps banks to circumvent monetary restraint. This makes it progressively harder for governments to control the money supply each time that tight money is needed for economic management (see Jessop 1985; Toporowski 1989). Unsurprisingly, monetarism was soon abandoned in favor of other neoliberal pursuits. The inverse effect, but for similar reasons, is seen in the limits to quantitative easing as an economic stimulus measure Second, by encouraging expansion in the financial sector, the neoliberal strategy increased financial claims on the real economy. In a period when financial investment in global equity markets is increasingly liquidity driven and based on increasingly opaque forms of leverage, industrial productivity and output do not keep pace with the growth of financial claims. This has been aggravated by other government policies under both Conservative and Labour governments that undermined industrial investment and growth (Toporowski 1989; Watson 1999; see also Guttmann 2008).

Third, in eschewing a "modernizing" interventionist economic policy, the Thatcher government systematically reduced its role in training and tried to bring education and research and development activities closer to the market. Overall, its policies (continued under New Labour) reinforced the low skill, low wage, low productivity character of British industry (Daniels and McIlroy

2009). Interestingly, one of the few areas where skills were allegedly in adequate supply is financial services (Davis and Latter 1989, 521). As the pace of technological innovation accelerates and ever-new demands are placed on the workforce, this problem became more severe, especially in the old industrial heartlands (Ashton, Green and Hoskins 1989). Fourth, in promoting popular capitalism and privatized Keynesianism, the Conservative and New Labour regimes acted irrationally, politically as well as economically. The Thatcher and Major governments pursued short-term asset stripping of the public sector for the sake of a share-owning democracy, cosmetic reductions in the Public Sector Borrowing Requirement and tax cuts—all to the detriment of long-term improvements in competitiveness. New Labour also claimed it was electorally imperative to continue the legacies of Thatcherism in low tax rates and enjoyed the (illusory) benefits of the housing bubble both in terms of political support and tax revenues from the housing boom and related economic activities.

Fifth, by privileging owner occupation in the hope of electoral benefit, both Conservative and Labour regimes boosted the financial services sector. But this also promoted a consumer boom on the basis of housing equity, aggravated the crowding-out effects of the housing sector borrowing requirement on productive investment, and discouraged regional labor mobility from areas of high unemployment to areas of labor shortage. Promoting owner occupation also created a vested interest that proves fickle during downturns in the housing market. Both Conservative and Labour governments suffered from this— most notably, of course, New Labour at the height of the NAFC. Sixth, much of the apparent success of the neoliberal strategy under Thatcher, Major, and New Labour depended on trends in the south-east. In the north of England and the provinces it triggered far more job losses in manufacturing (both in absolute and relative terms) than in the south. This occurred through the combined impact of general macroeconomic policies and specific microeconomic measures to restructure nationalized industries (which are overrepresented in the north). In contrast, the package of neoliberal measures was especially advantageous to the City, rentier, and producer service interests located above all in London and the south-east (Peck and Tickell 1995). Other government investment projects have also favored London and the rest of the south-east – the Olympic Games being another recent example.

Even in the 1980s and 1990s, then, the seeds of later financial crises and continuing economic decline were evident. Much of the financial expansion occurred through the increasing internationalization of the City and its ever closer integration into the global circuits of capital. Regulatory arbitrage played a key role here, when, following the "Big Bang" that liberalized and deregulated the City of London, opening the way for London to become the leading international center for international financial capital. In this regard, it is noteworthy that many of the biggest financial scandals that have transpired in 2007–2012 were generated through activities in the City, regardless of the nationality or primary seat of the financial institutions involved. This was linked in turn to a pattern of investment that was skewed towards sectors that service the consumption boom (retailing, distribution, personal financial services, and credit) rather than those involved in internationally tradable commodities. This trend continued, of course, into the New Labour years.

Hence, within two years of Thatcher's accession to power, fractionalism, and sectionalism reemerged, pitting the City against profit-producing capital, international capital with global horizons against capitals with strong interests in European integration, and north against south. The effects of this are evident in the poor performance of the neoliberalized UK economy in comparative perspective (e.g., vis-à-vis continental Europe), the greater vulnerability to financial crises than in Scandinavian and Rhenish coordinated market economies, and the continuing intensification of income and wealth inequalities. Thatcherism succeeded in rolling back the postwar social democratic and Conservative "one nation" postwar settlement but did not provide the basis for a new accumulation strategy that was not tied to deeper integration in the circuits of international financial capital and that could provide a stable "popular capitalist" social basis for this strategy. The Conservatives gained some respite in this regard, however, because the losers (of whom there were many) lacked the organizational and strategic capacities to develop and pursue an alternative strategy. New Labour reinforced this through its deliberate break with its social democratic and corporatist heritage in favor of the embrace of the City, further financial deregulation, deepening integration into global financial markets, enhanced labor market flexibility, and the outsourcing of the welfare state to the private sector or to "partnerships." As the economic distortions and social inequalities accumulated, under both party leaderships, however, the crisis within the power bloc intensified.

Consolidated Thatcherism (including here the Major government) combined a distinctive "two nations" authoritarian populist hegemonic project, a centralizing "strong state" project, and a neoliberal accumulation strategy. It is crucial to distinguish these three aspects of Thatcherism not only because they developed unevenly in the Thatcher–Major years; but also, and more important for our purposes, because the so-called "break" with Thatcherism initiated by New Labour's Third Way affected Thatcherism's hegemonic more than its state project[6] and left its neoliberal accumulation strategy more or less intact. Thus, whilst New Labour certainly retained an authoritarian populist approach in many areas, it equally clearly moved towards a more socially inclusive hegemonic project, at least rhetorically. This project claimed to address the limitations of the possessive individualism favored by neoliberalism and recognized the need to reembed market forces into a broader, more cohesive social order. It aimed to remoralize the neoliberal accumulation strategy around a populist "one nation" hegemonic project that would reduce social exclusion without undermining the economic well-being of "middle England," whose members delivered Blair and Brown three general election victories despite a loss of support in Old Labour's heartlands. This project reflected Blair's strong Christian socialist leanings and marked antipathy to collectivism and corporatism.[7] Social inclusion was to be secured primarily through labor market attachment and the economic regeneration of marginalized communities, and individual, family, and child poverty were to be alleviated mainly by a series of "stealthy" (rather than proudly proclaimed) redistributive measures that ideally involve redirecting revenues within what would still remain rigid fisco-financial parameters. However, communitarian themes and policies proved little more than flanking measures to ameliorate (none too effectively) the impact of neoliberal accumulation.

Following its election, the New Labour government was content to administer much of Thatcherism's legacy in regard to the six main planks of neoliberalism, as if considering their effects to date as so many economically or politically irreversible faits accomplis. In many ways, the three successive Labour Governments under Blair's continuing authoritarian plebiscitary tutelage deliberately, persistently, and willfully drove forward the neoliberal transformation of Britain rather than halting or reversing it. This can be seen in New Labour's firm attachment to the internationalization of the British economy, as evidenced in its welcome to inward investment, its active promotion of the international interests of British-based (but not always British-owned) financial, commercial, and industrial capital and its support for the Washington Consensus on the benefits of free trade in services on a world scale. Indeed, New Labour warmly embraced the logic of neoliberal globalization as a whole, proclaiming to all and sundry at home and abroad its inevitability, desirability, and truly global benefits. And, as Blair proudly proclaimed at the 2005 Labour Party Conference, every time that he had tried to introduce modernization, with hindsight he regretted that he had not been more radical.

However, just like the preceding Conservative governments, New Labour rejected the levels of taxation and public expenditure needed to pursue a consistent modernization strategy. It was more inclined towards a neo-Ricardian strategy oriented to weak competition based on deregulating enterprise and reducing relative unit labor costs in the interests of allocative efficiency rather than one that is oriented to greater dynamic efficiency based on developing strong competition around enhanced structural or systemic competitiveness. As profit-producing capital became weaker as a result, this reinforced the dependence of governments as well as national economic performance on the cultivation of financial capital as the last, best hope of the UK economy. In 2007–2008, however, this strategy hit the buffers. The NAFC was the coproduction of the neoliberal regimes and finance-dominated accumulation strategies in the US (the prime culprit by virtue of its weight in the global economy) and the UK (where financial capital has much greater weight in the national growth dynamic compared to its place in the US economy). It was also profoundly disorienting because deregulated, liberalized, financial capital was supposed to operate according to the principles of the efficient market hypothesis.

NEOLIBERALISM REDUX

The crisis *of* finance-dominated accumulation regimes in the UK and US did not produce a crisis *of* neoliberalism. Indeed, the only example where this occurred was Iceland, where the weight of the hypertrophied financial sector was even more excessive than in the UK, and where radical measures were taken to impose the costs of crisis management on financial capital (Cyprus came later as part of the Eurozone crisis). In the two Anglo-Saxon economies, however, while financial capital may have lost some credibility, it remained dominant in the accumulation regime, in the state apparatus, and, for the US, in the legislature. It was therefore able to exploit the crisis, making sure that it did not, in Rahm Emanuel's terms, "go to waste." Where finance-dominated accumulation drives economic expansion and financial capital is a significant part of the economy (and strongly interconnected with other sectors), financial crisis becomes a source of problems that must be addressed to restore the logic of accumulation. If financial capital is well entrenched in the state apparatus, then the capacity to rescue "too big to fail" financial institutions also exists when states can create fiat money and engage in other credit maneuvers to socialize toxic assets and losses. And when the financial capital is dominant in the power bloc, it can maneuver to delay, dilute, and otherwise weaken attempts to reregulate its operations. The costs for this are transferred to the state and this, in turn, provides the opportunity (also not to be allowed to go to waste) of doubling up on the neoliberal vilification of the state, to cut entitlement programs, and roll out further austerity measures. In short, a crisis *of* finance-dominated accumulation has been transformed into a drawn-out crisis *in* finance-dominated accumulation. This was possible because the neoliberal project experienced only a temporary crisis *in* its onward march.

Despite the passing of the neoliberal highpoint, and even after its contradictions came into play, as evidenced, inter alia, by the NAFC, which produced a new phase of "blowback" neoliberalism, the project still dominates world society thanks to the path-dependent effects of policies, strategies, and structural shifts that were implemented during that highpoint. This is seen in the continuing structural power of finance-dominated accumulation and accumulation through dispossession.

These path-dependent effects are political and ideological as well as economic. This is related, first, to the weight of the US economy in financial and economic terms (linked to its pathological codependence with China) in the world market, in spite (and, indeed, because) of the many disproportions with which it is associated on a world scale. Second, it is related to the continued attraction of the dollar as a world currency in the unfolding crisis. Third, it is related to the role of the US state in helping to displace and defer the contradictions of neoliberalism onto other spaces and times. This does not mean that the US case (itself heterogeneous and by no means confined, in any case, inside the US) is paradigmatic—it means no more (but no less) than that it is dominant. The UK economy and state are not so privileged in these respects. It is more exposed financially, sterling lost its role as world money more than 80 years ago, and it lacks the military and other capacities to act as a global hegemon. In this sense, the UK remains the junior partner of the US (even being encouraged by US economic and political interests to stay in Europe) and has less room to escape the constraints of the cumulative effects of finance-dominated accumulation and its neoliberal regime shift.

Notes

1. This and the following paragraphs draw on Jessop (2010).
2. The following draws on Jessop (2002).
3. On these important distinctions, see Jessop (2013b).
4. Rahm Emanuel, Chief of Staff for President-elect Obama. http://www.youtube.com/watch?v=_mzcbXi1Tkk&NR=1&feature=fvwp, November 19, 2008 [accessed 05.01.2014]. Emmanuel mentioned: health care cost control and expansion of coverage, energy security and alternatives, tax fairness and simplicity, education reform to train the workforce, financial regulatory overhaul with principles of transparency and accountability.
5. To wit: local congestion and regional imbalance always accompany growth; some financial services jobs are being decentralized; neither monetary nor regulatory policy are dictated or constrained by London's international role; and, compared with other European economies, financial intermediation is relatively efficient.
6. Thus, whilst New Labour had strong centralizing instincts, a penchant for centralized micromanagement of local social and economic policy initiatives, and a frenetic desire to discipline the Labour Party and control the wider political agenda, it also conceded—albeit reluctantly—some (at least potentially democratic) constitutional reforms at national, regional, and urban levels. Even in these regards, however, decentralization was marred by "control freakery."
7. Gordon Brown shared Blair's ethical socialism and commitment to the work ethic but, as can be seen from his expensive program of redistribution by stealth, is less hostile to an active role for the state. On the other hand, he continued to support the Private Finance Initiative, an expensive means of purchasing capital goods on annual rental from profit-making enterprises.

References

Ashton, David, Francis Green, and Martin Hoskins. 1989. "The Training System of British Capitalism: Changes and Prospects." In *The Restructuring of the UK Economy*, edited by Francis Green, 131-51. Hemel Hempstead: Harvester Wheatsheaf.

Blanchard, Oliver, and Daniel Leight. 2013. "Growth Forecast Errors and Fiscal Multiplier." Working paper. Washington, DC: International Monetary Fund.

Boyer, Robert, and Yves Saillard, eds. 2002. *The Theory of Régulation: State of the Art.* London: Routledge.

Clarke, Simon. 1988. *Keynesianism, Monetarism, and the Crisis of the State.* Cheltenham: Elgar.

Crouch, Colin. 2004. *Post-Democracy.* Cambridge: Polity.

Daniels, Gary and John McIlroy, eds. 2009. *Trade Unions in a Neoliberal World.* London: Routledge.

Davis, E. Philip and Antony R. Latter. 1989. "London as an International Financial Centre." *Bank of England Quarterly Bulletin* 29 (4): 516-28.

Deutsch, Karl. 1963. *The Nerves of Government.* New York: Free Press.

Dore, Ronald. 2008. "Financialization of the Global Economy." *Industrial and Corporate Change* 16 (6): 1097–112.

Gill, Stephen. 1995. "Globalization, Market Civilization and Disciplinary Neoliberalism." *Millennium* 24 (3): 399–423.

Guttmann, Robert. 2008. "A Primer on Finance-Led Capitalism and its Crisis." *Revue de la Régulation* 3-4: 1–19.

Habermas, Jürgen. 1984. *The Theory of Communicative Action.* London: Heinemann.

Hay, Colin. 1999. *The Political Economy of New Labour*. Manchester: Manchester University Press.

Ingham, Geoffrey. 1984. *Capitalism Divided? The City and Industry in British Social Development*. Basingstoke: Macmillan.

Krippner, Greta. 2005. "The Financialization of the American Economy." *Socio-Economic Review* 3: 173–208.

Jessop, Bob. 1985. "Prospects for a Corporatist Monetarism." In *Economic Crisis Trade Unions, and the State*, edited by Otto Jacobi, Bob Jessop, Hans Kastendiek and Marino Regini, 105–30. London: Croom Helm.

_____. 2002. *The Future of the Capitalist State*. Cambridge: Polity.

_____. 2007. "New Labour or the Normalization of Neo-liberalism?" *British Politics* 2 (3): 282–88

_____. 2010. "From Hegemony to Crisis? The Continuing Ecological Dominance of Neoliberalism." In *The Rise and Fall of Neoliberalism: The Collapse of an Economic Order?*, edited by Kean Birch and Vlad Mykhnenko, 171–87. London: Zed Books.

_____. 2013a. "Revisiting the Regulation Approach: Critical Reflections on the Contradictions, Dilemmas, Fixes, and Crisis Dynamics of Growth Regimes." *Capital & Class* 37 (1): 5–24.

_____. 2013b "Credit Money, Fiat Money and Currency Pyramids: Reflections on Financial Crisis and Sovereign Debt." In *Financial Crises and the Nature of Capitalist Money*, edited by Geoff Harcourt and Jocelyn Pixley. Basingstoke: Palgrave-Macmillan.

_____. 2013c. "Finance-dominated Accumulation and Post-democratic Capitalism." In *Institutions and Economic Development after the Financial Crisis*, edited by Sebastiano Fadda and Pasquale Tridico, London: Routledge.

Jessop, Bob, Kevin Bonnett, Simon Bromley and Tom Ling. 1988. *Thatcherism: A Tale of Two Nations*. Cambridge: Polity.

Lapavitsas, Costas. 2011. "Theorizing Financialization." *Work, Employment, and Society* 25 (4): 611–26.

Mudge, Stephanie Lee. 2011. "What's Left of Leftism? Neoliberal Politics in Western Party Systems, 1945–2008." *Social Science History* 35 (3): 337–80.

Nölke, Andreas. 2009. "Finanzkrise, Finanzialisierung und vergleichende Kapitalismusforschung." *Zeitschrift für Internationale Beziehungen* 16: 123–39.

Overbeek, Henk. 1989. *Britain in Decline*. London: Hutchinson.

Peck, Jamie. 2010. *Constructions of Neoliberalism*. New York: Oxford University Press.

Peck, Jamie, and Nik Theodore. 2012. "Reanimating Neoliberalism: Process Geographies of Neoliberalization." *Social Anthropology* 20: 177–85.

Peck, Jamie and Adam Tickell. 1995. "The Social Regulation of Uneven Development: 'Regulatory Deficit', England 's South East and the Collapse of Thatcherism." *Environment and Planning A* 27 (1): 15–40.

Rasmus, Jack. 2010. *Epic Recession: Prelude to Great Depression*. London: Pluto.

Sum, Ngai-Ling. 2010. "Wal-Martization and CSR-ization in Developing Countries." In *Corporate Social Responsibility and Regulatory Governance: Inclusive Development?*, edited by Peter Utting and José Carlos Marques, 50–76. Basingstoke: Palgrave.

Toporowski, Jan. 1989. "The Financial System and Capital Accumulation in the 1980s." In *The Restructuring of the UK Economy*, edited by Francis Green, 242-62. Hemel Hempstead: Harvester Wheatsheaf.

Watson, Matthew. 1999. "Rethinking Capital Mobility, Re-regulating Financial Markets." *New Political Economy* 4 (1): 55–75.

7 A Critical Juncture in EU Integration?

The Eurozone Crisis and Its Management 2010–2012

Mathis Heinrich and Amelie Kutter,
Lancaster University

INTRODUCTION

The Eurozone crisis articulates, to date, as the sovereign debt crisis of states in the European Union (EU) periphery that hold large current account deficits. It first surfaced in late 2009 when, after a change in government, the level of Greece's government debt was fully revealed and concern arose among investors that the Greek government might fail to service its debts. Successive downgrading of the creditworthiness of Greece sparked speculation on its default and the devaluation and breakup of the Euro currency. Greece was a likely first target of speculative attacks given its persistently high government debt, the little credibility of the Greek government in managing public finances, and the relative insignificance of the Greek economy both in the Single Market and global markets (Lapavitsas et al. 2012, 6). Had it occurred in isolation outside the currency union, the Greek sovereign debt crisis could have been resolved in ways similar to sovereign debt crises discussed in the other chapters of this volume—by devaluating the country's currency in combination either with government default or with loans from the International Monetary Fund (IMF) and other partners.

Yet the Greek sovereign debt crisis emerged in a monetary union that establishes a globally traded currency but lacks unitary fiscal and economic policies. The Greek crisis occurred in conjunction with sovereign debt crises of other Eurozone members such as Ireland, Portugal, Spain, and, later, Italy. These countries were considered to be under default risk after they had taken on excessive guarantees for ailing financial sectors and/or suffered stark recession in the aftermath of the 2007–2008 North-Atlantic financial crisis. Most of them also saw their financial accounts turned upside down with the halt of foreign capital inflow. As members of the currency union, these so-called PIIGS (Portugal, Ireland, Italy, Greece, and Spain) could not buffer downgrading by devaluation. Instead, their increased default risk showed in rising spreads in yields on their government bonds measured against the benchmark of German bonds. The appreciation of the Euro, which had allowed the public and private sectors in these countries to borrow at similarly low costs in the 2000s, regardless of differences in economic performance and government debt levels, no longer applied. Borrowing costs shot up in correspondence to new estimations of default risk that now priced in structural weaknesses of the economy, high national debt, recession, and little tax revenue as well as liabilities taken over from the financial sector. The downgrading of the government bonds of the PIIGS also affected holders of these bonds, most of them based outside of the PIIGS in EU countries such as the Netherlands, France, Germany, or the UK.[1] The mutual exposure of banks and states within the Eurozone translated into high volatility in bond markets and contagion via credit default swaps on government bonds and bank liabilities. These turbulences conjured up the threat of a domino default of the PIIGS and alarmed those holding government bonds of the PIIGS as well as those investing in and relying upon the stability of the Euro.

It is against the backdrop of this Eurozone "debt bomb" that EU governments got together in May 2010 and hectically set up rescue action for insolvent states and banks. They had to start from scratch. Until its reform launched from 2011 onwards, the Economic and Monetary Union (EMU) did not provide for short-term management and long-term prevention of sovereign debt crises. It stipulated that member states had to observe the criteria of the Stability and Growth Pact, notably the provision that government debt should not exceed 60 percent and public deficit should remain below 3 percent of a country's GDP. However, these criteria were neither consistently enforced nor bolstered by joint fiscal and economic policies. Automatic fiscal transfers or joint bailout funds, common in other currency unions for balancing the solvency problems of members, were ruled out by the "no-bailout" clause of the EU treaties. In addition, the competences of the European Central Bank (ECB) were restricted to targeting inflation in the Eurozone, while public debt targeting was left to national governments. Moreover, no provisions were in place to oversee and resolve large banks that operated transnationally within the Single Market, so that decisions on how to bail out these banks when they ran into difficulties during the North-Atlantic financial crisis were left to the discretion of the hosting countries.

The limitations of the EMU have attracted a great deal of attention among scholars who search to grasp and explain the Eurozone crisis, as have the contradictory strategies of the dominant intergovernmental player, the German government (Salines, Glöckler and Zbigniew 2012; Bulmer and Paterson 2010). This chapter seeks to introduce another line of inquiry. We argue that calamities in the Eurozone have challenged the regime of European economic integration as a whole. The Eurozone crisis marks a critical juncture of that regime in that it introduces uncertainty and opens avenues for fundamental revision. The fact that the adopted measures of crisis management locked in established policy sets, which match well with the interests of transnationally operating finance and business, is not only the result of German representatives' unilateralism. The particular outcomes of Eurozone crisis management reflect how actors, which emerged with economic integration, engage in ad hoc and institutionalized EU decision making. The outcomes also reflect dominant crisis narratives generated across contexts of multilevel political communication.

The argument is developed in five steps. In the ensuing step, Analyzing the Eurozone Crisis as Critical Juncture: Premises and Concepts, introduces the theoretical perspective from which we derive our argument, a combination of cultural political economy, international political economy, and discursive-institutionalist study of European integration. In the third step, The Political Economy of European Integration and the Eurozone Crisis, we will explicate in what respect the Eurozone crisis exposed and challenged the existing framework of European economic integration, reconstructing the political economy of European integration and the Eurozone crisis. In the fourth step, The Course of Eurozone Crisis Management, recapitulates the responses to this critical juncture. In the fifth step, An Opportunity for the "Usual Suspects"? Actors and Narratives, we explore two strands of explanation for the policy outcome: actor constellations within the multilevel setting of the EU and crisis narratives developed in multilevel political communication. In the conclusion, the argument will be taken up again for final discussion.

ANALYZING THE EUROZONE CRISIS AS CRITICAL JUNCTURE: PREMISES AND CONCEPTS

The analysis starts from the assumption that financial and economic crises imply more than cyclical deteriorations of business cycles. Crises of the scope of the Eurozone crisis render the taken-for-granted coherence of the economic regime problematic in which they occur, undermining how profit was generated and the way in which accumulation was institutionalized and believed to function (Kutter, forthcoming a). Such crises may trigger either a rupture, in which a new regime is introduced, or a period of experimental transition, in which different forces struggle over future patterns of coherence (Jessop 2002). The Eurozone crisis, in many ways a continuation of the North-Atlantic financial crisis, exposed EU-internal current account imbalances and unsustainable growth models based on them. It cast doubt on the rationality of the EMU and produced a moment of profound disorientation as crisis-management routines were missing. Thus, the Eurozone crisis marks a critical juncture as understood in historical institutionalism: a situation in which the structural (economic, cultural, ideological, organizational) influences on political action are significantly relaxed for a relatively short period and the range of plausible choices open to powerful political actors expands substantially (Capoccia and Kelemen 2007, 243).

However, to account for the policy choices made in that moment, looking into powerful actors' motivations and constraints will not suffice. Which opportunities actors see emerging with a crisis, and which preliminary fixes for crisis management they envisage will largely depend on the particular selectivities of the conjuncture they find themselves in: the politico-economic development, the policies and institutionalized routines they are aware of, and the constellation of actors they deal with. In addition, actors will employ representations of crisis and imaginings of economy that reduce the complexity of actual economic activities, practices, and regimes and their crisis tendencies so as to render them manageable objects (Jessop and Oosterlynk 2008). Crisis narratives are discursive selectivities as they attribute relevance to some phenomena of crisis rather than others and relatively unambiguously identify causes and responsibility for failure and remedy (Hay 1999).

In the context of the EU, selectivities will have a "multilevel" face. Actor-constellations and narratives emerge in a distinct hierarchical setting of codepending territorial levels and differently integrated policy fields. This multilevel arena makes up the institutional context and actor constellation of Eurozone crisis management. Crisis narratives will emerge from nationally integrated, but *Europeanized*, mass media that selectively translate proposals from the various arenas of decision making into terms of domestic political debate, thereby often amplifying intergovernmental polarization (Kutter, forthcoming b).

In the following, we will use these assumptions to reconstruct the political economy of the Eurozone crisis and the approach of crisis management adopted so far, as well as to consider explanations for its adoption. The analysis draws on secondary sources and primary analysis of EU policy documents (Heinrich 2012; Bieling and Heinrich 2013) and crisis narratives developed by the German press and government (Kutter 2012).

THE POLITICAL ECONOMY OF EUROPEAN INTEGRATION AND THE EUROZONE CRISIS

At the heart of the Eurozone crisis lies the divergent development of national economic performances and current account imbalances within the EU. Thus, the crisis is deeply rooted in the European integration process itself and certainly has a longer history, too.

With the breakdown of the international monetary and financial system of fixed exchange rates and nationally orientated (Keynesian) policies in the 1970s, the so-called Dollar Wall Street Regime (DWSR) emerged—a global system dominated by the dollar as the world currency and the Wall Street (with its outliers) as the leading global financial market (Gowan 1999). Carried by a strong market-liberal consensus of economic and political elites, barriers to the flow of goods, capital, and labor have been continuously removed, putting the attraction of global capital and its investment as primer policy aims of national and regional economies (ibid; Gill 2003). In this environment of expanding and liberal global markets, export-driven and finance-dominated (credit-based) accumulation strategies emerged as the dominant ways to generate economic growth (Stockhammer 2009; Becker and Jäger 2011). These two growth models complemented each other and led to a sharp increase of financial assets and investments managed by big financial players, such as investment banks, institutional investors, hedge funds, and private equity funds. Hence, financial claims in the form of interest rates, dividends, or property holdings became ever-more important, opening up the possibility to generate profits and overcome economic stagnation by the expansion of financial services and innovations (Huffschmid 2007).

European economic integration has to be seen in this global context. Starting with the introduction of the European Single Market in the late 1980s, European economies underwent neoliberal reorganization: provisions on the Single Market pushed the liberalization and deregulation of European markets to intensify European trade and direct investments. They introduced a method of regional integration that seeks to foster industrial productivity by means of competition, through negative integration and the abolition of nationally specific legislation (Ziltener 1999). This method was later on coupled with the doctrine of improving international competitiveness. The EMU further established a strict framework of monetary and fiscal discipline in which low inflation and high interest rates attract global capital. The European Financial Action Service Plan adopted in the 1990s set the basis for a further restructuring of European financial markets in line with Anglo-American strategies of shareholder-value-oriented accumulation and financial innovation (Bieling 2010, 216). Thus, European economic integration was and is primarily focused on restructuring the European economy in line with the DWSR. Consequently, existing national economic regimes within the EU transformed along the lines of globally dominant growth regimes. Today, European economies can be partitioned into three groups, organized around export- or finance-oriented accumulation strategies (Becker 2011, 13; Bellofiore, Garibaldo and Halevi 2010, 121):[2]

- The first group includes EU countries from northern and central Europe (Germany, Netherlands, Belgium, Austria, Finland, Sweden, and Denmark), which all have a substantial current account surplus mainly due to an export-driven economy with high productivity measures, enforced by strict wage regimes, restrictive and/or corporate forms of labor market regulation and social-welfare systems.
- The second group comprises the United Kingdom, Ireland (partially) and France. Their current accounts are rather balanced, but remain precarious due to the weight of the financial sector. They tend towards a trade deficit (UK and Ireland) or surplus (France). This group is characterized by elite-driven financial accumulation, which is combined with mass-based financialization of private debt in UK and Ireland. Correspondingly, industrial production is weak and less competitive.
- And the third group in so-called European (inner) periphery includes new EU members in central-eastern Europe, as well as countries in the South (Portugal, Spain, Greece, and, partially, Italy), which count for a big current account deficit and a high amount of finacialized household or private debt, while economic performance and national industrial production are weak. This group is highly dependent on foreign capital inflows and either linked to the first group via production chains, or to both groups via transnational trade and financial relations.

The gaps in economic performance and competitiveness between deficit and surplus countries have intensified within the EMU, not least because members could not adjust macroeconomic imbalances via national exchange rates, tariffs, or nontariff barriers (Schulten 2011). Thanks to competitive deregulation however, surplus countries continuously increased their intra-European exports to the detriment of the price competitiveness of products from remaining EU countries, which could not keep up their productivity through a "race to the bottom" of wages, labor, and social-welfare regulations. Instead, they pushed internal demand, boosting private and household debt through dependent external financialization (Becker 2011, 15).

Hence, deficit countries with high levels of domestic demand, financialized debt, and weak industries needed huge amounts of foreign credits, portfolio, or direct investments to sustain their economies while banks and multinational companies from EU core countries expanded lending, respectively, direct investments, into the EU periphery (Lapavitsas et al. 2012, 46). Consequently (and this is important to note), current account imbalances within the EU are not about trade relations and production only but result in unequal transnational creditor-debtor relations (Bieling 2010). Between 2003 and 2009, the gross external debt position increased by 56.4 percent in Greece, 43.6 percent in Ireland, 60.4 percent in Portugal, and 76.5 percent in Spain (World Bank 2013) and capital imports into all four countries kept rising since 1997 (see Figure 7.1).

When European interbank lending froze and financial institutions suffered liquidity shortages in 2008, capital inflows into Greece, Ireland, Portugal, and Spain broke down, after financial account surpluses had grown for the past twelve years (see Figure 7.1). European banks stopped investing in the periphery: after steady expansion during the 2000s, foreign claims of European private financial institutions in Greece, Ireland, Portugal, and Spain fell from \$2.3 trillion

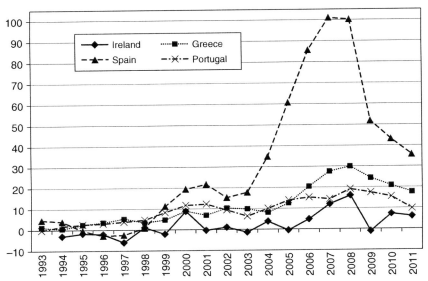

Figure 7.1   Financial Accounts in Ireland, Greece, Spain, and Portugal (in billion €)
Source: Eurostats, Statistics Database: Balance of payments by country [Data file] (Brussels: Eurostats), accessed 30 December 2012. http://epp.eurostat.ec.europa.eu/portal/page/portal/statistics/search_database.

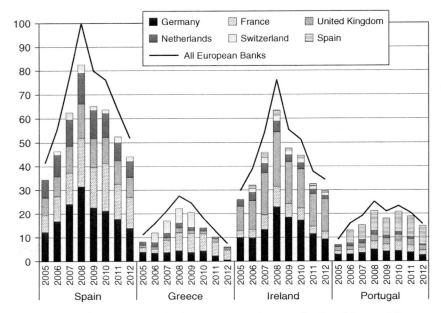

Figure 7.2 Foreign Private Bank Claims to Spain, Greece, Ireland, and Portugal (by nationality of reporting bank, in billion $)
Source: Bank for International Settlements, *Banking Statistics: Foreign claims by nationality of reporting banks* (Basle: BIZ), accessed 10 January 2013. http://www.bis.org /statistics/consstats.htm

in 2008 (of $2.5 trillion worldwide) to $1.1 trillion in 2012 (see Figure 7.2). This caused a massive shortage of capital assets. With slacking national economic performance, credibility for foreign investors further decreased and the costs of debt-servicing rose, which sharpened the general liquidity squeeze of these economies even further (Becker and Jäger 2011). Moreover, this vicious circle of low growth and increasing debt, in which deficit countries are caught, escalates crisis within the EU as a whole. The downgrading of the creditworthiness of some EU member states threatens surplus countries via transnational capital and trade relations (by increasing the risk of credit defaults, or demand fallout) and puts the credibility of the entire EMU at stake, as problems to refinance public debts expand to the center (Altvater 2012). In addition, mutual exposure of sovereign and bank risk in highly integrated financial sectors bears the constant threat of renewed banking and sovereign debt crises.

THE COURSE OF EUROZONE CRISIS MANAGEMENT

Proposals for adequate responses to the crisis related to two realms of crisis management: measures of state and bank rescue that aimed to stop the downgrading of the PIIGS' creditworthiness and related feedbacks into creditors' assets and the Euro currency, and EMU reform that would tackle institutional flaws of the currency union and reduce current account imbalances. The proposals played upon known crisis management routines and included suggestions for a fundamental revision of the framework of economic integration. Hypothetical options from which EU decision makers could have chosen to tackle the sovereign debt crises are listed below (Lapavitsas et al. 2012).

- Bridging loans for struggling states (and/or their banks) granted by third parties and coupled with austerity conditionality, which is meant to foster productivity and fiscal credibility so as to restore the creditworthiness of insolvent states (the neoliberal option following the Washington Consensus). The burden of adjustment is shifted on societies in debtor states via cuts in expenditure, tax increase, and fall in real wages; whereas creditors face minor losses as long as default is prevented. Risk of debt-default trap for debtor states with feedbacks into the EU.
- Direct transfers or collective rescue mechanisms such as a European monetary fund or Eurobonds, combined with stimulus that should induce growth and enhance creditworthiness in that way (the Keynesian option). The burden of adjustment rests on the collective and investors in the Euro. Risk of moral hazard and devaluation of the Euro.
- Default, possibly coupled with an exit from the Eurozone, which would charge off debt via haircuts and devaluation and reestablish financial sovereignty. The burden of adjustment rests on creditors and debtor society. Risk of domino default and EMU breakup.

Proposals for EMU reform corresponded to the rescue measures. The first option envisaged enhanced supranational supervision and coordination of otherwise decentralized fiscal and economic policies in order to (better) control current account imbalances and individual states' fiscal discipline and banking supervision. The second advocated a fully-fledged fiscal, transfer and banking union.[3] Finally, the breakup of the Euro into currency zones (a hard "northern Euro" and a soft "southern Euro"), or a roll-back to the European Monetary System were discussed as measures that would allow for devaluation (Peukert 2012; Fuest 2011).

EU representatives categorically excluded default as it was feared to induce domino default among PIIGS; they also did not want to dismantle the prestige project EMU. The approach the governments finally adopted was mixed, even though it favored "bridging loans and austerity conditionality" and "enhanced supranational supervision and coordination of fiscal and economic policy." Mechanisms for state and bank rescue developed from a first bilateral package of €110 billion for Greece in April 2010 into a temporary rescue fund for states in need of financial assistance, the European Financial Stability Facility (EFSF) in May 2010. The EFSF bundled guarantees by Euro Area members (€440 billion), the European Commission (€60 billion), and the IMF (€250 billion), which were used to back private financial institutions' interest-paying loans to debtor states. Since interest rates on the EFSF's loans increased faster than expected, EU governments agreed to transform the EFSF into a permanent European Stability Mechanism (ESM) in March 2011 and introduced a legal passage for its activation into the Lisbon Treaty, thereby watering down the "no-bailout" clause. The ESM now got its own supranational structure to bailout states and banks with an (additional) effective capacity of €500 billion (Grahl 2011). In addition, the ECB adopted a pragmatic approach and started purchasing government bonds (in total amount of €210 billion) that were hard to refinance on financial markets, thereby stretching its competences and de facto taking over the role of a lender of last resort.[4]

Provisions for greater supervision and coordination were adopted incrementally, starting with the *Europe 2020* strategy in March 2010. In this document, the European Commission stressed fiscal consolidation and stronger cooperation among Eurozone states as a means to facilitate "smart, sustainable and inclusive growth" (European Commission 2010a). Six comprehensive legislative proposals by the Commission followed in summer 2010 (the so-called six pack), which scheduled tight control measures and a modification of the Stability and Growth Pact (SGP) to adjust economic policies and macro-economic imbalances in the Eurozone (European Commission 2010b). In October 2010, an intergovernmental task force headed by the president of the European Council, Herman van Rompuy, plead for stronger preventive surveillance and the reestablishment of monetary and fiscal discipline in countries with high deficits (Council of the European Union 2010). These interventions eventually fed into adjustments of the EMU in the form of the "Euro-Plus Pact" and the "Fiscal compact" signed by the EU member states (apart from the Czech Republic and UK in the latter case), in March 2011 and 2012 (Council of the European Union 2012). The agreements provided for supranational surveillance and coordination of member states' budgetary, monetary, and fiscal policies, among other things, through automatic sanctions in case of lax fiscal management. Signature states were further obliged to coordinate their financial and economic policies within a "European semester," to bring their structural deficits below 0.5 percent of the GDP per year (Klatzer and Schlager 2011, 62). In December 2012, the European Council further proposed a Single Supervisory Mechanism as a first pillar of a European Banking Union. It grants the ECB direct supervisory powers over most banks in Eurozone countries and is meant to facilitate direct recapitalization of banks without burdening member states.

The adopted measures were never uncontroversial. The French government initially pledged for swift bailout, stimulus, and an encompassing reorientation towards a *gouvernance économique*, but faced fierce opposition by the German government that, in coalition with surplus states, insisted on the "no-bailout" clause as well as on the minimalist-monetary conception of EMU (Crespy and Schmidt 2012). The drastic implications of the Eurozone crisis have given rise to new criticism. While transnational debt relations could be stabilized temporarily, the risk for a deflationary spiral within the EU increased, with cleavages between the European center and periphery effectively deepening (Altvater 2012, 284). So far, costs have been exclusively dumped on the population, wage-earning and precariously employed workers as well as on recipients of welfare and social benefits, especially in the EU periphery. In addition, with institutional reform, supranational technocratic bodies have gained further powers that are not paralleled by structures of democratic control (Urban 2011). Both developments have triggered strikes and protests that question persisting social injustice and power relations within the EU. Hence, the Eurozone crisis deepens the "Post-Maastricht Crisis" of the EU, characterized by increasing factionalism, lack of political leadership, and decreasing legitimacy of the European project itself (Deppe 2011). However, alternatives have been crowded out comprehensively, such as programs of simultaneous democratization and definancialization of European economies, that is through stricter control of financial markets, the taxation of private equity, and a defense of achievements in the field of social and labor policies (Bieling 2011, 190). How and why this disarticulation has been produced will be shown in the next section.

AN OPPORTUNITY FOR THE "USUAL SUSPECTS"? ACTORS AND NARRATIVES

This section explores two lines of explanation for the selection and retention of the EU's mixed crisis management approach: the particular constellation of actors empowered through the EU's model of economic and financial integration and the way these actors made use of the intergovernmental-supranational decision-making procedures (economic-agential selectivities); and dominant crisis narratives that lend plausibility to the chosen approach of crisis management (discursive selectivities).

Reconstructing Actor-constellations and Politico-economic Selectivities

The global and EU-specific restructuring processes of financialization and deflationary competition, described in the previous sections, empowered those economic actors upon which European international export- and financial-market–based accumulations strategies mainly rely. Moreover, the subsequent liberalization and expansion of European markets intensified the regional cohesion of European capital and led to a constant increase in the strategic importance of multinational companies, export industries, as well as transnationally-oriented institutional investors and banks within European state formations and supranational institutions (Holman and van der Pijl 2003, 82, 83; Holman 1992, 19–21). Consequently, the emergence of those actors who serve as the transnational productive base and as external creditors and investors in the European economy also enhanced the dominance of surplus and finance-oriented countries in the center of the EU. Politically, this strategic selectivity is not only expressed in a strong Franco-German leadership but also in the privileged access and interest reflection of transnational business and financial conglomerates in European decision making and institutions (Van Apeldoorn 2002)—a bias, which can be also seen in the EU's reactions to the Eurozone crisis.

European state and bank rescue measures are mainly driven by intergovernmental dynamics, disputes and ad hoc decisions of European member states.

This is not only due to a lack of supranational mechanisms and routines in this policy area but also to the profound disorientation and uncertainty of economic and political elites at the beginning of the Eurozone crisis. Accordingly, bilateral rescue packages, as well as the establishment of the EFSF and ESM, were driven by progressive compromises under German and French mediation, with a strong German imprint. German representatives made sure that lending was taken out via guarantees for private bank's loans instead of Eurobonds and that rescue mechanisms were linked to strict austerity conditionality (Young and Semmler 2011; Dyson 2010, 604).

Hence, the rescue mechanisms and payment guarantees must be seen not only as biased in favor of surplus countries, but also as reflecting the interests of European creditors. European banks still had a total exposure of more than $1.7 trillion to banks, public and private sectors in Portugal, Greece, Ireland, and Spain in summer 2010 (see Table 7.1). Thus, state rescue mechanisms are primarily stabilizing transnational credit relations in order to secure the domestic financial system of those countries in the EU center whose banks heavily invested into the EU periphery (mainly Germany and France, but also the UK). Correspondingly, internationalized European banks intensely lobbied for concrete implementations of rescue mechanisms and even set at the table when they were negotiated.[5] As a result, any form of competitive devaluation in the European periphery (which would have threatened the competitiveness of surplus countries' export industries) has been avoided, while European banks have taken only a symbolic haircut to relieve financial institutions in deficit countries.

In contrast, the ECB's monetary policy reactions to the crisis are mainly driven by supranational dynamics and coordinative mechanisms of collectivized institutions. In particular, the ECB has put huge amounts of cheap credits into the European banking system, which banks in turn have used to lend to deficits countries with a much higher interest rate, while successively disposing their Greek, Irish, Spanish, and Portuguese government bonds to European public rescue funds (Richter and Wahl 2011, 11). Between 2010 and 2012, banks from the European center reduced their investments into government bonds of deficit countries by more than 50 percent, while especially bank exposures from Germany, the UK, and France to public sectors in Greece, Ireland, Portugal, and Spain shrank to less than $66 billion in summer 2012 (see Table 7.1). Thus, the ECB policy breaks with old routines of safeguarding internal European price stability and moves towards becoming a lender of last resort for the Euro Area. However, this move is not to support governments in financial trouble, but rather European banks. Hence, it reflects the priorities of European finance and lender states, but actually runs the risk of endangering the disinflationary strategy of export-oriented surplus countries by causing Euro appreciation tendencies—a reason why German Bundesbank representatives openly oppose the widened mandate of the ECB and a final decision about its (new) role is still to come (Reimann 2012).

Finally, the reforms of EMU governance structures in reaction to the Eurozone crisis are strongly embedded into coordinative European mechanisms

Table 7.1 Consolidated International Bank Exposures to Spain, Greece, Ireland, and Portugal (by nationality of reporting bank, in billion $)

Exposures to	Type of exposure	Bank nationality									
		2010 (Q4)					2012 (Q2)				
		GER	FR	UK	AEC²	ALL¹	GER	FR	UK	AEC²	ALL¹
Spain	Banks	75.4	38.8	21.1	199.3	223.5	38.4	22.8	12.0	110.4	130.2
	Public sectos	28.6	30.3	9.6	88.1	102.4	24.1	16.0	4.5	55.0	70.1
	Other private sectors	77.9	71.5	76.5	344.4	379.8	60.0	74.5	61.4	289.5	323.1
	Total exposures³	181.9	140.6	107.2	631.7	705.6	122.5	113.4	77.9	454.8	523.3
Greece	Banks	2.2	2.2	2.6	8.9	10.9	0.1	0.2	0.2	2.0	2.6
	Public sectos	14.7	15.0	3.4	44.3	46.3	0.3	1.0	0.1	3.8	4.1
	Other private sectors	9.1	39.6	8.1	75.1	80.5	5.1	38.9	5.3	61.9	65.5
	Total exposures³	26.1	56.7	14.1	128.3	137.7	5.5	40.1	5.6	67.7	72.2
Ireland	Banks	28.5	8.1	18.3	68.8	83.2	14.6	6.7	11.8	41.8	57.8
	Public sectos	3.1	4.0	4.5	15.4	19.3	2.5	1.8	3.7	10.2	12.1
	Other private sectors	86.5	17.5	112.4	290.6	354.9	69.0	19.4	109.8	259.4	321.4
	Total exposures³	118.2	29.6	135.2	374.8	457.4	86.2	27.8	125.2	311.4	391.3
Portugal	Banks	15.7	6.1	4.7	39.1	42.0	6.3	3.1	1.1	16.0	17.6
	Public sectos	7.8	8.2	2.1	32.4	34.6	5.9	3.5	1.8	21.7	22.2
	Other private sectors	12.9	12.7	17.5	121.8	124.4	11.7	11.6	15.0	105.2	108.4
	Total exposures³	36.4	26.9	24.3	193.3	201.0	24.0	18.1	17.9	142.9	148.2

Source: Bank for International Settlements, Banking Statistics.
¹ All reporting countries. ² All European countries. ³ Includes positive market values of derivatives contracts, guarantees extended, credit commitments and unallaocated claims by sector in addition.

and compromise structures in context of the EMU. As such, the reforms taken out in the "Euro-Plus Pact" and the "Fiscal Compact" in 2011–2012 primarily rely on the *Europe 2020* strategy renewing the Lisbon strategy from 2000. Here big European business networks in particular adopted a pace-setting strategy for technocratic surveillance and the coordination of member states' financial and economic policies in order to enforce European global competitiveness by enlarging strategies of competitive deregulation and austerity policy of surplus countries over the rest of the EU. The public consultation process shows that EU member states were rather divided about the necessity of consolidating public-sector budgets in early 2010 and clearly hold on to existing European instruments of (rather loose) fiscal policy advice (European Commission 2010c, 4, 10). In turn, European business stakeholders consequently requested the restoration of public finances and the promotion of the EU's global competitiveness. As part of this strategiey they argued for cuts in public expenditures, robust monitoring systems and strong peer pressure instruments at the EU level (ibid, 16, 20, 28; European Rountable of Industrialists 2010; Business Europe 2009, 9).

So, although national governments, especially German and French representatives, clearly push for the implementation of *Europe 2020* (e.g., in the van Rompuy task force), agenda-setting power in EMU reforms lies much more in the hands of transnational capital groups that interact with the European Commission and technocrats at the European level. According to external research, the European Roundtable of Industrialists (ERT), a conglomerate of European big businesses and multinational capital, played a key role in setting-up the Commissions' "six pack" in summer 2010 (Corporate European Observatory 2011). In addition, many recommendations by Business Europe, an interest group including central industrial and employers' federations of European states, found their way into the aims of the Euro-Plus Pact (Corporate European Observatory 2012). Hence, EMU reforms reflect the strategic priorities of multinational export companies and EU surplus countries by focusing on EU global competitiveness and by advancing the strategy of disinflationary devaluation over the entire Union.

Crisis Narratives in Multilevel Political Communication

The retention of the EU's crisis-management approach can also be related to complexity-reducing crisis narratives, that is dominant ways of accounting for the crisis (regarding origins, responsibility, and remedy) in mediatized public–political debate. In the multilevel context of the EU, such crisis narratives emerge from national mass media that selectively translate proposals from the various arenas of decision making into terms of domestic political debate (Kutter 2012). This section examines crisis narratives in different mainstream segments of the German public-political debate and assesses how they are connected with accounts presented by EU decision makers.[6] Crisis narratives can shape interpretation in three ways: they identify icon events as indicating a crisis tendency (possibly also calling for decisive-authoritative intervention or radical change), which henceforth suggests what events classify as crisis-relevant; they incorporate these events into existing rationalizations, raising truth claims about the causes of the crisis; and they pave the way for burden-shifting when attributing blame (Kutter, forthcoming b).

Default and contagion was not the key event through which representations of the Eurozone crisis developed in the German public, but rather the news that Greece's government had repeatedly fiddled statistics about its budget deficit.[7] This news set the scene and introduced the major protagonists of a heated blame-game between Greeks and Germans. It was scandalized by the tabloid *BILD* and taken up in other media and the German government in mitigated fashion. Greece emerged as the villain and the epitome of a backward, profligate and fraudulent southern European who destabilized the currency union through irresponsible behavior. By contrast, Germany emerged as the hero and the epitome of the prudent and immaculate European with a booming economy of higher virtues (Kutter 2012). This portrayal legitimized the punitive approach towards Greece in the beginning of the crisis. But the blame game could be varied, for example by rehabilitating Greece as victim and vilifying Germany as former violator of the SGP or as profiteer of the periphery's loss in competitiveness (Young and Semmler 2011). Merkel was juxtaposed as the Iron Lady to Sarkozy, the White Knight, who rushed in to the rescue of the humiliated (Crespy and Schmidt 2012). In short, the scandal about the fiddled statistics framed the debate about rescue measures in moral terms. Individual countries and their fiscal-economic policies appeared as the source of trouble, and news and evidence were accumulated to highlight the poor state of their public finances (Kutter 2012).[8]

Two discursive events transformed these causal stories later on: the rapid downgrading of PIIGS' creditworthiness in May 2010 and the revelation of massive exposures of countries in the EU center to the debt of the PIIGS, which Jean-Claude Trichet declared as a "systemic crisis" requiring extraordinary measures in October 2011. The first event set in motion a series of interventions for state and bank rescue and installed supranational actors like the ECB and the Commission as authorities in coordinated action. Through their interventions, the representations of the crisis were recontextualized in existing institutionalized competences and policy frameworks in the field of EU monetary and financial policy. It is not by chance that the first reaction of the Commission to the sovereign debt crisis, published in the *Europe 2020* strategy in March 2010, builds on earlier agreements reached in the Lisbon Treaty. Along with structural reforms fostering employment and education, *Europe 2020* highlighted macroeconomic stability in the Eurozone as precondition for "sustainable, smart and integrative growth." The Commission stressed the necessity to consolidate public budgets and cooperation among Eurozone members in order to overcome imbalances (European Commission 2010a, 24). With this and similar interventions, the Commission and other EU representatives embedded the formerly conflicting national interpretations of the crisis in established rationalizations of EU technocratic discourse that stressed truth claims rather than moral claims. By emphasizing national homemade problems of public expenditure, false competition, and labor market policies as common (rather than specifically Greek) causes for the Eurozone crisis, the Commission established a generalizing story. It implied that problems were endogenous and could be tackled within established policy frameworks of austerity and competiveness (Heinrich 2012).

The German government clearly adjusted to this causal narrative. From May 2010 onwards, rhetoric shifted from blaming Greece to merit claiming for the German government. The German government's actions were presented as using the sacrifice of German taxpayers to support PIIGS' recovery and enhance their competitiveness. In other segments of the German public, the Eurozone crisis was also reduced to issues of fiscal adjustment, whether portrayed as response to (Greek, etc.) fiscal overstretch and "living beyond their means" (German general opinion papers, initial statements of the German government), or to a lack of competitiveness (German think tanks, business and finance representatives and, later, statements of the German government), or as misplaced priority (counterpoint of the financial press, later reinforced by the IMF). Good and bad Europeans now qualified by whether they had done their "homework" in fiscal consolidation. And divergence in fiscal and economic performance was generally seen as reason why stricter control and/ or greater convergence in fiscal and economic policies had to be introduced (Kutter 2012). However, general opinion papers and the German government kept endorsing the established design of the EMU (Berghan and Young 2012). Only the financial press advocated a swift and lean supranationalization of fiscal policy and banking supervision early on. It thus preempted suggestions for far-reaching institutional reforms that were embraced by EU decision makers after Trichet, among others, had warned of systemic crash (Kutter 2012).

Common to all these crisis narratives is a view of the Eurozone crisis as problem of fiscal management, competitiveness, and EMU institutional design. The preceding banking crisis and rescue measures, which endangered the public finances of these states in the first place, are not part of the story. The sovereign debt problems of the deficit countries are thus effectively disconnected from the North-Atlantic financial crisis, as well as the crisis tendencies in financialization and the DWRS that it revealed. As a result, current account imbalances appear as a problem of competitiveness only, while the unsustainable involvement of peripheral growth models in the DWRS remains underexposed.

This complexity reduction seems to draw on the streamlining of the experience of the North-Atlantic financial crisis. It blanked out financialization and finance domination by privileging within-system crisis interpretations (the Eurozone crisis is seen to be manageable within established accumulation regimes); by naturalizing depictions of financial markets as opposed to state and politics that were assigned agency; and by shifting causation from systemic aspects of the economy to individuals by way of personalization, i.e. blaming bankers, managers, speculators, and new financial actors (Kutter 2012). Additionally, the reduction of the Eurozone crisis to issues of competitiveness and fiscal discipline apparently rests upon interpretations generated during the debate on regulatory policy and the role of the state that dominated the German public during the years 2008 and 2009. This debate reemphasized the interventionist state (after decades of advocating general state retreat), only to re-introduce its limits (limited to extraordinary circumstances) and underline opposition to a big engaging state. This lean "strong state" has also been projected onto the European level, when stressing the necessity of targeted supranationalization in the EMU or EU budget and deficit oversight. The debate also helped portray the sovereign debt crisis as problem of an overstretched state, thus implicitly justifying a crisis management concentrated on austerity policies and fiscal control. Within such a crisis narrative, protest and strikes appear primarily as an outcry against necessary adjustment and their protagonists as losers of such an adjustment process (Kutter 2012). In short, the narrative of fiscal adjustment and competitiveness not only aligns various segments of the German public, it also disarticulates entry points for alternative vision.

CONCLUSION

In this chapter, we have advanced a first attempt to reconstruct the Eurozone crisis and its management between 2010 and 2012 from a cultural political economy perspective. In doing so, we explicitly focused on the multilevel articulation of politico-economic and discursive selectivities, as they unfold with the dynamics of European economic integration during a moment of profound policy disorientation.

We have shown that the Eurozone crisis marks a critical juncture that challenges the policy framework of EU economic integration. It questions the way the EU periphery has been integrated into established models of negative economic integration, the conception of monetary union, and enduring restructuring of European financial markets.

A CPE perspective advocates that such revelatory moments unleash both discursive-interpretative and political-power struggles over plausible policy options, which contribute to the formation of new social coalitions or the reinforcement of existing forces. The Eurozone crisis opened up an opportunity to lock in established policy sets, which match well with the interests of transnationally operating finance and business, as well of those EU member states in the European center, which mainly host those actors. This can be put down to a range of selectivities of the conjuncture, in which the Eurozone crisis occurred.

First, policy-reactions to the crisis drew on existing export-oriented and financial-market–based accumulation strategies. However, the fact that far-reaching measures and reforms were implemented that reinforced these strategies related to specific actors' privileged access to decision making. Here, Eurozone crisis management appeared as an opportunity for the usual suspects: a strong axis between Germany and France insisted on further European economic integration in terms of permanent state rescue measures and a perspective European fiscal and banking union. At the same time, strong and mostly informal transnationally organized interest groups and advocacy coalitions pushed for a stretch of the legal competence of European institutions into formerly sovereign national areas of budgetary, macroeconomic, and fiscal policies, by mediating different national interests and ante-chambering the shape of further European economic integration.

Secondly, the adopted approach to Eurozone crisis management corresponds to selectivities of mediatized crisis narratives. They restored the coherence of competition-and-finance-driven accumulation in that they "indigenized" the crisis as a problem of missing competitiveness and rationality in the EMU. By omitting the wider implications of the DWSR and the North-Atlantic financial crisis and by reinvoking the narrative of the overstretched state, they also effectively disarticulated entry points for critique and alternative vision.

Notes

1. For the figures on mutual exposures of banks and states within the European Union, see Figure 7.2.
2. Note that the clusters are ideal types. Variation may occur within a group (e.g., central-eastern Europe), over time (e.g., France, Ireland) as well as within a country (e.g., Italy).
3. Both options may draw on an altered role of the ECB, stretching its competences to additionally target sovereign debt.
4. Such direct targeting of sovereign debt through the purchase of €210 billion privately held bonds of debtor states was enabled by the Securities Market Program established in May 2010.
5. "Finanzlobby prägt Entscheidungen des Euro-Krisengipfels," LobbyControl, http://www.lobbycontrol.de/2011/07/finanzlobby-pragt-entscheidung-des-euro-krisen-gipfels. [accessed 13 November 2011]
6. Sources included secondary and primary insights in tabloid and quality press, financial press, German government declarations, EU documents, as well as selected TV news shows.
7. This was revealed when government changed in October 2009.
8. The financial press, echoing representatives of the IMF and ECB, castigated intergovernmental quarrels, instead, and blamed lack of decisive action as driving the escalation.

References

Altvater, Elmar. 2012. "From Subprime Farce to Greek Tragedy: The Crisis Dynamics of Financial Driven Capitalism." In *Socialist Register 2012: The Crisis and the Left*, edited by Leo Panitch, Greg Albo and Vivek Chibber, 271–87. London: Merlin Press.

Bank for International Settlements. 2013. *Banking Statistics: Foreign claims by nationality of reporting banks*. Basle: BIZ. http://www.bis.org/statistics/consstats.htm.

Becker, Joachim. 2011. "EU: Von der Wirtschafts-zur Regulationskrise." *Z-Zeitschrift für Marxismus* 85: 10–29.

Becker, Joachim, and Johannes Jäger. 2011. "European Integration in Crisis." Paper presented at the 17th EuroMemo Workshop on Alternative Economic Policy, Vienna, 16–18 September.

Bellofiore, Riccardo, Francesco Garibaldo and Joseph Halevi. 2010. "The Great Recession and the Contradictions of European Neomercantilism." In *Socialist Register 2011: The Crisis This Time*, edited by Leo Panitch, Greg Albo and Vivek Chibber, 120–46. London: Merlin Press.

Bieling, Hans-Jürgen. 2010. *Die Globalisierungs- und Weltordnungspolitik der Europäischen Union.* Wiesbaden: VS-Verlag.

Bieling, Hans-Jürgen. 2011. "Vom Krisenmanagement zur neuen Konsolidierungsagenda der EU." *Prokla* 41(2): 173–194.

Bieling, Hans-Jürgen, and Mathis Heinrich. 2013. *Die Transformation des Europäischen Finanzsystems: Krisendynamiken, Initiativen und Konflikte.* Series "Analysen" of the Rosa-Luxemburg-Stiftung, Berlin, forthcoming.

Bulmer, Simon, and William E. Paterson. 2010. "Germany and the European Union: From 'Tamed Power' to Normalized Power?" *International Affairs* 86 (5): 1051–73.

Business Europe. 2009. *Putting Europe Back on Track: European Growth and Jobs Strategy Post 2010.* Brussels: Business Europe Report.

Capoccia, Giovanni, and R. D. Kelemen. 2007. "The Study of Critical Junctures: Theory, Narrative and Counterfactuals in Historical Institutionalism." *World Politics* 59: 341–49.

Corporate European Observatory. 2011. *Corporate EUtopia: How New Economic Governance Measures Challenge Democracy.* January. Brussels: CEO Report.

Corporate European Observatory. 2012. *Business against Europe.* http://corporateeurope.org/news/business-against-europe. [accessed 30 December 2012]

Council of the European Union. 2010. *Strengthening Economic Governance in the EU: Final Report of the Task Force to the European Council.* 21 October. Brussels: European Council.

Council of the European Union. 2012. *Treaty on Stability, Coordination and Governance in the Economic and Monetary Union.* 2 March. Brussels: European Council.

Crespy, Amandine, and Vivien Schmidt. 2012. *The Clash of Titans / the White Knight and the Iron Lady: France, Germany and the simultaneous Double Game of EMU Reform.* Paper prepared for the ECSA Canada meetings, April 27-28, 2012.

Deppe, Frank. 2011. "Der Weg in die Sackgasse: Eine Kurzgeschichte der Europäischen Integration." In *Europa im Schlepptau der Finanzmärkte*, edited by Joachim Bischoff et al., 9–29. Hamburg: VSA Verlag.

Dyson, Kenneth. 2010. "Norman's Lament: The Greek and Euro Area Crisis in Historical Perspective." *New Political Economy* 15 (4): 597–608.

European Commission. 2010a. *EUROPE 2020: A European Strategy for Smart, Sustainable and Inclusive Growth.* COM(2010) 2020, Brussels: EC.

———. 2010b. *Proposal for a Regulation of the European Parliament and of the Council on the Prevention and Correction of Macroeconomic Imbalances.* COM (2010) 527 final, Brussels: EC.

———. 2010c. *Europe 2020—Public Consultation. Overview of Responses.* Staff Working Document SEC(2010) 246 final, Brussels: EC.

European Roundtable of Industrialists. 2010. *ERT's Vision for a Competitive Europe in 2025.* February. Brussels: ERT Report.

European Central Bank. 2013. "ECB Announces Measures to Support Bank Lending and Money Market Activity." http://www.ecb.europa.eu/press/pr/date/2011/ html/pr111208_1.en.html. [accessed 15 January 2013]

Eurostats. 2012. *Statistics Database.* Brussels: Eurostats. http://epp.eurostat.ec.europa.eu/portal/page/portal/statistics/search_database. [accessed 30 December]

Fuest, Clemens. 2011. "Will the Reform of the Institutional Framework Restore Fiscal Stability in the Eurozone?" *CESinfo Forum* 12 (2): 34–9.

Gill, Stephen. 2003. *Power and Resistance in the New World Order*. Houndmills: Palgrave.

Gowan, Peter. 1999. *The Global Gamble: Washington's Faustian Bid for World Dominance*. London: Verso.

Grahl, John. 2011. "Politics and the Euro Crisis." Paper presented at the Rosa-Luxemburg Stiftung Workshop on "The Euro Crisis," Berlin, 15–16 December.

Hay, Colin. 1999. "Crisis and the Structural Transformation of the State: Interrogating the Process of Change." *British Journal of Politics and International Relations* 1 (3): 317–44.

Heinrich, Mathis. 2012. "Zwischen Bankenrettungen und autoritärem Wettbewerbsregime: Zur Dynamik des Europäischen Krisenmanagements." *Prokla* 42 (3): 395–412.

Holman, Otto. 1992. "Introduction: Transnational Class Strategy and the New Europe." *International Journal of Political Economy* 22 (1): 3–22.

Holman, Otto, and Kees van der Pijl. 2003. "Structure and Process in Transnational European Business." In *A Ruined Fortress? Neoliberal Hegemony and Transformation in Europe*, edited by Alan W. Cafruny and Magnus Ryner, 71–93. Lanham: Rowman & Littlefield.

Huffschmid, Jörg. 2007. "Internationale Finanzmärkte: Funktionen, Entwicklung, Akteure." In *Finanzinvestoren: Retter oder Raubritter? Neue Herausforderungen durch die Internationalen Kapitalmärkte*, edited by Jörg Huffschmid, Margit Köppen and Wolfgang Rhode, 10–50. Hamburg: VSA-Verlag.

Jessop, Bob. 2002. "The Political Scene and Politics of Representation. Periodising Class Struggle and State in 'the Eighteenth Brumaire.'" In *Marx' Eighteenth Brumaire: (Post)Modern Interpretations*, edited by Mark Cowling and Martin James, 179–94. London: Pluto Press.

Jessop, Bob and Sten Oosterlynck. 2008. Cultural political economy: On making the cultural turn without falling into soft economic sociology, *Geoforum*, 39(3), 1155-1169

Klatzer, Elisabeth, and Christina Schlager. 2011. "Europäische Wirtschaftsregierung – eine stille neoliberale Revolution." *Kurswechsel* 29 (1): 61–81.

Kutter, Amelie. 2012. "Return to the German model? Crisis Narratives in the German Financial Press." *CPERC Working Paper*, 2012 (4), http://www.lancs.ac.uk/cperc/docs/Kutter%20CPERC%20Working%20Paper%202012-04.pdf. [accessed 30 May 2013]

———. 2013. "Totgesagte leben länger. Die Fortschreibung ökonomischer Ordnung in Krisenlektionen der deutschen Finanzpresse." In *Ökonomie, Diskurs, Regierung: Interdisziplinäre Perspektiven*, edited by Jens Maeße, 95–120. Wiesbaden: VS Verlag.

———. Forthcoming a. "Zur Analyse von Krisendiskursen." In: *Sprachliche Konstruktionen sozial- und wirtschaftspolitischer Krisen in der BRD*, edited by Martin Wengeler and Alexander Ziem. Bremen: Hempen.

———. Forthcoming b. "A Model to the World? Polity-Construction During the EU Constitutional Debate in Poland and France." *Journal of Language and Politics*.

Lapavitsas, Costas. 2012. *Crisis in the Eurozone*. London: Verso.

LobbyControl. 2011. "Finanzlobby prägt Entscheidungen des Euro-Krisengipfels." http://www.lobbycontrol.de/2011/07/finanzlobby-pragt-entscheidung-des-euro-krisengipfels. [accessed 13 November 2011]

Peukert, Helge. 2012. *Die große Finanzmarkt-und Staatsschuldenkrise: Eine kritisch-heterodoxe Untersuchung*. Marburg: Metropolis.

Richter, Franziska, and Peter Wahl. 2011. *The Role of the European Central Bank in the Financial Crash and the Crisis of the Euro-Zone*. Berlin: Weed.

Reimann, Anna. 2012. "Euro-Krise: Bundesbank-Chef Weidmann warnt EZB vor Anleihekäufen." *Spiegel-Online.* 26 August. http://www.spiegel.de/wirtschaft/soziales/bundesbankpraesident-weidmann-warnt-ezb-vor-anleihekaeufen-a-852081.html

Salines, Marion, Gabriel Glöckler and Zbigniew Truchlewski. 2012. "Existential Crisis, Incremental Response: The Eurozone's Dual Institutional Evolution 2007–2011." *Journal of European Public Policy* 19 (5): 665–81.

Schulten, Thorsten. 2011. "Europäischer Tarifbericht des WSI 2010/2011." *WSI-Mitteilungen* 7: 355–362.

Stockhammer, Engelbert. 2009. "The Finance-Dominated Accumulation Regime, Income Distribution and the Present Crisis." *Papeles de Europa* 19: 58–81.

Urban, Hans-Jürgen. 2011. "Das neue Europa: stabil und autoritär? Europas Weg in einen neuen Autoritarismus." In *Europa im Schlepptau der Finanzmärkte*, edited by Joachim Bischoff et al. 30–64. Hamburg: VSA Verlag.

Van Apeldoorn, Bastiaan. 2002. *Transnational Capitalism and the Struggle over European Integration.* London: Routledge.

World Bank. 2013. *Data: External Debt stocks, Total.* Data file. Washington, DC: World Bank. Accessed 10 January 2013. http://data.worldbank.org/topic/economic-policy-and-external-debt.

Berghan, Volker, and Brigitte Young. 2012. "Reflections on Werner Bonefeld's 'Freedom and the Strong State' and the Continuing Importance of the Ideas of Ordoliberalism to Understand Germany's (Contested) Role in Resolving the Eurozone Crisis." *New Political Economy, iFirst* DO I(10), 2012.

Young, Brigitte, and Willi Semmler. 2011. "The European Sovereign Debt Crisis: Is Germany to Blame?" *German Politics and Society* 97 (29): 1–24.

Ziltener, Patrick. 1999. *Strukturwandel der Europäischen Integration: Die Europäische Union und die Veränderung von Staatlichkeit.* Münster: Westfälisches Dampfboot.

8 The Trouble with Economic Reform

Understanding the Debt Crisis in Spain and Italy

Jonathan Hopkin, The London School of Economics

INTRODUCTION

The Great Recession of the late 2000s began as the collapse of the Anglo-Saxon model of highly leveraged capitalism, but the countries that have suffered most have been the Southern European democracies, often referred to as the PIGS (Portugal, Italy, Greece, and Spain). The transformation of what started as a banking crisis into a sovereign debt crisis has ended up engulfing countries that, for the most part, were not particularly associated with the financial excesses of the boom years, and has allowed debate to move away from reform of the financial system in the Anglo-Saxon countries to the sustainability of government spending in Europe, and particularly Southern Europe, and the future of the euro currency.

A common view expressed ever since the euro crisis began has been that the euro was fatally flawed from its inception because of the presence of the EU's Southern fringe, whose economic backwardness and fiscal recklessness was bound to place the single currency under strain unless greater convergence with the North was achieved.[1] Even before the euro began to circulate, their histories of high inflation, frequent currency devaluations, difficult labor relations, and fiscal indiscipline called into question their commitment to the hard-money regime of the euro. Extensive structural reforms would be necessary if their economies were to integrate successfully with the more developed and "virtuous" North, reforms which would be politically costly and which most commentators were skeptical could be achieved.[2]

These fears—that the Eurozone would be "economically and politically divided between a northern hard core and flaky southern fringe" (Rachman, quoted in Verney 2009, 1)[3]—now appear to have been justified. The Southern European countries all face serious fiscal problems, and years of inflationary wage and price increases have made their products uncompetitive. The disciplined and productive North has to pick up the tab in order to hold the Eurozone together and avoid a chaotic default or exit of one or all of the Southern member states. If this is to work, it is argued, the Southern countries must rein back their public spending and adopt economic reforms to restore competitiveness. Austerity and reform are the order of the day.

This chapter proposes to revisit and carefully scrutinize this standard argument about national institutions and euro membership in Southern Europe. Although the failure of monetary union to induce effective convergence, the failure of Eurozone institutions to police national fiscal policies effectively, and the institutional weaknesses of the periphery nations are all very real, the conventional narrative on the causes of the crisis misses the point. A more plausible view is that the euro crisis is the result of the way in which the euro was designed, which inevitably generated imbalances between surplus and deficit countries but lacked the appropriate institutions to deal with them. Laying the blame on the institutional failings of the debtor countries is misleading and fails to take into account the extensive reforms already undertaken by these countries, both before and since euro membership.

In fact, this chapter argues that economic reform in Southern Europe has been not only extensive, it is to a degree part of the problem. Some aspects of the structural reform project promoted by European institutions (summarized in the Lisbon process) were useful, and to the extent that they were taken seriously by the Southern member states produced positive results. However, the broad program of promoting liberalization and greater openness may have been more risky than initially believed and may have made the current crisis far more acute. The Southern European political economies have distinctive institutional arrangements, and in the context of this particular regime type, liberalizing reforms may well have unexpected and perverse effects.

A comparison between Spain and Italy presented in this chapter suggests that a more closed economy with higher levels of state interventionism may in fact prove beneficial under the conditions of financial integration characteristic of the Eurozone. Italy was long seen as the main threat to the stability of the euro, while Spain won plaudits for its embrace of fiscal probity and openness to trade. Yet, the crisis has proved more acute in Spain than in Italy, with the latter suffering more as a result of its historical accumulation of government debt than because of recent policies. This chapter will therefore explore the hypothesis that the structural reform agenda in Southern Europe may have done more harm than good, given the absence of complementary institutions.

THE CONTOURS OF THE PROBLEM: SOUTHERN EUROPE AND THE CRISIS

The crisis of the euro is the result in the short term of the financial turbulence associated with the American subprime crisis, but its structural component is to be found in the rapid financial integration of the Eurozone—which took place without any real economic convergence. As predicted during the "optimal currency area" debates of the 1990s, differential productivity and wage/price increases, added to low levels of labor mobility, created strain that was visible initially as a persistent trade deficit of the South (and Ireland) and a surplus in the North (see Figure 8.1). In the 2000s, persistent trade surpluses

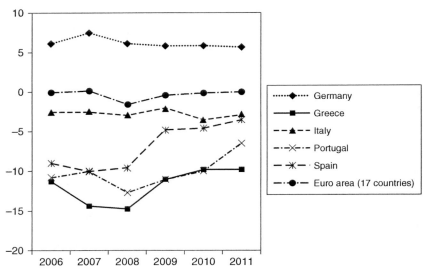

Figure 8.1   Selected Current Account Balances 2006–2011 (percentage of GDP)
Source: OECD Stat Extracts (http://stats.oecd.org/).

were run by the Eurozone's continental and Northern members, most notably
Germany, and persistent balance of payments deficits by the periphery (Ireland, Greece, Spain, and Portugal, with Italy also moving into deficit by the end
of the decade). This imbalance mirrored the imbalances in the global economy
as exporting nations (such as China) recycled their surpluses in the financial
markets of the deficit countries (such as the UK and US), for instance by buying government debt and real estate.

A related development in this period was differential productivity and wage
growth. While the anchor of the Eurozone, Germany, squeezed labor cost growth
and eked out productivity gains (a strategy also followed by Scandinavia and
the Benelux countries), unit labor costs grew more quickly in Southern Europe
and in Ireland. The failure to prevent wage growth exceeding that of the Eurozone anchor, and the appreciation of the euro in the mid-2000s, led to a
sharp increase in the real exchange rate for these countries. Southern Europe
was disproportionately affected by competition from emerging economies,
since its industries relied to varying extents on low-value-added, labor-intensive
production (Roubini and Mihm 2010, 32). Financial flows from surplus countries such as Germany both accentuated and disguised this problem: an excess
of available capital over investment opportunities maintained a buoyant labor
market and allowed divergent wage growth to continue, pushing wages and
prices beyond competitive levels and leaving Southern Europe exposed once
the downturn arrived.

At the heart of the problem was the collapse of the "competitive corporatism" (Rhodes 2001), which had been successful in the 1990s as Southern Europe strived to meet the convergence criteria for Eurozone membership. The

Maastricht Treaty required countries aspiring to join the European Monetary Union (EMU) to maintain interest rates, inflation and government deficits within strict parameters. For the Southern Europeans, this meant a dramatic reduction in nominal wage growth that could only be achieved with the collaboration of the trade unions, that signed up to painful wage restraint, at least until euro membership was secure. Social pacts were agreed to in Spain and Italy, which kept inflation and interest rates close to the European average, while tax rises and government spending restraint kept deficits within range. Once the euro came into circulation, these pacts began to break down. In the absence of effective coordination in wage bargaining, costs rose more quickly than productivity, a familiar problem in the past but for which the traditional remedy—competitive devaluation—was no longer available.

The absence of a tradition of collective bargaining, capable of delivering wage restraint, certainly exposed Southern Europe to competitiveness problems. However, what the conventional narrative tends to understate is that wage growth in the South and high savings rates in the North were two sides of the same coin. The excessive wage rises in Southern Europe were the consequence of excess capital accumulation in the North, which was recycled into net capital inflows for the South. These inflows had inflationary effects, generating increases in investment and consumption, both of which pushed up wages and prices. In a monetary union, national governments have no monetary policy instruments with which to curb such inflationary effects, and the relatively slow economic growth in Germany led the European Central Bank (ECB) to set interest rates at levels that were extraordinarily loose for the faster growing Southern economies. In other words, Germany's savings and the ECB's monetary policy led to an economic boom in the South, which quickly translated into large trade deficits and a higher real exchange rate for the Southern European economies. There was no way for the Southern Europeans to counter this, save running historically unprecedented budget surpluses.

From this perspective, the Southern European crisis becomes a typical case of volatile capital movements, with an investment boom followed by a "sudden stop," as in the Asian financial crisis of the late 1990s (Wade 2000). The speculative flow of capital into the Eurozone periphery accelerated through to the mid-2000s, fed by the confidence generated by initial high returns, before stopping dead as the global financial collapse took hold. As the resulting credit crunch hammered the Southern European economies, a reverse flow was generated by the "flight to safety" as investors tried to liquidate their positions and place their money in safe havens, such as Germany. The abolition of capital controls by the Single European Act meant that national governments could do nothing to stem this outflow, while the ECB made its own contribution by deciding a premature tightening of monetary policy in spring 2011, and the European Commission blamed the victims and demanded recession-inducing fiscal contraction to address the explosion of government deficits resulting from the crisis.

The European institutions' focus on government borrowing as a response to the crisis is the clearest demonstration of the design faults of the Eurozone.

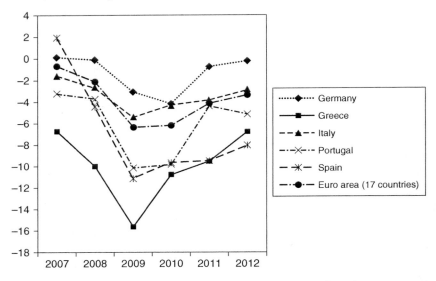

Figure 8.2   Selected Government Deficits 2007–2012 (percentage of GDP)
Source: OECD iLibrary, Key Tables (http://www.oecd-ilibrary.org/).

The Stability and Growth Pact established that governments should not run deficits of greater than 3 percent of GDP, but in the year after the financial collapse of autumn 2008 output collapsed by around 5 to 6 percent in most Eurozone countries. Even without adopting any kind of stimulus measures, deficits quickly rose towards 10 percent of GDP in countries such as Ireland and Spain, which had been running budget surpluses prior to the crisis. This rapid reversal was the result of bubble-related tax revenues collapsing while social spending rose to cope with higher unemployment, and in the Irish case, an unwise national government bailout of the banking system. The effects were catastrophic in Greece, which had been running clearly excessive deficits in the boom years, but fiscal policy had not been obviously reckless in the other cases (see Figure 8.2). Yet, European policy makers insisted that the fiscal damage caused by the crisis needed to be addressed immediately, pushing Southern Europe into a deep and sustained recession.

In short, the Southern European "problem" as such is not essentially a problem of fiscal profligacy leading to government deficits, except in the Greek case. That said, the Southern European countries' institutions have proved ineffective at managing the consequences of monetary union. Problems such as lax financial controls in the public administration, high rates of tax evasion, product and labor market rigidities, and endemic corruption have all been identified as obstacles to economic recovery. For this reason, bailouts and other forms of assistance are tied in the rhetoric of Northern European politicians and EU leaders to the need for "structural reform." But what exactly does structural reform mean, and can it contribute to saving the Eurozone? The rest of this chapter discusses the politics of structural reform in Southern Europe.

STRUCTURAL REFORM AND "EMBEDDED ILLIBERALISM" IN SOUTHERN EUROPE

The structural reform agenda in the EU, launched formally by the Lisbon summit of 2000, aimed to spur economic convergence in the EU by establishing a common approach to supply-side policies that would encourage efficient allocation of resources and promote greater economic integration (Hopkin and Wincott 2006). The Lisbon objectives revolved around more efficient market regulation and government intervention to improve human capital formation and innovation, with an emphasis on social cohesion as well as market liberalization. Alongside the measures to reform welfare provision and labor markets contained in the European Employment Strategy, and the fiscal and monetary convergence implied by EMU, a common European approach to economic policy was formalized around broadly market liberal principles, accompanied by a (less enthusiastic) recognition of the European tradition of social protection.

Progress in applying these principles could be assessed by consulting a variety of scorecards and league tables (some European in scope, some global) that measured the degree of consistency of national policies with the common framework.[4] Northern European, and especially Scandinavian, member states generally scored high, the UK and Ireland also performed relatively well, while the large economies of continental Europe lagged somewhat. Southern Europe consistently performed poorly in these analyses, and a number of observers identified this slow progress as a potential source of strain in European economic management (Sapir 2006; Tabellini and Wyplosz 2006).

This slow progress was, however, entirely predictable given the inconsistency of the aspirations of the Lisbon agenda with the entrenched institutional arrangements in Southern European countries. The Southern European countries exhibit features of "embedded illiberalism" (Hopkin and Blyth 2012). The distinctiveness of this model lies in its extensive use of regulation and complex (and sometimes corrupt) bureaucracy to control, distort, or suppress market mechanisms. To capture this institutional pattern and place it in a comparative context, Figure 8.3 presents aggregate scores on various measures of market regulation, which captures the bureaucratic hurdles that have to be overcome to set up a business. This is a reasonable proxy measure of the broad weight of regulatory intervention of the state in economic activity.[5] Low scores indicate lower and high scores indicate heavier regulation.

This map of market regulation in the member states of the Organization for Economic Cooperation and Development (OECD) yields some predictable and some less obvious findings. While it is no surprise to find New Zealand, Canada, the US, and the UK (which have enthusiastically adopted the deregulation agenda) at the light regulation end of the scale, it is significant that egalitarian Denmark has light regulation and that the other Nordic social democracies (Sweden and Finland) are also in the less intrusively regulated half of the sample. At the other end of the scale, the Southern European countries all have high scores reflecting their "statist" tradition of heavy government

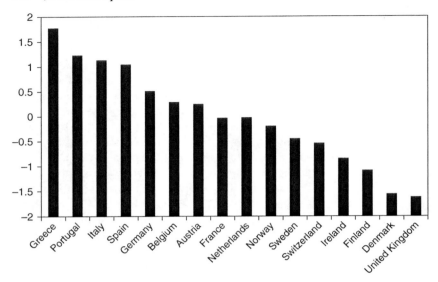

Figure 8.3   Market Regulation, Selected European Countries, Early 2000s
Market Regulation: Factor regression scores for 18 regulatory variables (higher scores imply
more restrictive regulation).
Source: Jonathan Hopkin and Mark Blyth (2012), "What Can Okun Teach Polanyi? Efficiency,
Regulation and Equality in the OECD." *Review of International Political Economy* 19 (1): 1–33.

intervention in the economy, [6] while Germany, Belgium and Austria all have
fairly high levels of regulation. In the middle of the scale we find France, the
Netherlands and Norway.

Analysis of product markets, labor markets, and financial markets confirms
that in many policy areas the OECD countries are divided between more "liberal" political economies, where economic activity faces lighter regulation, and
more "statist" political economies, where regulation is heavier (Hopkin and
Blyth 2012). Anglo countries have the lightest labor regulation, the Southern
European countries tend to have more rigid employment rules, while the other
continental and Northern European countries tend to be placed in between
(Botero et al. 2004). Similarly, in financial-market regulation, most of the
Anglo countries and Northern Europe have lower barriers to competition in
the banking sector, while Central and Eastern Europe have higher barriers,
with Southern Europe somewhere in between and Spain below average (De
Serres et al. 2006).

Southern European political economies are generally characterized by high
levels of economic regulation.[7] These consistent patterns have important consequences for Southern Europe's ability to meet the demands of structural reform emanating from the EU. The distance these countries were required to
travel in order to reach the benchmarking standards was much greater than for
the Northern countries of the EU, and, not surprisingly, most analyses placed
the four Southern countries way down the scale in terms of structural reform

performance. The World Economic Forum's 2010 "Lisbon Review" placed Italy twenty-fifth out of the twenty-seven EU member states (ahead only of Rumania and Bulgaria), with Greece twenty-third, Spain eighteenth, and Portugal sixteenth (Schwab 2010). To place these results in a global context, the World Economic Forum's Global Competitiveness Index for 2012–2013, which ranks 144 countries in terms of rather similar criteria (Schwab 2012), puts Spain thirty-sixth, Portugal forty-ninth, Italy forty-second, and Greece ninety-sixth.

In the light of this reluctance, or inability, to adopt measures recommended by a range of experts and international institutions, Southern Europe's current difficulties have been consistently interpreted as a failure to reform. In particular the failure to remove "rigidities" in labor markets is adduced as an important source of reduced competitiveness and external imbalances (e.g. Zemanek 2010). The structural reform agenda of course consists of a number of measures that are obviously desirable, all else equal, such as improving the transparency and efficiency of the public administration. But the notion that structural reform, and in particular deregulatory structural reform, is unambiguously positive irrespective of broad institutional and social conditions can and should be challenged. First, liberalization in search of flexibility (e.g. in labor markets) can be destabilizing, particularly in times of crisis. Moreover, the costs of structural reform in such an acute recession may end up politically undermining the whole idea of liberalization. The rest of this chapter explores the dynamics of reform, and nonreform, in Southern Europe, with particular attention to Spain and Italy.

HEROES AND VILLAINS: GROWTH AND REFORM IN SPAIN AND ITALY

Although a broad narrative about the problems of Southern Europe, the euro, and structural reform has developed over the last decade, important distinctions should be drawn between the various cases. First, their growth records under monetary union have differed markedly, with Spain and Greece enjoying consistently high growth from the mid-1990s until the crisis while Portugal and particularly Italy stagnated. Second, the nature of the crisis differs in the four cases. In Greece, a combination of growth, a large current account deficit (reaching up to 14 percent of GDP at its peak; see Figure 8.1), and simultaneously a large structural budget deficit and large total volume of public debt (visible even before the crisis) has created a desperate situation in which a collapse in output has coincided with unsustainable public finances. Greece, therefore, faces a competitiveness crisis and a fiscal crisis. In Portugal, growth was anemic and budget deficits were generally high, but total public and private indebtedness was more contained. In Italy, growth was anemic, but budget deficits remained broadly under control, despite the very high total volume of public indebtedness, and private indebtedness remained moderate. In Spain, in contrast, buoyant growth encouraged a consumer boom based on credit, and although the government finances were sound, the collapse in output has created a debt crisis in the private sector and (with a lag) in the public sector. In sum, all of these countries face high unemployment, low productivity growth, and varying degrees of fiscal strain. Still, there are important nuances.

The Italy–Spain comparison is particularly interesting. Although both countries have performed relatively poorly in the various benchmarking exercises carried out by international organizations, Spain was considered by most observers to be on a much more positive trajectory than Italy, reflecting its much higher growth rates as the European economy recovered from the currency crises of the early 1990s (the collapse of the exchange rate mechanism) (OECD 2005). Spain was applauded for its embrace of relative economic openness, a fairly high degree of financial liberalization, and comparative fiscal rigor. Spain was also successful in attracting foreign direct investment, which transformed Madrid into a major corporate and banking center. On the other hand, some large Spanish companies embarked on ambitious program of expansion, making acquisitions, particularly in South America. Spain still faced criticism for its dualistic labor market model, which offered some workers extraordinary degrees of job security while younger workers faced a succession of temporary contracts. Yet, notwithstanding Spain's limited ambition in structural reform, it developed a reputation as a dynamic and forward-looking economy through the 2000s, at least in comparison to the other Southern European countries. As the European Commission triumphantly claimed in 2005: "The story of the Spanish economy in EMU is a dazzling one" (European Commission 2005).

The Italian experience was very different. In the same period, Italy's stagnant growth rates were attributed to an inward-looking and sclerotic form of crony capitalism that was incapable of addressing its chronic decline in competitiveness. The comparison occasionally surfaced in public debate in Italy, with the poor Italian growth record being set against Spain's apparently vibrant economy as an indication of Italy's decline compared to its culturally and historically similar neighbors (e.g. Salvati 2003; Bosco 2005). While Spain appeared open to capital inflows and willing to integrate more closely with the European and global economy, Italy shut out foreign investors and sought to protect declining domestic industries. Foreign direct investment in Spain was almost twice as high in absolute volume as in Italy (see Figure 8.4). Aznar and Zapatero were lauded abroad for presiding over Spain's economic "miracle," while Prodi and Berlusconi were assailed in the international press as unfit to govern the European Commission and Italy, respectively (The Economist 2001). *The Economist* magazine, ever the bellwether of elite thinking on economic performance, stated baldly that Italy was "the sick man of Europe" and that its "economy was stagnant, its businesses depressed, and reforms moribund" (The Economist 2005).

Two brief vignettes—of the air-travel and banking sectors—bear this out. In the air-travel sector, both countries had national carriers under state control, which suffered from high costs and declining market share as the European market was liberalized in the 1990s. The Spanish response was to privatize Iberia and, through a combination of cost cutting and expansion (e.g., the acquisition of Aerolineas Argentinas), to restore its financial position. It ultimately

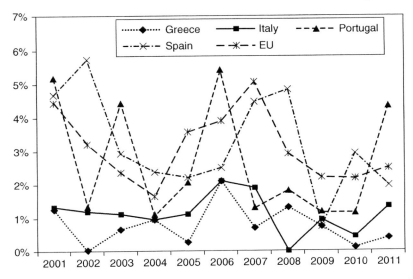

Figure 8.4   Foreign Direct Investment Inflows, Southern European Countries 2000s (percentage of GDP)
Source: OECD iLibrary (http://www.oecd-ilibrary.org/).

merged with British Airways, placing it in a position to survive in a radically restructured world market.

In Italy, tentative attempts were made to follow a similar strategy, but an increasingly politicized atmosphere led these efforts to break down. Alitalia was also suffering dramatic losses as European reforms undermined its national monopoly, and the political tensions between Rome and Milan prevented the emergence of any Italian airport as major hub (the botched launch of Milan Malpensa as a Northern hub being an object lesson in inept and clientelistic management, and the costs of political opportunism; Hine 1999). A decision was half-heartedly taken to privatize and encourage a merger with one of the emerging conglomerates of national carriers, with Air France-KLM being favored. However, the weakness of the center-left government of Romano Prodi prevented this move going through. The government fell in early 2008, and the center-right under Silvio Berlusconi launched a populist campaign to "save" Alitalia as a national carrier. It rejected foreign acquisition and instead promoted an Italian merger with the loss-making Air One, subsidized by the government and by air travelers (with Alitalia being accorded monopoly rights on the Milan-Rome route for a period of time to help finance the deal).

A similar contrast can be observed in the banking sector. The Spanish financial sector had long been consolidated into a small number of large, national banks that had ambitions of overseas expansion. However, the Spanish market was also opened to foreign acquisitions relatively early, with British mortgage lender Abbey National opening in Spain in the early 1990s and Barclays acquiring the Banco Zaragozano. Liberalization measures in the 1990s encouraged a substantial growth of mortgage lending and consumer credit, facilitating a housing boom that began in the late 1990s and ended only in 2007, with property prices in Madrid reaching levels to rival the most expensive cities in the world. The boom in prices also fed a construction boom, with huge housebuilding projects along the length of Spain's Mediterranean coastline (often fuelled by local-level political corruption, as building permits were exchanged for money or political favors; the scandals surrounding Valencia regional president, Camps, being an eloquent example). Properties were bought by many foreign buyers, often retirees or small investors from Northern Europe (financing a substantial part of the emerging trade deficit). Although the Bank of Spain regulated the banks relatively tightly (enforcing countercyclical reserve requirements) the small regional savings and loans (*cajas de ahorros*) were able to build up unsustainable exposures to the housing market, which was very clearly in an Anglo-Saxon style bubble.

The Italian banking sector has a different history. Until the 1990s it was highly fragmented, with few large national-scale banks and many small regional and local institutions with close ties to local politics (many of them state owned, to some degree). The period since has seen rapid consolidation, with regional savings banks absorbed into emerging conglomerates, such as Unicredit and Intesa-San Paolo. However, the sector remains relatively inward looking and politicized, as one recent episode illustrates clearly. When Dutch bank ABN-Amro sought to expand into Italy by buying the Venetian Banca Antonveneta in 2005, Bank of Italy governor Antonio Fazio pulled out the stops to block the deal. He first used regulatory powers inappropriately, and then mobilized contacts in the Italian financial world to generate an unsuccessful counter bid, which allegedly used insider trading to raise the capital for an alternative deal (the banker leading the consortium, Fiorani, was jailed). The affair seemed symptomatic of everything that was dragging the Italian economy down: regulatory inefficiency, inflexibility, corruption, and cronyism. Yet when the financial crisis hit, ABN-Amro (now owned by the Royal Bank of Scotland in a deal involving the Spanish Banco Santander) found itself forced into the arms of the British taxpayer by insolvency. In an ironic twist, Antonveneta was sold off by Santander back to another Italian bank, Monte dei Paschi di Siena (see Messori 2006). Again, the national model of capitalism was protected by political interventionism, in contrast to the relative openness of the Spanish political elite to international economic and financial integration.

These two examples serve to make the point that, within the broad pattern of "embedded illiberalism" we can observe in Southern Europe, Spain appears much more open to integration than does Italy, and received plaudits (at least until 2008) from international organizations and the financial press as a result. The catastrophic collapse of the Spanish economy in the last two years is therefore a remarkable outcome. Spain's impressive growth performance was, it turned out, a mirage resulting from an unsustainable property bubble. The resulting building boom spilled over into the rest of the economy, bringing unemployment down to unprecedented levels, while speculative property investments from Northern Europeans helped generate a trade deficit that reached around 10 percent of GDP at its peak. Just as we saw in the other bubble economies, investors overreached themselves, leaving deserted building sites, at least a million unsold homes, and a 4 percent drop in output in 2009. Despite running fiscal surpluses and provisioning for future losses in the banking sector in the good years, Spain very quickly found itself running fiscal deficits of around 10 percent of GDP.

In contrast, Italy, which has not run a budget surplus for over quarter of a century, is surprisingly in a better (or less disastrous) position. The current government deficit for 2012 was, at just over three percent of GDP, within touching distance of the Eurozone's much maligned Stability Pact, and although the overall levels of government debt remain high (over 120 percent of GDP), Italy is still running primary fiscal surpluses even in the midst of the recession. Output has certainly shrunk sharply, and unemployment is rising, but not on a scale comparable to Spain—and although Italy has not embarked on anything approaching a recovery, it is not suffering the free fall facing its Mediterranean neighbor. The next section will draw out some of the political implications of the comparative trajectories of these two countries.

THE DARK SIDE OF STRUCTURAL REFORM

This chapter has argued that the liberalizing structural reform agenda is no panacea for the imbalances within the Eurozone, and it may even have brought more damage than benefit to Southern European countries. Although all of the Southern European countries have been condemned at various points as structural reform "laggards," there are grounds for dismissing the widely held view that this failure to reform is an important cause of the crisis. Moreover, if this is the case, by extension the widely touted remedy for the crisis—financial aid coupled with a commitment to structural reform on the part of the debtor countries—is unlikely to bear the expected fruit. This section examines why structural reform is so difficult to achieve, and why its results are so often disappointing.

The first point to be made is that liberalization measures interact with other economic and social institutions, sometimes with perverse effects. This suggests a "dark side" to structural reform, with its emphasis on flexibility in the labor market and openness in product and financial markets. Although the big Spanish banks adopted a conservative approach to capital requirements, Spain's openness to foreign capital flows allowed the overconfidence and excessive risk taking in the international financial system to stoke a housing boom to match those in the US, the UK, and Ireland. On a macro level, the supposedly sound budgetary position of the Spanish government also masked the accumulation of household debt, while the euro hid the symptoms of an unsustainable trade deficit. The partial liberalization of the labor market— Spain has the highest proportion of temporary workers of any EU country— allowed the effects of recession to feed into the labor market rapidly and acutely. Spain's embrace of some of the key features of the economic policy orthodoxy of the early twenty-first century—financial innovation, balanced government budgets, labor market flexibility (at least for part of the workforce), openness to trade, and foreign investment—did not avert a disastrous crisis. The high levels of indebtedness of Spanish households, a major break with tradition, are particularly problematic given the limits of the Spanish welfare state and the importance of the family as a social shock absorber.

While Spain was prospering, Italy was supposedly doing everything wrong. Outside capital—whether industrial or financial—was shunned.[8] The stories of Antonveneta and Alitalia are evocative of broader trends in the Italian economy. This protectionist and mercantilist style has clear efficiency costs. Yet, rejection of open markets, long criticized by outsiders as a drag on growth, proved an asset when the global financial system imploded. Hostility towards foreign investment protected Italy from the direct effects of the crisis, as there were limited flows of hot money to dry up. Italian output suffered as a result of the collapse of its export markets, as much as from a fall in domestic demand. In sum, despite the apparently dysfunctional nature of Italian economic institutions, it can be argued that these institutions proved helpful in protecting Italy from international financial turbulence (Quaglia 2009).

Not only did (partial) structural reforms fail to produce clear benefits on economic performance, the political implications of the crisis undermine the reform agenda still further. The crisis has discredited the Anglo-Saxon model of capitalism, which inspired at least in part the Lisbon process and the push for reform from institutions such as the IMF and OECD. To the extent that structural reforms are associated in the public debate with the excesses of financialization, the case for these reforms is weakened. The severe imbalances of the Spanish economy were ignored because Spain ticked the correct boxes according to the orthodoxy of the boom years: fiscal probity, openness to financial flows, a booming real estate market, and an acquisitive and outward-looking corporate sector. The collapse of this model can only discredit these policies.

In Italy, the crisis is also likely to reinforce economic policy conservatism. The Italian elites' determination to retain control of their economy by curbing markets was theorized by Giulio Tremonti, Berlusconi's treasury minister, in a book, *La Paura e la Speranza* (2008). For Tremonti and his allies on the Italian right, globalization was always seen as a threat rather than an opportunity. The Italian left, ironically, has increasingly embraced a "third way" style of politics that accepts many features of market liberalism, such as flexible labor markets (Alesina and Giavazzi 2007). But after the experience of the Monti government, which combined attempted structural reforms with tax increases and restrictions on spending, the Italian electorate's suspicion of liberalization remains strong.

In sum, structural reform has failed in Southern Europe. It has failed in that most of the agenda remains unfulfilled, but it has also failed because to the extent that liberalization measures were taken, they cannot be defended politically as unqualified successes. Given the political difficulties of pushing through reforms, which in many respects would be inconsistent with entrenched social and economic institutions, this suggests an increasing rejection of reform. The association of reforms with austerity policies imposed by supranational institutions, under the threat of punishment by the bond markets, seems almost designed to mobilize electoral support for protectionist policies. The Southern European countries and Ireland have seen the biggest drops in popularity of the European project over the years since the crisis (Serricchio, Tsakatika and Quaglia 2013). For the EU to blame the crisis on these countries' reluctance to reform, and impose strict procyclical fiscal policies, is courting further popular hostility to European integration.

CONCLUSION

This chapter has drawn on the experiences of the two largest Southern European democracies—Italy and Spain—to argue that the sovereign debt crisis in the Eurozone has been misinterpreted. Northern European politicians and European Union leaders have focused on the alleged fiscal irresponsibility and inflationary wage rises in Southern Europe as causes of the crisis, neglecting to take seriously the role of financial flows within the Eurozone as the real cause of the problem. Although Southern Europe's characteristic institutional arrangements have many flaws, they are not the sole cause of the crisis, and in some respects, may have helped mitigate its effects. The comparative analysis of Italy and Spain illustrates that the rush to open peripheral economies to capital flows from surplus economies in the North was the real threat to the integrity of the Eurozone. The protectionist instincts exhibited by Italian political and business elites may have contributed to containing the effects of global instability for Italy, while Spain's more enthusiastic embrace of financial integration exposed it to the bubble dynamics generated by unrestrained and unregulated capital movements.

There are at least two possible explanations for this misinterpretation of the nature of the crisis on the part of European elites. The first is that it is politically easier to blame the victims of the crisis, and helps avert the risk that the response to the crisis would threaten the interests of the creditor nations within the Eurozone. After all, blaming the failings of the debtor nations deflects attention away from the reckless and inept management of the North's financial surplus by its financial institutions. A focus on the failings of the financial sector would increase the pressure on Northern European creditors to consider debt restructuring and would also build momentum behind the push for stronger regulation of the European financial system, a thorny political issue that European leaders seem reluctant to address.

The second interpretation emphasizes the ideological blinkers afflicting European policymakers in the current context. The design of EMU reflected the dominant thinking in elite circles about economic governance in the 1990s and, in particular, the dominant view on how the economy works amongst German political and financial elites. These dominant views emphasized the efficiency of financial markets (which justified unrestricted capital flows, allowing money to be invested in ways which would supposedly maximize returns), the undesirability of exchange-rate flexibility and inflation, the importance of fiscal probity, and a preference for "light touch" regulation in the financial, product, and labor markets. These views reflected in part the broad Washington consensus centered around US elite thinking and in part the preferences of the dominant actors within the European Union. The response to the crisis was naturally conditioned by the assumptions made by the designers of the monetary union.

Given these assumptions, the crisis in Southern Europe could not possibly be the consequence of financial markets' inherent instability or the dangers of excessive monetary rigidity. Instead, the problems lay in the reckless behavior of Southern European politicians who spent too much public money and the greed of Southern European trade unions who bid wages way beyond competitive levels. Given this interpretation of the crisis, it is only natural that European policy makers should identify greater restraints on national fiscal autonomy and structural reforms of labor markets as the way forward. Moreover, it follows from these assumptions that countercyclical macroeconomic policy is out of the question, since it would only worsen the problem of government indebtedness while likely sparking inflation. Hence, the only response to the crisis, save last minute bailouts when the Eurozone appears close to collapse, is to impose austerity and demand structural reforms. If the analysis presented here is correct, these policies are entirely misplaced and fail to address the real problems of the institutional framework of the Eurozone. Not only will these policies most likely fail, they may well prove politically self-defeating, encouraging a populist, anti-European backlash in the periphery countries.

The threats to political stability in Southern Europe are clear, and they are closely related to the structural reform agenda. Economic reforms face a classic political dilemma: the costs are concentrated and immediate whereas the benefits (where they exist) are diffuse and delayed. For this reason, opponents of reform are more likely to mobilize than the potential beneficiaries, leaving reformist governments exposed to high political risks with very uncertain rewards (Stokes 2002). In the midst of a severe economic crisis, structural reforms will likely face even greater opposition than in normal conditions, since losers from reform stand to lose more, given the scarcity of economic opportunity. In the first three to four years of the crisis, protests against austerity policies were not of the order of magnitude necessary to threaten political stability. As the recession continues and even deepens, the potential for disorder increases, and government proposals for structural reforms that would deprive some social groups of their livelihoods can be expected to provoke a response.

At the time of writing, political tensions in Spain and Italy are building rapidly, and each country currently faces destabilizing threats. In Spain, one clear effect of the crisis is the sharpening of the territorial cleavage, with a strong rise in proindependence sentiment in Catalonia, and the strategic shift of the mainstream nationalist party, Convergence and Union, in favor of a referendum on Catalan statehood. In the presence of a conservative Spanish nationalist party (the Popular Party) in the central government, this development has the potential to disrupt interterritorial solidarity at a moment when the Spanish state is demanding spending cuts of its regional governments. As well as the heightening territorial tensions, Spain's spectacularly high unemployment interacts with the build-up of household indebtedness to produce serious social strains. Spain's personal bankruptcy laws are very restrictive, and mortgage defaults are severely penalized, with banks enjoying the right to repossess properties without giving up their claims to repayment of the outstanding mortgages. This has led to the practice of 'escraches', imported from the Argentine experience, whereby protestors mobilize outside the homes of politicians that have opposed reforms to these regulations. Youth unemployment of over 50% has driven a number of mass mobilizations emulating the US 'Occupy' movement, christened as the 'indignados'. The collapsing support of the two main political parties in opinion polls confirms the threats to political stability (Orriols 2013).

In Italy, where elections were held in February 2013, the backlash has taken the form of the dramatic rise of an "antipolitics" party, the Five Stars Movement led by comedian Beppe Grillo, which won a spectacular 25 percent of the vote in its first national election (Hopkin 2013). The marked decline in the vote shares of the two main parties – the Democratic Party on the centre-left and Silvio Berlusconi's People of Liberty on the right – meant that there was no clear majority for any coherent coalition in the Italian Parliament, placing Grillo's movement under the spotlight. The Five Stars Movement has few policy ideas, and most of its program consisted of cuts in the salaries of elected politicians and experiments with direct democracy, although one of its commitments is to a referendum on euro membership. Added to the increasingly euroskeptic stance of Berlusconi's party and its coalition partner the separatist Northern League, which also campaigned on an antiausterity theme, this amounts to a majority of Italy's parliamentarians blaming the European Union for Italy's fiscal problems. At the time of writing there is no government in Italy, and the economic situation is becoming increasingly desperate. But the poor showing of Mario Monti's centrist alliance confirms that the policy mix advocated by the European Union institutions lacks sufficient political support to have any chance of being implemented in Italy.

Imposing further austerity and structural reform in these circumstances is fraught with risk. The euro crisis and the troubles of Southern Europe are developing into a kind of political economy experiment, testing the resilience of the social order and the political institutions of some of Europe's youngest democracies. The austerity program places all the burden of adjustment on the Eurozone's debtor nations, while the recommendations of the European institutions for structural reforms require key elements of the social settlement of Southern European countries to be dismantled in the midst of the worst economic crisis for decades. The slow-motion collapse of the Greek political system and social order provides a stark warning of the possible consequences of this experiment.

Notes

1. The economic woes of southern "Club Med" countries have illustrated the untenable tensions of linking nations of vast economic disparities in a currency zone without a central fiscal authority or unified budget to address imbalances.
2. See, for example "Rising Deficits in Portugal, Italy Rattle Eurozone," *Financial Times*, 17 May 2005.
3. An excellent analysis along these lines can be found in Hall (2012).
4. For example, the Centre for European Reform's annual "Lisbon Scorecard": http://www.cer.org.uk/publications/archive/report/2010/lisbon-scorecard-x-road-2020.
5. For a more thorough analysis of the data, see Hopkin and Blyth (2012). Much of this data is drawn from the World Bank Institute's "Doing Business" data collection project. See Djankov et al. (2002).
6. On statism, see Schmidt (2002).
7. In this analysis, for reasons of simplicity of exposition we neglect the important observation of authors such as Vogel that market liberalization generates the need for new regulation, so that talk of "more" or "less" regulation can be misleading (Vogel 1998).
8. Another example is the disastrous investment made by BG Group (British Gas) in Brindisi, in the Apulia region. A planned €500 million liquefied natural gas terminal was ultimately shelved after environmental approvals were withdrawn and local managers charged with corruption. See "Italy Halts BG Group Plan for Brindisi." *Financial Times.* 8 October 2007. http://www.ft.com/cms/s/0/b5f1e6ac-75da-11dc-b7cb-0000779fd2ac.html#axzz2I4lsvava[4].

References

Alesina, Alberto, and Francesco Giavazzi. 2007. *Il liberismo e di sinistra*. Rome: Il Saggiatore.

Botero, Juan C., Simeon Djankov, Rafael LaPorta, Florencio Lopez-de-Silanes and Andrei Schleifer. 2004. "The Regulation of Labor." *Quarterly Journal of Economics* 119 (4): 1339–82.

Bosco, Anna. 2005. *Da Franco a Zapatero: La Spagna dalla periferia al cuore d'Europa*. Bologna: Il Mulino.

Cohen, Roger. 2010. "Greece, Europe and Alexander Hamilton," *New York Times*, 1 March.

De Serres, Alain, Shuji Kobayakawa, Torsten Sløk and Laura Vartia. 2006. "Regulation of Financial Systems and Economic Growth." *OECD Economics Department Working Papers* 506.

Djankov, Simeon, Rafael LaPorta, Florencio Lopez-de-Silanes and Andrei Schleifer. 2002. "The Regulation of Entry." *Quarterly Journal of Economics* 117 (1): 1–37.

European Commission. 2005. "Country Study: Spain in EMU: A Virtuous Long-Lasting Cycle?" *Occasional Papers*, 14. Brussels: European Commission Directorate Generale of Economic and Financial Affairs.

Hall, Peter. 2012. "The Economics and Politics of the Euro Crisis." *German Politics* 21 (4): 355–71.

Hine, David. 1999. "Malpensa 2000." In *Italian Politics: The Return of Politics*, edited by David Hine and Salvatore Vassallo, 209–26. Oxford: Berghahn.

Hopkin, Jonathan, and Mark Blyth. 2012. "What Can Okun Teach Polanyi? Efficiency, Regulation and Equality in the OECD." *Review of International Political Economy* 19 (1): 1–33.

Hopkin, Jonathan, and Daniel Wincott. 2006. "New Labour, Economic Reform and the European Social Model." *British Journal of Politics and International Relations* 8 (1): 50–68.

Hopkin, Jonathan. 2013. " Italy Did Not Just Send in the Clowns". *Foreign Affairs* March 11. http://www.foreignaffairs.com/articles/139051/jonathan-hopkin/italy-did-not-just-send-in-the-clowns

Messori, Marcello 2006. "The Bank Takeover Bids and the Role of the Bank of Italy." In *Italian Politics: The End of the Berlusconi Era?*, edited by Grant Amyot and Luca Verzichelli, 139–63. Oxford: Berghahn.

OECD. 2005. *Policy Brief: Economic Survey of Spain. 2005*. Paris: OECD.

Orriols, Luis. 2013. "Se muere el bipartidismo PPSOE?". *El Diario.es. Piedras de Papel*, 27 March. http://www.eldiario.es/piedrasdepapel/fin-bipartidismo-PPSOE_6_115198484.html

Quaglia, Lucia. 2009. "The Response to the Global Financial Turmoil in Italy: 'A Financial System that Does Not Speak English.'" *South European Society and Politics* 14 (1): 7–18.

Rhodes, Martin. 2001. "The Political Economy of Social Pacts: Competitive Corporatism' and European Welfare Reform." In *The New Politics of the Welfare State*, edited by Paul Pierson, 165–94. Oxford: Oxford University Press.

Roubini, Nouriel, and Stephen Mihm. 2010. *Crisis Economics: A Crash Course in the Future of Finance*. New York: Penguin.

Salvati, Michele. 2003. "Italia-Spagna: Un Confronto." In *La Lezione Spagnola*, edited by Víctor Pérez-Díaz. Bologna: Il Mulino.

Sapir, André. 2006. "Globalization and the Reform of the European Social Model." *Journal of Common Market Studies* 44 (2): 369–90.

Schmidt, Vivien. 2002. *The Futures of European Capitalism*. Oxford: Oxford University Press.

Schwab, Klaus, ed. 2010. *The Lisbon Review 2010*. Geneva: World Economic Forum.

Schwab, Klaus, ed. 2012. *Global Competitiveness Report 2012/13*.Geneva: World Economic Forum.

Serricchio, Fabio, Myrto Tsakatika and Lucia Quaglia. 2002. "Euroskepticism and the Global Financial Crisis." *Journal of Common Market Studies* 51 (1): 51–64.

Stokes, Susan. 2002. *Public Support for Market Reforms in New Democracies*. Cambridge: Cambridge University Press.

Tabellini, Guido, and Charles Wyplosz. 2006. "Supply-side Reforms in Europe: Can the Lisbon Strategy Be Repaired?" *Swedish Economic Policy Review* 13: 101–56.

The Economist. 2001. "Fit to Run Italy?". 26 April. http://www.economist.com/node/593654

The Economist. 2005. "Italy: The Real Sick Man of Europe". 19 May. http://www.economist.com/node/3987219?story_id=3987219

Tremonti, Giulio. 2008. *La paura e la Speranza. Europa: La crisi globale che si avvicina e la via per superarla*. Milan: Mondadori.

Verney, Susannah. 2009. "Flaky Fringe? Southern Europe Faces the Financial Crisis." *South European Society and Politics* 14/1 (2009): 1–6.

Vogel, Stephen. 1998. *Freer Markets, More Rules: Regulatory Reform in Advanced Industrial Countries*. Ithaca, NY: Cornell University Press.

Wade, Robert. 2000. "Wheels within Wheels: Rethinking the Asian Crisis and the Asian Model." *Annual Review of Political Science* 3: 85–115.

Wise, Peter, Adrian Michaels and George Parker. 2005. "Rising Deficits in Portugal, Italy Rattle Eurozone," *Financial Times*, May 17.

Zemanek, Holger. 2010. "Competitiveness within the Euro Area: The Problem that Still Needs to Be Solved." *Economic Affairs* 30 (3): 42–7.

9   Greece and the Recent Financial Crisis
Meltdown or Configuration?

Sotirios Zartaloudis, University of Manchester

INTRODUCTION

The ongoing financial crisis has put the so-called EU cohesion countries (Greece, Portugal, Ireland, and Spain)[1] at the center of a borrowing cost cyclone. Their ever-increasing borrowing costs and recourse to the Troika for financial support has meant that they have had to implement extensive fiscal consolidation measures. This chapter discusses the impact of the ongoing (2008–2012) financial crisis on Greek politics. It first provides a succinct overview of Greek politics before the commencement of the financial crisis, arguing that Greece enjoyed one of the most stable, popular, and widely legitimated democratic regimes of its modern history. Second, it discusses Greece's response to the financial crisis, arguing that the latter constituted a critical juncture for the country's politics and public policy (Collier and Collier 1991). Third, it examines the impact of the financial crisis on perceptions (Blyth 2002), arguing that the crisis has led to the rise of populism, extremism, violence, and nationalism. Fourth, it assesses the impact of the financial crisis on Greek politics, arguing that it led not only to a significant rise in protests, strikes, and public discontent—and also to the dramatic reconfiguration of the Greek political system, characterized by the rise of extreme antisystemic parties and the fall of mainstream ones. The chapter concludes by arguing that these political developments have further exacerbated the Greek crisis.

GREEK POLITICS BEFORE THE CRISIS: DEMOCRATIC CONSOLIDATION THROUGH PUBLIC DEBT?

In 1974, Greece's seven-year dictatorship collapsed due to the Cyprus debacle instigated by the Colonels' regime. The colonels themselves invited the previous premier, Konstantinos Karamanlis, back to the country. Karamanlis had led the country back to democracy by conducting free elections and legalizing the then-outlawed Greek Communist Party. Karamanlis created a new center-right party, New Democracy (ND), which was in office between 1974 and 1981. During that time, a new leftist party—the Pan-Hellenic Socialist Movement

Table 9.1   Electoral Results (%)—Greece

	1981	1993	1996	2000	2009	2012
PASOK	48	47	41	44	44	12
ND	36	39	38	43	34	30
KKE	11	4.5	5	5	7	4.5
SYN/SYRIZA	-	2.9	5	3	4	27
GD	> 0.2	> 0.2	> 0.2	> 0.2	> 0.2	7

Source: http://ekloges.ypes.gr; results given in rounded figures.

(PASOK)—gained popularity among the Greek electorate with its populist anti-Western (against US, NATO, and EU) and anticapitalist discourse. In 1981, PASOK was elected to office and initiated a period of almost total dominance in Greek politics. It dropped its pre-1981 radical discourse and assumed a clearly pro-Western and pro-EU stance. PASOK remained in government for more than twenty-three years of the thirty-eight-year-long democratic period that commenced in 1974 (1981–1989; 1993–2004; 2009–2012). The ND was in power the remaining fourteen years[2] (1974–1981; 1990–1993; 2004–2009). In other words, both parties dominated Greek politics until 2012. They governed the country in turns and enjoyed an overwhelming majority of over 70 percent of the combined popular vote (see Table 9.1).

The 1974–2009 Greek political system was complemented by small parties of the extreme left and right that tended to have Eurosceptic and anti-Western orientations (Verney 2011). The Greek Communist Party (KKE) has been a constant member of the Greek parliament since 1974, facilitating the incorporation of a long-persecuted part of society to the Greek political system. In addition, since 1993, a splinter group of the Communists—most of them Euro-Communists and/or anti-Soviet/Stalinist—has been represented in almost all parliamentary terms (with the exception of 1993–1996) as SYN (Coalition of the Left and Progress). In 2003, SYN joined SYRIZA (Coalition of the Radical Left-Uniform Social Front). SYRIZA is a coalition, formed by SYN (the largest group) and numerous leftist factions (SYRIZA 2012a). In June 2010, most of the moderate pro-European members of SYN left SYRIZA and formed a new party with the acronym DHMAR (Democratic Left), which favors Greece's EU membership and supports a social-market economy based on a strong welfare state. Since 2003, SYRIZA adopted a more leftist and anti-systemic discourse than SYN (see the following ideational narratives on crisis causes and solutions). In addition to the mentioned parties, the Greek political system also had a number of splinter parties from PASOK and ND. As they lasted for only one to three elections, they will not be discussed in this chapter (Nicolakopoulos 2005).

Despite the shift in the Greek political system, economic policy in the post-1974 period remained surprisingly similar to the postwar one. More specifically, the dominant policy model during this period was statism (state intervention in economic and social activities) accompanied by clientelism, which marginalized any autonomous political organization of disadvantaged classes or groups (Diamandouros 1983). Furthermore, the public sector had a predominant role in providing employment, which resulted in its strategic use by political elites who used employment provision as a way to satisfy voters and/or expand their electorate. Finally, trade unions were highly subordinate to party politics, and civil society groups in favor of progressive redistribution were weak (Petmesidou 1991).

As stated previously, ND and PASOK have dominated Greek parties since the return to democracy (a period known as "metapolitefsi"). These parties continued on the same statist and clientelistic path, but with a major difference: monetary and fiscal stability were largely ignored by the postdictatorship governments, as the expansion of the state was the main tool for democratic consolidation (Pagoulatos 2005). Public debt consequently increased from 17.6 percent of GDP in 1970 to 28.3 percent in 1981, and reached 112 percent in 1986 (Ioakimides 2001, 77). During this period, public-sector effectiveness and efficiency were completely neglected as the public administration was controlled by party cadres and thus converted to a fundamental component of "bureaucratic clientelism" (Lyritzis 1984). Additionally, the 1980s were characterized by strong government intervention in setting higher minimum wages that were not always in line with changes in productivity or levels of employment, but rather with the political promises and ideological convictions of the new PASOK government (Venieris 2006). This policy had a negative effect on unemployment, which became an acute problem, especially among the young and women (Katrougalos and Lazaridis 2003, 59).

In the 1990s, both PASOK and ND governments implemented a number of privatizations and labor market reforms (which were opposed by the unions) (Featherstone 2003, 2006; Pagoulatos 2005; Mitsopoulos and Pelagidis 2012; Featherstone and Papadimitriou 2008) to gain entry to the Economic and Monetary Union by the end of the decade (Pagoulatos 2005, 360). Despite these reforms, none of the post-1990s' governments curtailed the hiring process in the public sector. Thus, despite some modest efforts towards fiscal consolidation, Greek public debt and deficits remained high (see Tables 9.2 and 9.3). Moreover, the trend of pay rises and generous pensions along with early retirement schemes remained in place (Tsakalotos 1998, 121) and tax revenues remain low (Greece had consistently lower tax revenues than the

Table 9.2 General Government Public Deficit/Surplus as a Percentage of GDP

	1981	1988	1995	1997	1999	2000	2007	2008	2009	2010	2011
Greece	-11	-12.8	:	:	:	-3.7	-6.5	-9.8	-15.6	-10.7	-9.4
Euro-17	:	:	-7.2	-2.8	-1.5	-0.1	-0.7	-2.1	-6.4	-6.2	-4.1

Source: Eurostat; 1981 and 1988 data retrieved from Dornbusch and Draghi (1990, 2).
(:= unavailable data)

Table 9.3   *General Government Public Debt as a Percentage of GDP*

	1981	1988	1995	2000	2007	2008	2009	2010	2011
Greece	28.8	73.6	97.0	103.4	107.4	112.9	129.7	148.3	170.6
Euro-17	:	:	:	69.2	66.3	70.2	80.5	85.4	87.3

Source: Eurostat; 1981 and 1988 data for Greece, retrieved from: Dornbusch and Draghi 1990, 2.
(: = unavailable data)

Table 9.4   *Total Unemployment Levels (%)*

	1995	2000	2007	2008	2009	2010	2011
Greece	:	11.2	8.3	7.7	9.5	12.6	17.7
Euro-17	10.5	8.7	7.6	7.6	9.6	10.1	10.2

Source: Eurostat. (: = unavailable data)

EU-27 average) (Meghir, Vayanos and Vettas 2010, 10–13). The low levels of tax revenues were due not only to public-sector inefficiency and corruption but also to the structure of the economy, as the black economy and proportion of self-employment and family businesses is larger in Greece than the EU average (Katrougalos and Lazaridis 2003). Despite the media coverage of public-sector profligacy (Featherstone 2011; Verney 2009), clientelism did not lead to an overstaffed public sector in absolute numbers. Still, it was plagued by persistently low efficiency and had a relative high number of public-sector workers compared to the EU average—its size was similar to that of most European countries but provided lower-quality services despite gradual improvement during the period 1990–2000 (Afonso, Schuknecht and Tanzi 2005).

As a result of the previously stated policies, Greece was plagued by persistently high public debt, deficits, and sluggish growth during the 1980s. Nonetheless, when fiscal consolidation was coupled with privatization in the early and mid-1990s to achieve European Monetary Union (EMU) entry, growth picked up and Greece enjoyed a period of increasing prosperity, with high economic growth, falling unemployment, and rising incomes until 2007, which led to achieving 94 percent of EU-27 average GDP per capita in Purchasing Power Standards (PPS) (see Tables 9.4, 9.5, 9.6). Unsurprisingly, the two main parties that led the country's democratization, PASOK and ND, were highly popular and dominated Greek politics for the whole 1974–2009 period.

Table 9.5   *GDP Change from Previous Year (growth/recession)*

	1996	2000	2007	2008	2009	2010	2011
Greece	2.4p	3.5p	3.0p	-0.2 p	-3.1 p	-4.9 p	-7.1 p
Euro-17	:	3.8	3.0	0.4	-4.4	2.0	1.4

Source: Eurostat (p = provisional value; : = unavailable data)

Table 9.6   GDP per PPS Compared to the EU-27 Average

	1996	2000	2004	2008	2009	2010	2011
Greece	83	84p	94p	92	94	90	82
Euro-17	115	115	113	111	110	110	110

Source: Eurostat (p = provisional value)

GREECE'S RESPONSE TO THE CRISIS: DENIAL, INERTIA AND INFIGHTING

When the economic crisis began in 2007, Greece was enjoying a period of economic growth and falling unemployment. The incumbent ND government proudly proclaimed that Greece was "safe" and protected from the crisis because Greek banks were not involved in the subprime mortgage crisis. The authorities further professed that the country was in a better situation that most of their EU counterparts and accused the foreign press of witch hunting when it reported Greece's increasing borrowing costs (*Kathimerini* 2008a, 2008b, 2008c). This was for the most part true, as only one financial institution[3] had invested in the toxic financial products that were at the root of the financial crisis in the US and the Eurozone, and the overwhelming majority of the Greek financial institutions was not affected by the financial crisis in the early stages. However, this was only a half truth. Although Greece was not directly affected by the subprime mortgage crisis, it was indirectly affected by the lack of confidence in global financial markets and the increasing borrowing costs among financial and nonfinancial institutions. Borrowing costs for Greece had started to increase slowly but surely since 2007. Still, the country did not face difficulties in financing its increasing deficits and debts from financial markets because its high growth rates secured confidence in the country.

Despite the relative calm before the upcoming storm, Greek politics was already sliding into a crisis. The ruling party ND was floundering because it only held a marginal majority in parliament. Additionally, numerous scandals involving key ministers and members of the party shook the government. The political crisis escalated in December 2008 when a teenage student was shot by a policeman in Athens. Riots spread as young people protested against the police, the government, and the state. Along with severe clashes between protesters and the police, the riots resulted in the widespread destruction of public and private property. The country appeared completely ungoverned as the government, in order to prevent the loss of lives, gave specific orders for the police to remain passive and allow the crowds to release their anger without any serious repression (Andronikidou and Kovras 2012, 721).

The endgame of the ND government began in 2009 when Premier Karamanlis ordered an early end of the parliamentary session, ahead of the general elections of October 2009. This move rendered Greece almost ungoverned for more than six months while the financial crisis escalated. Concurrently, the recession that hit in 2008 caused the deficit to skyrocket and Greek finances to deteriorate dramatically (see Table 9.2). Even though both prime ministerial candidates (Karamanlis from ND and Papandreou from PASOK) were aware of this state of affairs,[4] the situation went unreported as Greek officials once again provided false figures about its finances (European Commission 2010). In October 2009, PASOK won the elections on an agenda of economic expansionism based on pay and pension rises, tax cuts, and renationalizations. Although the crisis had already hit and the deficit hit a double-digit figure, the new government remained inactive until April 2010, at which point it sought financial support from Europe and the IMF to finance its deficit and debt. It is argued that the request for external support and the signing of the Memorandum of Understanding (MOU)[5] constitute a critical juncture for Greek public policy and politics. It meant the end of a long period when Greece was becoming wealthier and politicians for the most part followed an expansionary fiscal policy (with some exceptions during 1990–1993 and 1996–2000) financed by state borrowing (Mitsopoulos and Pelagidis 2012). After the signing of the Troika bailout in May 2010, the recession intensified alongside the significant and widespread cuts in public spending and benefits along with an unprecedented rise in taxation. In addition, Greece implemented a series of unpopular supply-side reforms, reformed its health and tax collection services, restructured its state apparatus, and proceeded with mass-scale privatizations. The recent crisis thus created a radically new economic reality that had a profound impact on Greek public policy.

The Troika–Greece deals and the subsequent MOUs had three main goals: 1) eliminate fiscal imbalances by achieving fiscal surpluses, 2) improve Greek competitiveness, and 3) provide liquidity for Greece until it returned to the financial markets. Given the large fiscal imbalances of the country when it requested official support (see Tables 9.2 and 9.3), the MOUs initially focused on achieving fiscal consolidation by cutting public-sector spending and increasing tax revenues. Greece implemented repeated rounds of public spending cuts including (European Commission 2012a, 2012b): the reduction of public investment; a gradual abolishment of the two so-called 13th and 14th salaries (Christmas, Easter, and summer bonuses) for public-sector workers; the establishment of a uniform system of public-sector remuneration; the introduction of a pay ceiling for general government employees (starting from approximately €3,000 per month in 2010 and currently being set at €1,900); reduction of allowances by approximately 30 percent; the introduction of a 1:5 hiring ratio—meaning that only one employee could be hired only for every five that left; and introduction of a labor reserve scheme whereby approximately 150,000 public-sector workers would be fired or forced into early retirement (Zartaloudis, 2011). In November 2012, the newly elected coalition government implemented the latest austerity measures that included, inter alia: the halving of all remuneration of local government officials; the further reduction of allowances for all public-sector employees; the reduction of pay for all high-level bureaucrats and political personnel; inclusion of more employees of the wider public sector in the common remuneration system; and further reduction of public-sector employees paid via special arrangements (e.g. judiciary and army).

In addition, a series of pension cuts were implemented for all (public and private) pensioners: the 13th and 14th pension was gradually abolished for pensioners earning above €2,500 monthly or those below 60 years of age; all pension entitlements were frozen until 2014; pensioners earning more than €1,400 would pay an additional tax (3 percent–9 percent); the retirement age was increased to 67 years of age for all employees; many occupational funds providing more favorable conditions were merged with the main social-security fund of the private sector, which transformed the Bismarkian Greek pension system to a multipillar pension system with separate contributory and noncontributory elements (Matsaganis 2011). Moreover, in November 2012, most pensioners lost a great amount (on average, 25–50 percent) of the lump-sum pay they received when they retired, and a regressive reduction of pension remuneration was implemented (5 percent cut for pensions from €1,000–€1,500 up to 25 percent for pensions above 4,000).

The above cuts were combined with a series of rises in taxation. More specifically, in the first year of the MOU a number of indirect taxes were introduced along with the steep rise in the Value Added Tax (VAT). Having previously had the most generous scheme (€12,000) in the Organization for Economic Co-operation and Development (OECD) (Garello 2010), Greece gradually harmonized its ceiling for taxable income with the EU average. Additionally, all Greeks earning above a certain income had to pay an extra tax called the Social Solidarity Tax, which would finance a cash benefit for the poorest Greeks. All homeowners also had to pay an additional property tax. Another key aspect of all MOUs involved the reform of the tax-collection system through the reduction of the number of agencies responsible for tax collection, the reduction of the staff numbers and bureaucratic processes, and the modernization of the tax-collection system. The latter part of the reform remains to be seen in Greece and has proven to be the most difficult to implement (European Commission 2012a, 2012b).

With regard to increasing competitiveness, Greece had to reduce its labor costs that were unnecessarily high as it had been granting constant pay rises above productivity since the early 1980s. The Greek government introduced a series of pay freezes in the private sector as well as a new framework of lower minimum salaries and lower pay levels than the national minimum for young workers. Furthermore, it implemented a series of labor market reforms that resulted in the flexibilization of employment relations by allowing collective agreements at the local, sectoral, and firm level. Another key component of the MOUs was a requirement linked with a number of EU directives regarding the opening up of the so-called closed professions (many professions, e.g. lawyers, pharmacists, taxi drivers, and engineers, were heavily regulated with restrictions on entry, operation, and service fees). Greece also implemented a series of mass-scale privatizations. However, on this front, little progress has been observed, given the dire economic situation of the country along with the unwillingness of the Greek government to privatize because of the fierce opposition of the trade unions and other actors who argued that the MOUs aimed to sell off the country (see section on the ideational impact of the crisis below).

The above measures not only constituted a critical juncture for Greek public policy and politics but also created tension between Greek governments and the Troika, as they were quite unpopular among the Greek public. The Papandreou government took the position that the MOU measures were against the party's ideology but were a necessary evil for saving the country from bankruptcy. Still, many members of the party, MPs, and ministers who had a more statist approach and favored the policies of the 1980s, openly criticized the Troika measures. As a result, some of the cuts and reforms that were voted through by the parliament were inadequately implemented (European Commission 2012a, 2012b). For instance, many restrictions on the closed professions remained until November 2012, the one-in-five hiring ratio was not maintained, many public-sector employees were not included in the uniform pay system, and there were few redundancies.[6] The Papadimos government had a relatively less confrontational relationship with the Troika given the premier's profile and the government's commitment to implementing the required austerity measures in February 2012, which were a precondition for Greece's second bailout (European Commission 2012b). During the last two elections, uncertainty about Greece's commitment to the MOU and Eurozone entry increased, and the Troika left the country until the formation of the new government. The current coalition government is based on a consensual agreement between three parties (formerly adversaries—ND, PASOK, and DHMAR) that are jointly pursuing a pro-EU and probailout agenda, and appear openly committed to implementing the MOU measures. This can be considered an achievement given the considerable antagonism shown by the current premier (Samaras) to the MOU while he was in the opposition (see the following section) and the low degree of consensus in Greek politics since the beginning of the crisis (Afonso, Zartaloudis and Papadopoulos 2012).

THE IDEATIONAL IMPACT OF THE FINANCIAL CRISIS ON GREEKS

The third part of this chapter examines the impact of the financial crisis on Greek perceptions (ideas, rhetoric, symbols, narratives, and other accounts of the social production of intersubjective meaning). It argues that the crisis resulted in the exacerbation of preexisting trends in Greek politics (namely, political violence, populism, and nationalism) (Clogg 1993; Stavrakakis 2002; Andronikidou and Kovras 2012) along with the rise of extremism. Greek elites and the public initially denied the crisis. Premier Papandreou consistently argued that Greece was attacked by "speculators" and "financial predators" who were unjustifiably and excessively betting on a Greek default in order to attack the euro. This view was widely reproduced by Greek media until the signing of the MOU in April 2010. It is argued that this state of denial had a very negative impact on the management of the crisis, as Greece was portrayed as an innocent victim of a global currency war which weakened voices highlighting the structural deficiencies of the economy that put Greece in the spotlight of the financial crisis.

If the Greek government was ambivalent about having to turn to the IMF and the EU, the opposition was clearly against it. With the exception of the small, populist, right-wing Popular Orthodox Rally (LAOS), which supported the first bailout and then opposed the second, all other parties were openly against the signing of the MOU. The most surprising adversary of the MOU was ND, which arguably played a key role in the worsening of Greece finances and competitiveness when in office during 2004–2009. The new leader of ND—Antonis Samaras—rejected the MOU and argued that Greece needed another "policy-mix" to promote growth (ND 2010; XO 2012). The remaining opposition parties (KKE and SYRIZA) were openly and vehemently against the MOU, calling it a neoliberal onslaught against workers devised to save the elites and the banks. KKE argued that there is no bailout in capitalism and that only a workers revolt would save Greece. It proposed that this could be achieved by withdrawing from the EU and NATO (KKE 1996, 2012). SYRIZA adopted for a less anticapitalist and anti-European discourse, but openly attacked the government for signing the MOU and denounced the IMF for its harsh neoliberal stance (*Tanea* 2012a; *Enet* 2010; SYRIZA 2010). Notably, all parties and opponents of the MOU followed the same logic and focused predominantly on the involvement of the IMF in the bailout, which ended up embodying the Troika while the EU was forgotten. It is argued that this was a strategic choice, as most Greeks were predominantly pro-European (Pagoulatos 2012).

Another strategic decision of the opposition was to focus on the MOU and the conditions demanded for Greece to receive support rather than the whole bailout deal. The aim of this strategy was to uncouple the demand for unpopular measures in return for new loans that would help Greece finance its public and trade deficits until its return to the financial markets. The opposition thus criticized the government (by stressing the negative impact of the measures on incomes), but not the reward (the Troika loans). As a result, two informal camps gradually formed in Greek public discourse: those who supported the MOU (memorandians or, in Greek, μνημονιακοί) and those who opposed it (antimemorandians, or in Greek, αντί-μνημονιακοί). This distinction is rather misleading as it ends up in an arbitrary and Manichaean divide. For instance, both camps have favored tackling tax evasion, cutting waste, and improving Greece's institutional, legal, and bureaucratic framework. And while the antimemorandum camp rejects austerity and the recession, it is more than certain that without the MOU, Greece would have to implement even further austerity measures. Hence, this division not only obfuscated the real policy dilemmas facing Greece (i.e. what kind of measures Greece must implement to improve its economic situation) but also escalated the denial over the country's systemic problems.

The cuts and the signing of the MOU provoked a number of general strikes and protests. The antimemorandum camp gained a street-like character where social media, daily protesters, and nonparty groups became the focal point of the opposition to the MOU as austerity and the recession intensified from late 2011 on. One of the first such groups to emerge was a social movement named Sparkle. The movement claimed that the MOU was unconstitutional and that Germany wanted to steal Greek land, monuments, and natural resources (*Zougla* 2010). Sparkle held rallies against Papandreou and the MOU in many cities and portrayed the government as subordinate to Germany and treacherous. Another group that shaped Greek perceptions about the crisis were the so-called indignant, which was inspired by the Spanish *indignados* movement. The Greek indignant took over Athens' Constitution Square and protested outside the parliament for several months—something unprecedented in Greek politics. Even though the indignant were very diverse and had many demands, they agreed on demanding a referendum for the MOU, a reversal of austerity, the punishment of corrupt politicians, and the protection of the most vulnerable citizens. Many political groups from the extreme left and right advantageously joined the indignant in their protests. After several weeks, two informal camps within the indignant were formed: the "upper Syntagma square" (the area of the square where nationalists were gathering) and the "lower Syntagma square" (the area of the square where leftists were gathering) (Tovima 2011). All of the protesters united whenever the parliament had to vote on a new austerity package. Shockingly, most protesters were chanting that the parliament building should be set ablaze, that the politicians should be hung in public for stealing public money, and that they were defending the country from a dictatorship.

Protest groups were joined by almost all trade unions (e.g. public-sector workers, taxi drivers, pharmacists) that repeatedly demonstrated in the streets of Athens. Parties from the extreme left and right with no parliamentary representation seized the opportunity to mingle with the protests to gain popularity and legitimacy. The most successful was the neo-Nazi organization Golden Dawn (GD), which predominantly focused on the issue of migration and campaigned vocally against immigrants. Given the economic recession, the massive rise in unemployment, and the increase of the number of immigrants, asylum seekers, and refugees, GD succeeded in legitimizing its antiforeigner hate speech and actions. The GD also argued that Greece was governed by corrupt traitors who sold out their country to its creditors without defending the national interest (*Ethnikismos* 2012).

Violent protests, a common feature in Greek politics since 1974 (Andronikidou and Kovras 2012) became more frequent. Almost every demonstration involved street violence, and many politicians were attacked or ambushed by protesters. This period of instability and increasing violence reached its peak in October 2011 when protesters stopped the ceremonies commemorating the decision not to surrender to the Axis powers during World War II in many cities throughout Greece. In these protests, public officials were heckled and attacked. Alarmingly, the president of the Hellenic Republic was heckled and attacked as a traitor that had sold out to the Germans and the MOU. Given the social, economic, and political turmoil, Premier Papandreou, in a desperate attempt to fend off internal party opposition and increase the legitimacy of his government's actions, called for a referendum on whether Greece should sign the second bailout package.

The opposition (especially SYRIZA and Sparkle) described the second bailout deal the final nail in Greece's coffin and denounced the debt-relief process as legal theft that would favor the banks. Papandreou's referendum never took place due to both internal (PASOK and ND) and external (Merkel and Sarkozy) opposition. Instead, after weeks of deliberations, a coalition government between PASOK, ND, and LAOS was formed with a mandate to complete the debt-relief process by negotiating with private bond holders, known as Private Sector Involvement (PSI), and then call for snap elections. The government was led by the appointed premier, Lucas Papadimos, who was the widely respected former European Central Bank (ECB) vice-chancellor. During the Papadimos government, the debate turned even more vitriolic, especially from the far left. SYRIZA branded him as a neoliberal banker who worked for the profits of his bosses against the interest of Greek citizens (*Skai* 2011). Both the left and the right denounced Papadimos's government as a dictatorship of the banks, the ECB, and the neoliberal elite of Brussels (*Axia* 2012). Numerous strikes and demonstrations were held, albeit in a more low-key fashion.

Papadimos resigned when the PSI was completed and Greece entered one of its most divisive electoral periods since 1974. The memorandian and anti-memorandian divide reached its peak, as all parties positioned themselves on the pro/anti-MOU axis. Two large informal blocs were created: on the one hand ND, PASOK, and the small Democratic Left (DHMAR) were in favor of continuing the course that Papandreou and the PASOK government chose (implement the MOU terms in order to receive financial and technical support from the Troika); on the other hand, SYRIZA, LAOS, ANEL,[7] KKE, and other extraparliamentary extreme parties, including GD, were against the it.

The debate during the two subsequent elections in May and June 2012 was rancorous. The promemorandum camp argued that the MOU and the implementation of the bailout were the sine qua non for Greece to remain in the EMU and claimed that the opposition was leading the country to international isolation through bankruptcy and a certain euro exit. In order to fight the rising popularity of the antimemorandum camp, all promemorandum parties vowed to "renegotiate" the terms of the bailouts on the implicit assumption that they could agree a deal that would lessen the burden of austerity. The antimemorandum parties vowed to end the MOUs and Greece's "destruction" by the so-called rescues. According to SYRIZA's leader, Alexis Tsipras, the EU policy was creating a "humanitarian" crisis (*The Guardian* 21 May 2012). The accusations against incumbent politicians of being traitors, neoliberal, and sell-outs continued while the promemorandum Greeks were on the defensive, arguing that they were forced to accept these agreements to save Greece and keep it in the Eurozone. This debate reflected to a great extent the divided and confused Greek public opinion. Even though more than 80 percent of Greeks were in favor of Eurozone membership, approximately 70 percent were against the MOU and the austerity imposed to remain in the EMU (*Lifo* 2012). The inability of the majority of Greek citizens to link the austerity and internal devaluation process with EMU membership can be considered a victory for the opposition, which either accepted the Troika loans or requests for better terms (mainly lower interest rates) but argued that the measures required as a condition for the loans were unnecessary, counterproductive, imposed by Germany, and would lead to Greece's destruction (*Aggelioforos* 2012b). Because most promemorandum parties (especially PASOK and ND) had been winning elections for the last 40 years through clientelistic practices (cf. Lyritzis 1984; Mitsopoulos and Pelagidis 2012; Nicolacopoulos 2005), austerity could only be presented by them as a necessary evil imposed by outsiders in order to remain in the Eurozone. Hence, both pro- and antimemorandum camps were generally negative towards the measures that are necessary for Greece to return to the financial markets.

The most commonly used scapegoat for the unpopular austerity measures and reforms has been Germany. Initially, the harsh and sometimes offensive German press coverage of the crisis and German politicians' statements on the issue (e.g., German magazines with offensive images and comments on ancient Greece, along with claims on the need to annex some Greek islands to Germany as a return for the bailout) hurt the population's national pride. The shock expressed by Greek public opinion was leveraged by Greek politicians like the vice president of the 2009–2011 PASOK government, Theodore Pagkalos, who argued that Greece may end up being the victim of potentially new German racism against Southern Europe. Furthermore, both PASOK and ND claimed that Greece was being unjustifiably punished by Northern Europe as Greece was not responsible for the Eurozone crisis (a position repeatedly supported by Papandreou and Samaras). Tellingly, Papandreou consistently argued that Europe (referring mainly to Merkel and Sarkozy) adopted a clearly conservative approach to the Eurozone crisis, while Samaras argued that the Troika recipe was doomed to failure.

Thereafter, Germany (Merkel in particular) was used as the scapegoat for Greece's quandary in an opportunistic fashion. More specifically, ANEL adopted most of the Sparkle's positions by arguing that it had fallen under foreign occupation and become a "Merkelite-protectorate" after the bailout (*Aggelioforos* 2012a; *Zougla* 2012). Similarly, although SYRIZA is a far-left party, it adopted a very nationalistic discourse. For instance, its leader denounced the Papadimos government as not Greek enough and repeatedly ascribed treacherous motives to the promemorandum camp. In addition, he adopted a nationalistic discourse against Germany and Merkel. On the 19 November 2012, he called Samaras a "Merkel-collaborate" and accused the president of being silent and failing to state a position or express an opinion on the legislation he ratified, thus transforming Greece into a "debt-colony" (*Skai* 2012b). Leading figures of both parties consistently argued that Germany owes money to Greece and not vice versa due to: 1) the World War II reparations that have not yet been repaid; and 2) a loan that the Nazis issued during Greece's occupation by Hitler that had not been given. Any Greek that was in favor of the bailout and the MOUs was thus unpatriotic (Barber 2012; Deutsche-Welle 2012). In many ways, therefore, the discourse of the left and the right often intersected with each other in their accusations against incumbent politicians and their adoption of a nationalistic discourse that blamed an external enemy (Halikio-poulou, Nanou and Vasilopoulou 2012).

In light of the nature of the political debate, it appeared that very few Greeks were critical enough to realize that Greece, through a clientelistic in-terplay between citizens and elected politicians, had created an unsustainable economic model whereby the government kept borrowing to finance its an-nual public and trade deficits (Meghir, Vayanos and Vettas 2010). In addition, the competitiveness of the Greek economy had gradually deteriorated by the unorthodox socialist experiment of the 1980s. Many Greeks therefore resorted to a blame-shifting discourse, where the country's predicament was somebody else's responsibility: for some it was the Germans and Merkel who wanted to once again enslave Southern Europe (and Greece in particular); for others it was the corrupt and treacherous elites (mainly politicians and bankers) who stole public money and sent the bill to ordinary people.

In sum, the financial crisis fuelled tendencies within Greek society that lurked in the background such as populism, nationalism, extremism, and vio-lence—evidence of the incomplete and defective democracy of the Metapo-litefsi. Moreover, Greek public opinion was divided over how to respond to the crisis: for some the MOU was a necessary evil that Greece had to accept in order to stay in the Eurozone; for others it was an unacceptable punishment to Greece that should have never been accepted. Hence, even though the vast majority of Greeks remained in favor of the EMU membership, there was great disagreement over the right way to move forward.

THE IMPACT OF THE FINANCIAL CRISIS ON GREEK POLITICS

After the MOU signing in 2010, Greece entered a period of path-breaking pol-icy characterized by the economic and discursive shifts discussed previously. These shifts deeply affected Greek politics, as they led to a radical reconfigura-tion of the post-1974 political system. Greek politics had been dominated by two parties since the 1981 elections: the center-left PASOK and the center-right ND, which jointly accounted for more than 70 percent of the votes in Greek national elections since 1981. However, in the June 2012 elections, PASOK witnessed a catastrophic decline in its voter share (from 44 percent to 12 percent), while (for the first time in Greek history) the share of the votes of parties from the extreme left and right rose considerably. SYRIZA's share of the vote jumped from approximately 3 percent to 27 percent, and GD's vote rose from 0.2 percent to 7.5 percent. Research on electoral preferences shows that there is a stark intergenerational divide among the Greek electorate: Greeks up to 35 years of age tend to vote predominantly antimemorandum parties such as SYRIZA and GD, while Greeks under 40 (and especially above 50) years of age tend to vote predominantly for ND, PASOK, and DHMAR (*Eklogika* 2012; Vernadakis 2012). This division can be explained to a great extent by the huge unemployment rates among young Greeks—over 50 percent for 16-to 25-year-olds—and the harsh economic conditions for young families with children.

Unsurprisingly, the two big winners of the crisis (SYRIZA and GD) have campaigned on a populist antiausterity/antibailout strategy. They also accuse PASOK and ND of being traitors, corrupt, neoliberal elites, or a combination thereof, who had to be overthrown by the people. This strategy was favored by a considerable section of the Greek electorate who were angered by the suffering caused by the country's predicament. Furthermore, both parties have adopted an economic populist agenda that resonates among desperate and disappointed Greeks (Dornbusch and Edwards 1991). For instance, SYRIZA has given false hope to most Greeks by promising a reversal of the austerity measures, as its leader Alexis Tsipras promised that he would return salaries and pensions to precrisis levels, abolish any additional taxation measures imposed after 2010, and increase hiring in the public sector due to staff shortages when in office (*Capital* 2012). These policies are rather unrealistic, given Greece's financial hardship, but they also resemble the precrisis clientelistic policies (e.g. income rises not directly linked to productivity, low taxation, strategic use of the public sector by governments in providing employment) that resulted in Greece's insolvency. GD has adopted a more hands-on clientelistic practice of offering protection from "illegal criminals" to older people walking in some areas of Athens, and providing free food and other safety nets to Greeks only (*Tanea* 2012b). However, it is argued that these political developments may further exacerbate the Greek crisis as neither party is offering realistic alternatives to Greece's problems. Furthermore, both parties follow a populist blame-shifting agenda towards the EU, Germany, global capitalism, and Greek and European elites while they seemingly neglect Greece's fundamental weaknesses, such as widespread tax evasion, unsustainable public finances, structural problems in pension and labor markets, and low competitiveness (Kalyvas, Pagoulatos, and Tsoukas 2013; Featherstone and Papadimitriou 2008; Meghir, Vayanos and Vettas 2010; Featherstone, 2006; Kazakos 2004).

Ironically, some of these developments can be considered as evidence of continuity instead of change for Greek politics. For instance, SYRIZA resembles the pre-1981 PASOK party, as the latter had until 1981 some radical factions and adopted an extremely populist discourse of rising incomes through socialism and abolishing capitalism (Pappas 2010). Moreover, SYRIZA has adopted a statist and populist approach like the PASOK of the 1980s. Subsequently, many PASOK MPs and members have moved to SYRIZA due to ideological differences with PASOK's new policy of austerity.

Despite the rise of the extremes in the 2012 elections, Greece succeeded in forming a pro-EU and promemorandum government that passed another austerity package in November 2012—the toughest until the time of writing (April 2013). It is expected that with these reforms Greece will achieve a budget surplus by 2013. However, unless the government, in liaison with its Eurozone partners, implements policies to stimulate growth, it seems unlikely that the recession will abate—which is something that will result in even more unemployment, poverty, and political turmoil. In addition, it is becoming increasingly obvious that Greece needs substantial debt relief in order to reduce its debt levels below 100 percent, given the unprecedented recession. The current EU response to the Greek crisis thus needs urgent revision to prevent total meltdown.

CONCLUSION

The financial crisis constituted a critical juncture for Greek politics. After signing the first MOU in 2010, Greece entered a period of path-breaking policy, economic, and rhetorical/symbolic shifts. These shifts affected Greek politics immensely. The immediate impact of the crisis was a dramatic rise in protests, strikes, and public discontent. The long-term impact seems to be the radical reconfiguration of the post-1974 political system: in the June 2012 elections, Greece's two major parties witnessed a dramatic decline in their vote share, while (for the first time in Greek history) the popularity of extremist parties at both ends of the political spectrum rose considerably. It remains to be seen whether this trend will hold and, therefore, if Greece will enter a process of political meltdown—or if there will be a significant but manageable reconfiguration of the political system.

Regrettably, it seems that a large section of the Greek electorate has turned to extreme and populist parties (SYRIZA, GD, and ANEL) as the post-1974 established parties (PASOK and ND) are unable to attend to their demands: personal prosperity through tax evasion, public-sector employment, early retirement, and increasing public investment financed by EU funds and loans from financial markets. In other words, a significant part of Greek society has not critically appraised the post-1974 economic and the political modus operandi that led to the country's current predicament. Instead, it votes for any party that promises to return Greece to the pre-2010 situation (as SYRIZA, GD, and ANEL do). This lost opportunity for achieving consensus on the long-standing deficiencies of the Greek economy, state, and society is arguably the worst impact of the financial crisis on Greek politics.

Notes

1. They were named cohesion countries because in the 1990s they were the poorest EU members, and a dedicated EU regional policy fund was created named the Cohesion Fund. The fund was set up to facilitate their economic convergence with their developed EU partners and joining with the Economic and Monetary Union (EMU) by the late 1990s (Rodriguez-Pose 2002).
2. During 1989–1990, Greece had an ecumenical government because no party could gain majority and form a government.
3. This was the state owned Hellenic Postbank (http://www.ttbank.gr/en/home).
4. The governor of the Bank of Greece had informed Karamanlis and Papandreou in January 2009 and again before the elections that the country's deficit would be approximately 12% for 2009 (Skai 2012a).

5. There have been two programmes of financial support and subsequent economic adjustment for Greece that have been financed and overseen by the Troika. The first one was agreed in May 2010 and the second one in February 2012. In return for the bailouts Greece had to agree with the Troika to a series of austerity packages and reforms—outlined in the MOU—and then implement them in order to receive the necessary bailout funds. The austerity package following the first Troika bailout was announced in May 2010, the second in June 2011, the third in October 2011, the fourth in February 2012, and the fifth in November 2012.
6. The only measure to reduce public-sector staff was the nonrenewal of short-term staff.
7. ANEL is the Greek acronym of the right-wing Independent Greeks party. ANEL is led by a former ND MP (Kammenos), who along with some leading Sparkle members and some former ND MPs are protesting against the bailout, calling the EU loan sharks and the pro-MOU politicians traitors. ANEL has adopted most of the positions of Sparkle, arguing that after the MOU, Greece is under foreign occupation as it has become a "Merkelite-protectorate" (*Aggelioforos* 2012a; *Zougla* 2012). It should be noted that ANEL's leader was a leading ND member and former minister of the government that led Greece to bankruptcy. However, ANEL received about 7.5% of the votes in the June 2012 elections.

References

Afonso, Alexandre, Sotirios Zartaloudis and Yiannis Papadopoulos. 2012. "Birds of a Feather? Comparing Austerity Reforms in Greece and Portugal in Times of Crisis (2010–2012)." *ECPR Joint Sessions of Workshops*. Antwerp, Belgium, 10–15 April.

Afonso, Antonio, Ludger Schuknecht, and Vito Tanzi. 2005. "Public Sector Efficiency: An International Comparison." *Public Choice*, 123: 321–47.

Aggelioforos. 2012a. "ANEL: With the Second Memorandum We become a Protectorate." http://www.agelioforos.gr/default.asp?pid=7&ct=10&artid=156693.

Aggelioforos. 2012b. "Request for a Parliamentary Inquiry against the First MOU Rejected." http://www.agelioforos.gr/default.asp?pid=7&ct=10&artid=161173.

Andronikidou, Aikaterini, and Iosif Kovras. 2012. "Cultures of Rioting and Anti-Systemic Politics in Southern Europe." *West European Politics*, 35 (4): 707–25.

Axia. 2012. "Kamenos: Papadimos Was Appointed by Goldman." http://www.axiaplus. gr/article/3754/kammenos-o-papadhmos-diioristhke-apo-thn-goldman.

Barber, Tony. 2012. "Greeks direct cries of pain at Germany." Financial Times, February 14, 2012, http://tinyurl.com/blx9a6q.

Blyth, Martin. 2002. *Great Transformations: Economic Ideas and Institutional Change in the Twentieth Century*. New York: Cambridge University Press.

Capital. 2012. "Tsipras: We Will Reverse the Cuts In Salaries and Pensions with One Law." http://www.capital.gr/news.asp?id=1667462.

Clogg, Richard, ed. 1993. *Greece 1981–89: The Populist Decade*. London: Macmillan Press.

Collier, Ruth B., and David Collier. 1991. *Shaping the Political Arena*. Princeton: Princeton University Press.

Diamandouros, Nikos. 1983. "Greek Political Culture in Transition: Historical Origins, Evolution, Current Trends." In *Greece in the 1980s*, edited by Richard Clogg, 43–69. London: Palgrave Macmillan.

Deutsche-Welle. 2012. "No letup in anti-German sentiment in Greece." http://www. dw.de/no-letup-in-anti-german-sentiment-in-greece/a-16151449.

Dornbusch, Rudiger, and Mario Draghi, eds. 1990. *Public Debt Management: Theory and History*. Cambridge: Cambridge University Press,

Dornbusch, Rudiger, and Sebastian Edwards, eds. 1991. *The Macroeconomics of Populism in Latin America*. Chicago, IL: University of Chicago Press.

Eklogika. 2012. "Party Voting According to Age." http://www.eklogika.gr/elections_results/9992.

Enet. 2010. "Demonstration against the IMF from SYRIZA of Thessaloniki." http://www.enet.gr/?i=news.el.article&id=230440.

Ethnikismos. 2012. "Golden Dawn: The Traitors Who Led Greece to the MOU Will Be Punished!" http://tinyurl.com/c2yxp8d.

European Commission. 2010. "Report on Greek Government Deficit and Debt Statistics." Brussels, Belgium: European Commission. http://epp.eurostat.ec.europa.eu/cache/ITY_PUBLIC/COM_2010_REPORT_GREEK/EN/COM_2010_REPORT_GREEK-EN.PDF.

Featherstone, Kevin. 2003. "Greece and EMU: Between External Empowerment and Domestic Vulnerability." *Journal of Common Market Studies*, 41 (5): 923–40.

Featherstone, Kevin. 2006. *Politics and Policy in Greece: The Challenge of Modernisation*. London: Routledge.

Featherstone, Kevin. 2011. "*The Greek Sovereign Debt Crisis and EMU: A Failing State in a Skewed Regime*." JCMS, 49 (20): 193–217.

Featherstone, Kevin, and Dimitris Papadimitriou. 2008. *The Limits of Europeanization: Reform Capacity and Policy Conflict in Greece*. Basingstoke: Palgrave Macmillan.

Garello, P., ed. 2010. *Taxation in Europe 2010, Paris, France*: Institute for Research in Economic and Fiscal Studies. http://www.irefeurope.org/en/content/taxation-europe-2010

Guardian. 2012. "Alexis Tsipras interview: 'Greece is in danger of a humanitarian crisis.'" http://www.guardian.co.uk/world/2012/may/21/alexis-tsiparas-greece-interview-syriza.

Halikiopoulou, Daphne, Kyriaki Nanou and Sofia Vasilopoulou. 2012. "The Paradox of Nationalism: The Common Denominator of Radical Right and Radical Left Euroscepticism." *European Journal of Political Research*, 51 (4): 504–39.

Ioakimides, Panagiotis C. 2001. "The Europeanization of Greece: An Overall Assessment." In *Europeanization and the Southern Periphery*, edited by Kevin Featherstone and George Kazamias. London: Frank Cass.

Kalyvas, Stathis, George Pagoulatos and Haridimos Tsoukas, eds. 2013. *From Stagnation to Forced Adjustment: Reforms in Greece, 1974–2010*. New York: Columbia University Press.

Kathimerini. 2008a. "The Tranquil Mr. Alogoskoufis." http://news.kathimerini.gr/4dcgi/_w_articles_economy_2_13/07/2008_277537.

Kathimerini. 2008b. "The Greek Banking System Is Stable and Reliable." http://news.kathimerini.gr/4dcgi/_w_articles_economy_2_24/09/2008_285830.

Kathimerini. 2008c. "Conspiracy Theories from the Ministry of Finance about the Spread Rise." http://news.kathimerini.gr/4dcgi/_w_articles_economy_2_04/12/2008_294591.

Katrougalos, George, and Gabriella Lazaridis. 2003. *Southern European Welfare States: Problems, Challenges and Prospects*. Basingstoke: Palgrave Macmillan.

Kazakos, Panos. 2004. "Europeanisation, Public Goals and Group Interests: Convergence Policy in Greece, 1990–2003." *West European Politics*, 27 (5): 901–18.

KKE. 1996. "The Program of KKE." http://www.kke.gr/15o_synedrio/to_programma_toy_kke.

KKE. 2012. "Weapon in the Hands of the People." http://tinyurl.com/bqjwjnr.

Lifo. 2012. "Against the Memorandum 68% of Greeks." http://www.lifo.gr/now/greece/16166.

Lyritzis, Christos. 1984. "Political Parties in Post-junta Greece: A case of Bureaucratic Clientelism?" *West European Politics*, 7 (2): 99–118.

Matsaganis, Manos. 2011. "The Welfare State and the Crisis: The Case of Greece." *Journal of European Social Policy*, 21 (5): 501–12.

Meghir, Costas, Dimitri Vayanos and Nikos Vettas. 2010. "The Economic Crisis in Greece: A Time of Reform and Opportunity." *Greek Economists for Reform*, http://greekeconomistsforreform.com/wp-content/uploads/Reform.pdf.

Mitsopoulos, Michael, and Theodore Pelagidis. 2012. *Understanding the Crisis in Greece: From Boom to Bust.* Basingstoke: Palgrave Macmillan.

ND. 2010. "Antonis Samaras about the Crisis." http://tinyurl.com/dyymyl2.

Nicolacopoulos, Ilias. 2005. "Elections and Voters, 1974–2004: Old Cleavages and New Issues." *West European Politics*, 28 (2): 260–78.

Pagoulatos, George. 2005. "The Politics of Privatisation: Redrawing the Public-Private Boundary." *West European Politics*, 28 (2): 358–80.

Pagoulatos, George. 2012. "Reinventing Europe: A Euro-crisis View from Greece." *European Council on Foreign Relations.* http://ecfr.eu/page/-/ECFR_Greece_paper_20122.pdf.

Pappas, Takis. 2010. "Macroeconomic Policy, Strategic Leadership, and Voter Behaviour: The Disparate Tales of Socialist Reformism in Greece and Spain during the 1980s." *West European Politics*, 33 (6): 1241–60.

Petmesidou, Maria. 1991. "Statism, Social Policy and the Middle Classes in Greece." *Journal of European Social Policy*, 1 (1): 33–48.

Rodríguez-Pose, Andrés. 2002. *The European Union: economy, society and polity*, Oxford: Oxford University Press.

Skai. 2011. "SYRIZA: Obedient Technocrat Mr. Papadimos." http://www.skai.gr/news/politics/article/188752/suriza-o-prothupourgos-einai-enas-upakouos-tehnokratis/.

Skai. 2012a. "G. Provopoulos: They Knew since January 2009 about the Deficit." http://www.skai.gr/news/politics/article/197696/g-provopoulos-ixeran-apo-ton-ianouario-2009-gia-to-elleimma.

Skai. 2012b. "Collaborator of Merkel—Mr. Samaras." http://www.skai.gr/news/politics/article/217512/tsipras-sunergatis-tis-merkel-o-samaras-epithesi-kai-ston-papoulia.

Stavrakakis, Yannis. 2002. "Religious Populism and Political Culture: The Greek Case." *South European Society and Politics*, 7 (3): 29–52.

SYRIZA. 2010. "Immediate Response from the Left about the IMF Crime." http://syriza-petralona.blogspot.co.uk/2010/04/blog-post_24.html.

SYRIZA. 2012a. "SYRIZA: Fractions." http://tinyurl.com/dx44y52.

Tanea. 2012a. "War for the (First) Memorandum." http://www.tanea.gr/ellada/article/?aid=4771815.

Tanea. 2012b. "Golden Dawn: Blood, Food and other Support only to Greeks." http://www.tanea.gr/ellada/article/?aid=4752234.

Tovima. 2011. "The 'Upper' and the 'Lower' Square." http://www.tovima.gr/politics/article/?aid=404735.

Tsakalotos, Euclid. 1998. "The Political Economy of Social Democratic Economic Policies: The PASOK Experiment in Greece." *Oxford Review of Economic Policy*, 14 (1):114–38.

Venieris, Dimitris. 2006. "The Virtual Reality of Welfare Reform." In *Social Policy Developments in Greece,* edited by Maria Petmesidou and Elias Mossialos. Aldershot: Ashgate.

Vernadakis, Xristoforos. 2012. "The 17 June Elections and the New Divisions of the Electorate." http://www.avgi.gr/ArticleActionshow.action?articleID=697536.

Verney, Susannah. 2009. "Flaky Fringe? Southern Europe Facing the Financial Crisis." *South European Society and Politics*, 14 (1): 1–6.

Verney, Susannah. 2011. "An Exceptional Case? Party and Popular Euroscepticism in Greece, 1959–2009." *South European Society and Politics*, 16 (1): 51–79.

XO. 2012. "Samaras: We Need Another Policy Mix." http://tinyurl.com/bmx484c.

Zartaloudis, Sotirios. 2011. "Public Sector Cuts in Greece and Portugal: The Sooner the Better?" paper presented at RECWOWE Final Conference, Brussels, June 15-17 2011, http://www.recwowefinalconference.eu/streams/stream-c-more-jobs-better-jobs/c-5-the-public-sector-in-recession-era-workforce-patterns/.

Zougla. 2010. "Defiance against the Memorandum by Mikis." http://www.zougla.gr/politiki/article/anipakoi-sto-mnimonio-zitise-o-mikis.

Zougla. 2012. "ANEL Protest against Merkel's Visit to Greece." http://www.agelioforos.gr/default.asp?pid=7&ct=10&artid=156693.

10 The Promise and Peril of Smallness in World Markets[1]

The Case of Financial Crisis in Denmark

Martin B. Carstensen, Copenhagen Business School

INTRODUCTION

Following the freeze of financial markets in 2008, and the ensuing Great Recession that has been with us since, studying national varieties of financial crises has become a veritable growth industry in social science. In the first part of the crisis, larger states such as the United States and the United Kingdom, or the dramatic blowups of small states such as Iceland and Ireland, took most headlines. Recently, however, both academics and policy makers are showing growing interest in the fate of small states that did not blow up but rather did relatively well. Sweden is an obvious candidate, since it got out of the crisis fast and practically unscathed. Denmark is another case that is catching the interest of the international regulatory community, for the sector-financed bailout model issued in 2008 as well as its ambitious resolution regime introduced in 2010 to replace the general state guarantee. Denmark is an outlier because—at least in the knowledge of this author—it is the only Western state that was hit by the crisis that made the banking sector pay. As a contrast, the common approach to bailing out banks was that the state socialized bank-sector debt through issuing state guarantees that were not financed by the sector itself. For example, there are different versions of this model in countries such as the Netherlands and Belgium (Kickert 2012a, 2012b) and a more extreme version in Ireland—where the state ended up having to ask the International Monetary Fund for help—or Iceland, which defaulted on its private bank debt. The chapter asks how Danish policy makers were able to get the Danish banking sector to participate so relatively actively in the handling of the crisis. In short, it is argued that an institutional setting for cooperation and negotiation between peak organizations and the state, a tradition in the banking sector for cooperation during crises combined with specific well-consolidated ideas about bank crises, created a setting conducive for policy learning and burden sharing.

Why should we care about a small state like Denmark? The Danish handling of the recent crisis is primarily interesting because it exhibited a substantially more demanding approach to sector involvement than it was the case in most other Western states. This was seen most clearly in the way that the Danish banking sector and the Danish policy makers agreed that the state would take on the risks of the sector as a whole if the sector shouldered winding down expenses up to 35 billion Danish kroner (DKr) (approximately €4.69 billion). So far, the Danish approach has kept expenses for winding down the banks that collapsed in the crisis below 25 billion DKr (approximately €3.35 billion), which is a remarkable achievement compared to the expenses incurred among both large states (like the US) or small states (like Ireland). Though of course some of the developments in the Danish case are mostly a matter of luck—to take one example, the consistently low interest rate that kept a large number of Danes in their overindebted houses—the Danish policy makers successfully avoided a meltdown of the Danish banking sector that could have been socialized and ended up as sovereign debt.

The following section presents the Danish "negotiated economy" (Pedersen 2006) as an example of a small state able to prosper in world markets due to a collective perception of vulnerability that breeds an ideology of cooperation and institutions of negotiation (Katzenstein 1985). Section three connects the theoretical framework to the history and concrete institutional setup of the Danish banking sector to show why from the outset policy makers and the Danish banking sector were particular well positioned to craft a crisis response in which the banking sector would play a relatively active role in financing and organizing the effort. Section four describes how the Danish financial sector was hit when international money markets started to freeze up in 2007, while sections five and six analyse how the four so-called bank packages that make up the primary crisis response of the Danish authorities are explicable with reference to the institutional and ideational structures established through the handling of earlier crises. The final section concludes.

IDEAS AND INSTITUTIONS FOR COOPERATION IN SMALL STATES

The ability of policy makers in a small state such as Denmark to substantially integrate the banking sector in the response to the financial crisis fits well with Katzenstein's (1985) classic theoretical framework on the promise and peril of smallness in world markets. Katzenstein famously argued that the relative success of small vis-à-vis larger states originated in an ability to craft reactive, flexible adjustments with the support of powerful groups in society, in the process gaining a high degree of political efficacy and legitimacy. The small states' "democratic corporatist" approach to policy making is predicated on three traits. First, an ideology of social partnership—that "integrates differing conceptions of group interest with vaguely but firmly held notions of the public interest" (Katzenstein 1985, 6)—permeates relations between different interest groups and the state. Second, domestic adjustments to international circumstances are agreed between the state and centralized and concentrated interest groups that are both hierarchically structured and highly inclusive. Third, these peak organizations serve to further a particular style of political bargaining that is voluntary, informal, and continuous and which "achieves a coordination of conflicting objectives among political actors" (Katzenstein 1985, 6). The Danish state is one example of such a system. According to Pedersen (2006), in the Danish "negotiated economy" that emerged in the course of postwar developments, effective economic governance is achieved through organized negotiations among actors in the public and private sector. The system is characterized by a combination of institutionalized learning, organized negotiations, and a shared conception among elite actors about the most pressing problems facing the Danish economy. Consensus is achieved through power struggles between state and other societal groups based on the deliberative shaping of preferences.

The need to cooperate and negotiate on a regular basis in many instances leads to a pragmatic, experimenting, and incremental approach to policy making that is well suited to adjusting to unforeseen developments in world markets. As Katzenstein (1985, 79) puts it, "the small European states continually improvise in living with change." The result is not necessarily effective or in all instances egalitarian, because political power is concentrated in elites whos interests are framed by the common knowledge (Culpepper 2008) they have come to agree on, but it enhances a spirit of a common purpose, enabling elite groups to commit to contributing to the solution of political problems. Thus, the ideology of working together for a common good is believed to facilitate much policy learning, cooperation, and flexible adjustment to the various challenges with which policy elites of small states are confronted.

This understanding of state–market relations contrasts with the standard account of the relation between the state and the financial sector, which has been dominated by a focus on the capture of authorities and the political system by the big players of finance (Stigler 1971; Crouch 2011; Warwick Commission 2009; Baker 2010; Mügge 2010; Pagliari 2012). Implicit to this approach is often the normative distinction between state and market that the two should be separated and the state regulate the market without much sector interference. However, the Danish case shows that there are indeed ways in which the state and the sector can interact, other than as adversaries. According to Mansbridge (1992), such situations come close to deliberation institutionalized through a corporatist setting. That is, one way to avoid self-serving rent seeking of interest groups is to build a neocorporatist system of interest representation. In such settings, both power and persuasion matter, but building a system of interest representation based on inclusion and traditions of cooperation may structure interaction in a way in which "the parties involved not only maneuver for advantageous positions but try to understand what the other really wants in order, for example, to offer what may be the cheaper satisfaction of wants than the other is demanding (Mansbridge 1992, 500). Cooperation in a stable institutional setting thus not only provides the authorities with much needed market information (Schwartz 2010), it also enhances the possibility of getting political actors to credibly commit to a "contested political space which creates the opportunity for domestic actors to learn and adapt" (Katzenstein 2003, 18).

The pragmatic and cooperative spirit that the small states are supposed to harbor becomes all the more important in times of crisis because a stable, long-lasting institutional setting for cooperation offers a greater potential for creative reactions to a crisis than circumstances where coordination and traditions for cooperation is less institutionalized and more ad hoc. Thus, in handling crises effectively it matters whether a discursive community is united on the basis of shared ideas inside cooperative settings. To put it simply, if institutions and ideas have been developed over the years to handle banking crisis—as they had been in Denmark in the banking crisis of the 1980s and early 1990s—it makes it easier to create a setting for cooperation and high-level policy learning. Thus, effective reform efforts are often premised on the ability of the policy elites to agree on a coordinative discourse as a basis for constructing a policy program that may serve as the foundation for cooperative negotiations (Schmidt 2003).

THE INSTITUTIONAL AND IDEATIONAL SETTING OF THE DANISH BANKING SECTOR

Though Katzenstein (1985) argues that the traits discussed above are characteristic of many Western European small states, they remain ideal typical traits. Therefore, to determine the role of such institutions in the way the Danish response to the financial crisis was organized, it is necessary to see what institutions and ideas have historically developed in the banking sector. As we will see in the following, the Danish banking sector has a long history of cooperation and a set of ideas and institutions for handling crises developed during and as a response to the Danish bank crisis of the 1980s and early 1990s. This institutional and ideational heritage in turn enabled the authorities to include the sector more actively in their crisis response.

Broadly speaking, the Danish bank sector is characterized by both concentration and decentralization: A few big players primarily placed in the capital sit on most of the market while a large number of small and midsize banks remain strongly represented locally. This country/city cleavage is a reminiscent of banking traditions developed in the eighteenth and nineteenth centuries, where local and regional financial institutions exclusively entered into engagements with farmers, small firms, and households in their region, and on the other hand, three big banks in the capital focused on larger enterprises and established few branches outside the Copenhagen area (Høpner 1999). Since then, increased competition in the sector and rising demands for credit financing since the 1960s set in motion a trend of mergers between small credit institutions that resulted in a number of relatively large banks outside the Copenhagen area. Concentration became even stronger during the 1990s, when two big mergers let to the creation of Denmark's two by far largest lenders: Unibank (later Nordea) and Danske Bank. The concentrated and decentralized structure of the Danish banking system has had important consequences for the interest representation of Danish banks. According to Ronit (1997), the political organization of the Danish banking sector has developed from network based to formal organization. During the twentieth century, the small and midsize banks started organizing into interest organizations, while the three biggest banks remained formally unorganized and instead coordinated and exerted their influence through personal contacts and in an ad hoc fashion. It took until 1950 for the Danish banks to organize within one organization (Den Danske Bankforening) that in 1990 merged with the interest organization for savings banks (Danmarks Sparekasseforening) to form the Danish Bankers Association (Finansrådet) that now serves as the primary interest group of the Danish banking sector.[2]

The development from network to formal organization is also seen more specifically in the area of handling banking crises (Hansen 1997). In the banking crises of the 1800s, the handling was more or less improvised and only weakly institutionalized. Thus, for example, in the crisis of 1907–1908, the Minister of Finance, the Danish National Bank, and four of the biggest Danish banks stepped in to guarantee creditors and so avoided a run on the banks in crisis. During the 1980s, the banks took on a more active role in handling crises. Most important was the institutional innovation of a privately funded but publicly regulated Deposit Guarantee Fund (Indskydergarantifonden). The fund was reformed in 1994 to enable it to offer guarantees to help a smooth transition of ownership in cases of bank collapse, but because these measures turned out to conflict with EU legislation regarding state subsidies, in 2007 the banking sector collectively created the Private Contingency Association. The aim of the association is to support the takeover of distressed banks by stronger competitors, for example by issuing guarantees on some of the assets acquired. The association was a continuation of the facility under the depositor guarantee scheme, which could assist members in covering extraordinary charges in relation to takeovers or mergers in distressed institutions (Kluth and Lynggaard, forthcoming). The Private Contingency Association also represented the financial sector in the negotiations with the government concerning the bank packages. The association can thus be viewed as an integrated part of solving banking crises in Denmark and constitutes the institutionalization of an old tradition of cooperation between banking sector and state in Danish banking crises.

Both before and after the creation of the Deposit Guarantee Fund, the approach to handling banking crises in Denmark was developed on the back of a norm of collaboration between public authorities and the banks. Traditionally, mergers between weak and strong banks was the dominant instrument in both the 1920 and 1933-crises and the more recent crisis in the end of the 1980s. Generally, the authorities employed a more-or-less improvised strategy of quick mergers between distressed and healthy banks, and when deemed necessary, public guarantees for specific institutions were issued. Fundamental for the strategy was that the state should not take ownership of the banks, neither fully nor partly (Ministry of Economy 1995), one argument being that a practice of bailing out a destitute bank by taking ownership would "distort incentives" and create "moral hazard." According to Høpner (1999, 121), the rationale underlying the authorities' attitude was based on a desire to avoid expensive liquidations, as in the 1920s, fearing that both the population and international markets would lose confidence in the Danish banking system. The banks on their side also supported private solutions. Thus, according to Ronit (1997, 130) a silent agreement existed between the banks—especially the big banks—and the interest organizations that no bank should be allowed to collapse. The motivation was to avoid the increased political influence on the sector that banking crises could spur as well as the negative reputation it could create for the Danish sector internationally. Taken together, the state played an active role in fostering private solutions between banks in trouble, and it did so by putting pressure on the banks to take on an active role, for example by offering considerable tax deductions to incentivize the banks to take over their weaker competitors.

Overall, then, the chapter presents two interconnected reasons why the Danish authorities were particularly well placed to get the banking sector to take on a relatively active role in the crisis response. First, the relation between the banks and the state is relatively well organized, and the way banks are orga-nized—whether in an informal network or in an institutionalized and formal representation through peak organizations—matters greatly for how political actors handle a crisis. As argued by Grossman and Woll (forthcoming), coun-tries where banks have strong interbank ties and collective negotiation capacity are often characterized by business–government relations that are more apt to a collective solution than systems where governments interact bilaterally with individual banks. However, put in the words of Schwartz (2010, 368), a central-ized system of organized interests is simply a machine; "the important issue is the shared sense of social purpose animating the machine." Thus, secondly, the capacity for collective action builds on a set of broad norms about the state as a facilitator of a fundamentally self-reliant banking sector and a range of more specific policy ideas and principles about how bank crises should be handled through mergers, if necessary with public support, but never through public ownership. Thus, the institutional setting and the shared norms of solidarity between the banks enabled a learning environment focused less on rent seek-ing and more on deliberation and cooperation.

THE CRISIS HITS

With a cumulative economic decline in 2008–2009 of −6.3 percent of GDP and −4.1 percent for the three years, 2008–2010, the Danish economy was clearly hard hit by the crisis (Goul Andersen 2011). Although Danish policy mak-ers at first insisted that the financial crisis was an exogenous event for which they had little responsibility, it has since been acknowledged that there were a number of endogenous reasons why Denmark suffered much from the crisis, the primary culprit being a relatively large housing bubble. The overheated housing market had been fueled by a freeze of property taxes (Mortensen and Seabrooke 2009) combined with a number of partly or wholly unfinanced tax breaks as well as procyclical credit liberalizations (Goul Andersen 2011). The credit liberalizations consisted of the creation of so-called interest-only loans and loans with flexible interest rates. The latter had already been implemented in 1996 by the previous government, but it took until the beginning of the 2000s for people to really make use of them. From that point, however, they became much more popular than anticipated when they were first created. Thus, at the peak in the second quarter of 2009, about 90 percent of all new loans were flexible loans (Goul Andersen 2011, 125) and Danish household debt had reached a level equal to 132 percent of GDP, against 106 percent at the end of 2003 (Østrup 2010, 82). Moreover, homeowners were granted unrestricted access to supplementary loans in the equity of their houses, which could be spent for any purpose, including simple consumption.

Unsurprisingly, the Danish financial sector exploited the credit liberalizations and the low interest rates to embark on a rapid credit expansion. In 2008, the banks had built a historically unprecedented deposit deficit: from a small deposit surplus around the year 2000 to a massive deposit deficit of 624 billion DKr (approximately €83 billion) or 40 percent of GDP in 2008. Danish banks financed the boom in lending between 2003 and 2008 in large part by raising short-term liquidity on the international money markets. Between the first quarter of 2004 and the first quarter of 2008, the share of deposits from foreign banks in midsize Danish banks grew from 30 percent to 50 percent (Ejerskov 2009, 51). Perhaps a small number compared to, for example, the Icelandic case, but the dependence of Danish lenders on foreign funding to finance this deficit made the sector vulnerable to the instabilities in the international money markets that began in the summer of 2007 and culminated in September 2008. Additional vulnerabilities stemmed from the by-far largest Danish bank, Danske Bank's, aggressive expansion into the Irish and Finnish markets, buying National Irish Bank in 2005 and Sampo Bank in 2007.

The first Danish bank to get into trouble following the instability that started in 2007 was the small bank Trelleborg, which was quickly sold to the fourth largest bank in Denmark, Sydbank. Things did not go easy when Roskilde Bank started showing weaknesses in the beginning of 2008. Roskilde Bank, at that point Denmark's seventh largest bank, was among the banks that had expanded most aggressively during the upturn, but with housing prices falling, its overly risky business model with exposure to the stagnating building sector led the bank to insolvency. To avoid any more bad publicity among international investors, the Danish state and the Private Contingency Association guaranteed all debt obligations incurred by the bank except subordinated debt. Because it was impossible to find a bank that was willing to merge with Roskilde Bank, total assets and liabilities of Roskilde Bank was transferred to a new company jointly owned by the state and the banking sector (Østrup 2010). The Private Contingency Association committed to paying 750 million DKr (approximately €100 million), with the state paying the remaining costs (so far a bit over ten billion Dkr, approximately €1.34 billion). However, much damage had already been done in terms of bad publicity, and from this point it only became harder for Danish banks to obtain funding from international wholesale markets. Another problem was the large-scale Irish and Baltic adventures of Danske Bank, which made investors unsure about what was actually on the bank's balance sheets and how it would be affected by an imminent devaluation of its Baltic assets. With the freezing of international money markets following the bankruptcy of Lehman Brothers in September 2008, Danish banks were heavily pressured for liquidity to roll over their huge deposit deficits.

BANK PACKAGES I–II: STABILIZATION MEASURES

On 30 September 2008, the Irish government issued a blanket guarantee for the debt commitments of the six largest Irish-owned banks. This put strong pressure on Danske Bank, because its bank, National Irish Bank, was not covered by the guarantee, and the bank experienced a massive withdrawal of funds. After negotiations with the Private Contingency Association and the Danish Bankers Association, and with the support of all parties in parliament except the socialist party Enhedslisten (the Unity List), on the 5 October 2008 the Danish government presented a two-year blanket guarantee of all deposits (excluding covered bonds), what was popularly called Bank Package I. In effect, the Danish state guaranteed deposits amounting to 259 percent of GDP, which puts Denmark ahead of most Western states, including Ireland (Grossman and Woll, forthcoming). What is most remarkable about the guarantee is its financing: The banking sector—represented by the Private Contingency Association—committed a total of 35 billion Dkr (approximately €4.7 billion). If the expenses from liquidating collapsed banks under the guarantee scheme exceeded this amount, the Danish state would shoulder the remaining costs. If, on the other hand, the cost of liquidation turned out less than what the fund contained, the state would reap the leftovers.[3] Bank Package I contained an additional significant innovation, namely the establishing of the winding up company Finansiel Stabilitet (Financial Stability), which had as a primary task to secure the payment of creditor claims to wound-up institutions and handle the controlled dismantling of financial institutions that no longer met solvency requirements.

Bank Package I served as an initial stabilizing measure that enabled Danish banks to reenter the national and international money markets. However, it did not help solve the additional problem of raising capital that the banks were experiencing and that threatened the solvency of a number of banks. With a contracting economy and a struggling building sector, losses began to mount in the banks. This caused fear that a large number of banks were close to collapsing, including Denmark's largest bank, Danske Bank (Østrup 2010), and that a credit squeeze would put even greater pressure on the real economy. Thus, in the effort to support bank lending and keeping the banks afloat, in February 2009 the Danish parliament (again, excluding the Unity List) agreed on Bank Package II, which broadly consisted of two measures. First, individual solvent financial institutions could apply Financial Stability for injections of hybrid core capital that if necessary to meet solvency requirements could be converted into common equity.[4] Financial Stability negotiated with each institution and decided on an individual interest rate reaching an average of 10.1 percent. When the deadline for applications from individual institutions expired on 31 December 2009, forty-three applications had been received, leading to a payout of 46 billion Dkr (approximately €6.17 billion). Second, with the aim of enhancing the ability of financial institutions to obtain liquidity after the end of Bank Package I, financial institutions could apply for individual state guarantees on bond issuance. When the application period expired at the end of 2010, individual guarantees had been granted to 64 institutions, amounting to 337 billion Dkr (approximately €45 billion).[5] The potential losses incurred on the capital injections and individual state guarantees of Bank Package II is financed through interest income and guarantee commissions (ranging 0.96–1.35 percent), respectively.[6]

Bank Package I and II are clear examples of the workings of the negotiated economy in the small state of Denmark, and how the development of a common ideology of cooperation and the founding of a generalized system of negotiations facilitate collective learning and policy flexibility (Pedersen 2006). First, as noted by Kluth and Lynggaard (forthcoming), the two first bank packages constituted a compromise reached through negotiations: In return for industry participation in financing rescuing efforts—primarily in the form of funding the winding up of the eleven banks that collapsed during the state guarantee—the state's subsequent re-capitalization program implied a very limited loss of control by banking executives, and shares were not diluted. This solution was not reached without political battles—since the banking sector fought bravely and succeeded in getting a model for capital injections where the state would buy shares in the banks off the table—but the battles took place as institutionalized negotiations between the state and sector and received full support from both sets of actors.[7]

Second, the two bank packages were built on existing norms and institutions but also in important ways extended these. As already mentioned, the norm of active sector involvement in banking crises and a clear commitment for the state to keep out of the banks was upheld, but more specifically, the policy ideas about how to handle banking crises was put to use in radically new circumstances. For example, the central role of the Private Contingency Association—as an organ of representation and funding by the sector—developed on the back of the more and more institutionalized role the sector (in the form of the Deposit Guarantee Fund) had been given during and after the previous banking crisis of the 1980s. Moreover, the construction of a fund that would contain up to 35 billion Dkr was decided through a form of policy learning based on the experience of winding down Roskilde Bank with only little support from the sector and at a very high cost for the state. This institutionalized model for crisis handling was further and significantly developed with the advent of Financial Stability that came to constitute a central institution for negotiations between the state and the sector about capital injections, individual state guarantees and winding up of destitute banks. In the banking crisis of the 1980s, the Danish National Bank had been the primary arbiter between the financial sector and the state, a role that in the current crisis was taken over and in time significantly changed by Financial Stability. Though the company is officially run by a director and board, the company has direct reference to the Minister of Economics and Business Affairs, offering possibilities for the government to intervene in specific cases of banking crisis. That being said, Financial Stability remains a relatively depoliticized setting for negotiations between state and sector in unwinding collapsed banks (see also Carstensen, forthcoming).

BANK PACKAGES III–IV: "FUTURE-PROOFING" THE SECTOR

In 2010, about a half a year before the state guarantee would expire, work started on creating a special bank resolution regime in Denmark. The exit-model that came to be Bank Package III looked a lot like the resolution model that had been in practice before the crisis, but with certain add-ons. Following the experience of unwinding Roskilde Bank, the authorities had two primary priorities in their work on the new regime: That it should ensure that normal costumers were reasonably covered by a deposit guarantee, and that they could access their account and use credit cards while the resolution procedure took place; and that creditors could be bailed in and pay for resolution relieving the tax payers from paying the bill for resolving ailing banks. Relating to the latter challenge, the resolution regime was designed—as the only scheme in Europe at that time—to ensure senior bondholders suffer losses, when a bank is unwound. The scheme was constructed so that if a bank chooses to be unwound under the scheme, a subsidiary company is established under Financial Stability that takes ownership of assets and some liabilities, wiping out shareholders and making senior bondholders take a hair-cut on their investment. Like in Bank Package I, the scheme is financed by the financial sector through the Private Contingency Association and the Public Deposit Fund.

The new regulation, implemented in October 2010, was first tested when Amagerbanken, at the time Denmark's fifth largest bank, turned insolvent in February 2011 after losing money on property investments, currency speculation and wind-energy projects. The bank was nicknamed "Armageddonbank" because creditors for the first time in Europe's history suffered hair-cuts on their investment. In accordance with Bank Package III, Amagerbanken was selectively bailed out with a transfer of assets and a partial transfer of liabilities. Holders of the bank's senior unsecured debt swallowed a 41 percent haircut on their investment (*Bloomberg* 7 February 2011). The money markets were quick to respond. With the possibility of encountering a significant hair-cut, investors were suddenly reluctant to lend most Danish banks money. The credit rating agency Moody's followed suit and in May 2011 downgraded six Danish lenders, including the country's biggest bank, Danske Bank, citing explicitly the lack of "systemic support" for the banks. For the few banks actually able to loan money, funding costs soared.

These developments made the Danish authorities wary. Supposedly, as reported by *Financial Times* (27 May 2011), making things tougher for surviving banks "was not the idea" when the Danish authorities allowed a state guarantee of bank liabilities to lapse two years after it was introduced. Thus, in a broader perspective, the authorities wanted a so-called "consolidation" of the Danish banking sector—meaning basically fewer small banks (Carstensen, forthcoming). Even though the authorities could easily do without the weak banks that were unwound using Bank Package III, the closing down of the international money markets worked against the aim of building a strong and competitive Danish banking sector. Policymakers wanted fewers banks, but they did not want all the mess that seemed to follow from shutting down banks without compensating creditors. Thus, in summer 2011 a first step was made to avoid using the resolution regime by creating a supplementary "dowry-scheme" that made it possible to supply a dowry to cover the expenses of a distressed bank's creditors and depositors for a healthy bank interested in taking over the bank. However, in June 2011 it turned out that the dowry-scheme was not effective in getting a buyer for the small bank Fjordbank Mors that then entered the normal winding-up process, once again grabbing the attention of the international money markets.[8]

Following the painful realization that the Danish bail-in scheme had been too ambitious at that point of the crisis—exposing Danish banks to unwanted pressure from the money markets—in August 2011 a new policy—called Bank Package IV, or "the consolidation package"—aimed as an alternative to the bail-in scheme was passed in agreement between opposition and government. The aim of the new scheme was to subsidize takeovers in an effort to ensure that troubled banks were not forced to resort to the new resolution framework. The bill contained two parts. First, the existing dowry-scheme was expanded. Now a healthy bank could take over either the whole of the distressed bank—where the state offers a dowry of the size of the costs that the state would have incurred had the distressed bank been unwound using the new resolution model—or only take over the good parts and leave the toxic assets to the state. In the latter case, the dowry pays the expenses that the state incurred in winding down the bad loans. The transaction is subsidized by the Deposit Guarantee Fund, which, as noted already, is financed collectively by the Danish banking sector.

Second, a state guarantee can be granted in two instances: either where a fusion between two banks leads to the maturing of loans taken out by the distressed bank that the state then guarantees for the remaining period, or when two banks merge and one of the banks already has an individual guarantee as part of previous crisis measures, in which case the banks can obtain a new state guarantee with maturity up to three years. The initiative explicitly sought to facilitate consolidation in the banking sector by reducing the risks connected with a merger. The small insolvent lender, Max Bank, became Denmark's first test of the ability of the new dowry scheme to sidestep the bail-in laws of the Danish resolution regime. As such, the authorities were successful as the mid-size bank Sparekassen Sjælland ended up taking over the healthy parts of Max Bank and the state assumed the bank's bad loans. Senior creditors were thus spared, while shareholders lost their investments.

The development from Bank Package III to Bank Package V is interesting for a number of reasons. First, it constitutes both a continuation and adjustment of the strategies developed through the 1980s and 1990s. As argued previously, the Danish authorities have consistently supported a consolidation of the Danish banking sector by letting larger banks buy out their weaker competitors. In the last banking crisis, this goal was accomplished without directly subsidizing the consolidation process, because it was possible to find interested buyers among the healthier banks. This also seems to have been the wish behind Bank Package III, which sought to normalize the relation between the state and the banking sector. This strategy quite clearly backfired because it put such great pressure on the international funding possibilities of both small and large banks; consequences that were subsequently sought alleviated by creating a new dowry scheme through Bank Package IV.

Second, the dowry scheme constitutes a further institutionalization of a praxis that goes back to the mid-1990s. Thus, Bank Packages III and IV enshrine the principle that the banking sector takes care of its own crises, but with the central role of Financial Stability as an institution for unwinding collapsed banks, the Danish state now takes a more active position in the process. Just as in the case of Bank Package I, Bank Package III requires that the banking sector finances the unwinding process. Although one could expect this to be the standard procedure in the resolution regimes that are being built around Europe in recent years, the self-financing principle sets Denmark apart once again. One example could be the Irish institution for unwinding financial institutions—the National Asset Management Agency—which was used to overtake bad loans for property and land development from the books of Irish banks. Besides being an extremely complex construct, the scheme does nothing to include the banks in it its financing. Additional examples could be the German or British resolution regimes that are silent on the matter of financing resolution by the banking sector.

Third, the case of Bank Package III demonstrated first how vulnerable small states are to international pressures and that they ignore these pressures at their own peril, but also how a relatively effective and flexible response can be churned out quickly. The effectiveness of the Danish response seems in part to hinge on the ability to base it on a strong and institutionalized tradition for cooperation. A case in point is the dowry scheme of Bank Package IV, which constitutes a formalization and strengthening of a praxis of actively supporting takeovers using tax deductions and guarantees. As argued by Hansen (1997), there has long existed a strong political wish in Denmark that collapsing banks should be merged with healthy institutions to avoid an expensive and unpractical collapse, and an important supporting mechanism has been tax deductions for the buying bank. A government report written in wake of the previous Danish banking crisis (Ministry of Economy 1995, 61) even explicitly admits that deductions without sound legal basis were offered in fusions during the crisis. Bank Package IV is thus a pragmatic but also more formal solution built on existing informal institutions and ideas from precrisis times.

Finally, the idea that the banking sector needs consolidation is interesting because it points to an important power battle inside the Danish banking sector. As noted by Katzenstein (1985, 87), the predictability of small states' politics created by the inclusion of all major producer groups and political actors in corporatist arrangements may often come at the cost of the exclusion of other political elites. This is seen in the focus on consolidation, where Danish authorities concurred on a strategy of "future proofing" the Danish banking sector by supporting the takeover of weak competitors by larger banks with the aim of creating yet bigger and more professional banks with better access to international money markets. Beyond the point that bigger banks are not necessarily the best response to the financial crisis—since in Denmark size was not the distinguishing factor for whether or not banks experienced significant difficulties—the aim of increasing concentration in the industry probably helps the big players more than the small. This seems to indicate that although an effective small-state approach to handling the crisis secures the credible commitment of the industry to partake in the financing, it does not necessarily support equality between small and big players in the sector. Put differently, because of the mutual dependence of state and the big players in the sector, policy elites included in the handling of the crisis will be reluctant to rock the boat through mutual critique. In that perspective it is hardly surprising that an elite consensus has been created around the necessity of "consolidating" the sector.

CONCLUSION

Table 10.1 presents an overview of the distribution of risk and financing in the four bank packages.[9] It illustrates nicely the division of labor between state and sector in the Danish handling of the financial crisis: With a relatively

Table 10.1 *Distribution of Risk and Financing in Bank Package I–IV*

	Bank Package I	Bank Package II	Bank Package III	Bank Package IV
Description	General state guarantee of all deposits	Capital injections and individual state guarantees on bonds	Exit scheme for destitute banks	Dowry scheme as alternative to Bank Package III
Who carries the risk?	The state	The state	The deposit guarantee fund	The deposit guarantee fund
Financing	Up to 35 billion DKr paid by the sector through the Private Contingency Association	Interest payment and guarantee commission	The deposit guarantee fund. Losses on guarantees and capital injections born by the state	The deposit guarantee fund

comprehensive guarantee of deposits, the state took on the risks of the sector while the banks collectively committed to financing the winding down of collapsed banks. However, in a long-term perspective, both risk and financing has—at least formally—been taken over by the collective organs of the banking sector. The evaluation of the Danish case has generally been positive. As argued previously, the Danish approach to stabilization and future-proofing of the banking sector that made the sector an active player in handling the crisis was built on existing institutions and ideas about banking crises that through negotiations between state and peak organizations were developed to fit the concrete circumstances of this crisis.

Though the Danish case provides an interesting alternative to other models of crisis handling used in the recent crisis, the positive evaluation comes with important caveats. First, the Danish authorities have not only been blessed with well-established institutions for cooperation and negotiation, they have also been blessed with a low interest rate—supported by the popularity of Danish government bonds among international investors—as well as relatively low unemployment rates floating around the 6 percent mark. This has played an important role in keeping a lot of home owners with risky variable interest rate loans as well as overindebted farmers afloat, which again has been fortunate for a number of otherwise shaky banks. Without low interest rates, the losses from the state guarantee could easily have exceeded the 35 billion DKr that the sector had committed to paying.

Second, the Danish political system still has not dealt with a number of the most important reasons for why the Danish banking sector was relatively hard pressed by the international financial crisis, most notably the credit liberalizations implemented in the end of the 1990s and the beginning of the 2000s. Among the most important reasons for the lack of fundamental reform is probably a fear of the electorate (Carstensen 2011; Kjar, forthcoming).

Third, perhaps the state could have made more money if it had chosen a different model than capital injections through loans of hybrid core capital. Recently, a public debate has reignited as to whether the Danish state should rather have bought shares in the banks and thereby made money from the upside that the increased value of bank stocks would have generated.

Finally, building on ideas from precrisis times and supporting the "consolidation" of the sector—meaning fewer small banks—is probably not the most progressive strategy. Handling the uncertainty of a crisis by adjusting existing ideas and institutions necessarily leads to a certain degree of conservatism, since the approach is predicated on the beliefs and interests of the actors and groups that wielded power before crisis struck. In some cases this might turn out be a strategic advantage, since the actors have over a long period of time nurtured and refined these ideas and institutions, and being well acquainted with them, they can perhaps use them more efficiently. But there is also a process of power at play, where other actors and organizations are effectively excluded from participating in the construction of the collective problem and solutions. In this way Denmark is a classic small state, because it does not seek an ambitious reordering of its economy but rather muddles through with reactive, flexible, and concerted adjustments.

Notes

1. The author would like to acknowledge the generous financial support from the Carlsberg Fund that partly financed the writing of this chapter.
2. The small credit institutions are still represented by the Association of Local Banks, Savings Banks, and Cooperative Banks in Denmark.
3. The banks ended up paying 25 billion Dkr (approximately €3.35 billion). Though the costs of the bank package remains unclear, it looks like it will balance, depending on how you count. If the banks' tax deductions connected to contributing to the scheme are not included, the scheme seems to end up in a small plus to the state. If tax deductions are included, there probably will be a deficit of a couple of billion Danish kroner. Compared to other countries, however, the Danish bailout scheme stands out as the most profitable among the Western states (Grossman and Woll, forthcoming).
4. Hybrid core capital is capital that may, under certain conditions, be included in the banking institutions' core capital. Hybrid core capital is loan capital subject to requirements, including that the maturity must not be fixed, and that interest on debt lapses if the banking institution has no free reserves (Danish National Bank 2008, 90). This obviously contrasts to a so-called upside-model, where the state purchases stocks in a financial institution and then sells it again when the institution (hopefully) is stabilized.
5. In the end, the actual issuance of bonds was 194 billion DKr (approximately €26 billion).
6. So far the outcome of Bank Package II is positive, amounting to almost 7 billion DKr. However, there are still a number of individual state guarantees that need refinancing in 2013.
7. As mentioned, the small socialist party, the Unity List, did not participate in the negotiations, but all other parties stood behind the agreement. On the side of the sector there were some that were very critical of financing the solution for banks that had behaved stupidly, but these opinions were never voiced strongly. In other words, the two bank packages enjoyed widespread support.
8. Senior creditors of Fjordbank Mors were expected to suffer haircuts of around 26 percent on their principal and about 450 of the bank's 73,000 customers facing a similar loss on deposits above the €100,000 threshold guaranteed by Danish deposit insurance rules.
9. There is actually a fifth and so far final bank package, which the government issued in March 2012. Though the term *bank packages* alludes to a certain degree of generality in the policy, it was actually specifically aimed at strengthening one bank, FIH Erhvervsbank (the fifth largest bank in Denmark), and for that reason it has been omitted from the present analysis (but see Carstensen, forthcoming).

References

Baker, Andrew. 2010. "Restraining Regulatory Capture? Anglo-America, Crisis Politics and Trajectories of Change in Global Financial Governance." *International Affairs* 86 (3): 647–63.

Carstensen, Martin B. 2011. "New Financial Regulation in Denmark after the Crisis— or the Politics of Not Really Doing Anything." *Danish Yearbook of Foreign Policy 2011* 106–129.

————. Forthcoming. "Projecting from a Fiction: The Case of Financial Crisis in Denmark." *New Political Economy*.

Crouch, Colin. 2011. *The Strange Non-Death of Neo-Liberalism*. London: Polity Books.

Culpepper, Pepper. 2008. "The Politics of Common Knowledge: Ideas and Institutional Change in Wage Bargaining." *International Organization* 62 (1): 1–33.

Danish National Bank. 2008. *Financial Stability 2008*. Copenhagen: Nationalbanken.

Ejerskov, Steen. 2009. "Pengemarkedet under den finansielle krise og pengeinstitutternes udlånsrente." *Kvartalsoversigt, 1. kvartal 2009*. Copenhagen: Nationalbanken.

Goul Andersen, Jørgen. 2011. "From the Edge of the Abyss to Bonanza—and Beyond: Danish Economy and Economic Policies 1980–2011." *Comparative Social Research*, 28: 89–165.

Grossman, Emiliano, and Cornelia Woll. Forthcoming. "Saving the Banks: The Political Economy of Bailouts." *Comparative Political Studies*.

Hansen, Per H. 1997. "Bankredninger i Danmark—en stabil tradition." In *Den danske Banksektor—mellem tradition og forandring*, edited by Torben Andersen and Karsten Ronit, 37–76. Aarhus: Systime.

Høpner, James. 1999. "The Danish Banking System: Concentration, Local Autonomy and the Financing of Small and Medium-Sized Enterprises." In *Mobilizing Resources and Generating Competencies: The Remarkable Success of Small and Medium-sized Enterprises in the Danish Business System*, edited by Peter Karnøe, Peer Hull Kristensen and Poul Houman Andersen, 113–35. Frederiksberg: Copenhagen Business School Press.

Katzenstein, Peter J. 1985. *Small States in World Markets: Industrial Policy in Europe*. Ithaca: Cornell University Press.

————. 2003. "Small States and Small States Revisited." *New Political Economy* 8 (1): 9–30.

Kickert, Walter. 2012a. "State Responses to the Fiscal Crisis: Belgium." *Public Money & Management* 32 (4): 303–10.

————. 2012b. "How the Dutch Government Responded to Financial, Economic and Fiscal Crisis." *Public Money & Management* 32 (6): 439–43.

Kjar, Iver. Forthcoming. "Still in the Market for Change: The Mass Public as a Veto Player in US and Danish Mortgage System Reform." In *Great Expectations, Small Transformations: Incremental Change in Financial Governance*, edited by Manuela Moschella and Eleni Tsingou. Colchester: ECPR Press.

Kluth, Michael, and Kim Lynggaard. Forthcoming. "Explaining Policy Responses to Danish and Irish Banking Failures during the Financial Crisis." *West European Politics*.

Mansbridge, Jane. 1992. "A Deliberative Perspective on Neocorporatism." *Politics & Society* 20 (4): 493–505.

Ministry of Economy. 1995. *Redning af pengeinstitutter siden 1984*. Copenhagen: Ministry of Economy.

Mortensen, Jens Ladefoged, and Leonard Seabrooke. 2009. "Egalitarian Politics in Property Booms and Busts: Housing as Social Right or Means to Wealth in Australia and Denmark." In *The Politics of Housing Boom and Busts*, edited by Herman M. Schwartz and Leonard Seabrooke, 122–45. Basingstoke: Palgrave Macmillan.

Mügge, Daniel. 2010. *Widen the Market, Narrow the Competition: Banker Interests and the Making of European Capital Markets*. Colchester: ECPR Press.

Pagliari, Stefano. 2012. *The Making of Good Financial Regulation: Towards a Policy Response to Regulatory Capture*. London: International Centre for Financial Regulation.

Pedersen, Ove Kaj. 2006. "Corporatism and Beyond: The Negotiated Economy." In *National Identity and the Varieties of Capitalism: The Danish Experience,* edited by John L. Campbell, John A. Hall and Ove Kaj Pedersen, 245–70. Montréal, Canada: McGill-Queen's University Press.

Ronit, Karsten. 1997. "Udviklingen af interesseorganisationer som alternativt styrings-system i dank bankvæsen." In *Den danske banksektor—mellem tradition og forandring,* edited by Torben Andersen and Karsten Ronit, 111–40. Aarhus: Systime.

Schwartz, Herman. 2010. "Small States in the Rear-View Mirror: Legitimacy in the Management of Economy and Society." *European Political Science* 9: 365–74.

Schmidt, Vivien A. 2003. "How, Where and When Does Discourse Matter in Small States' Welfare State Adjustment." *New Political Economy* 8 (1): 127–46.

Stigler, George. 1971. "The Theory of Economic Regulation." *Bell Journal of Economics* 2 (1): 113–21.

Warwick Commission. 2009. *The Warwick Commission on International Financial Reform: In Praise of Unlevel Playing Fields.* Warwick: Warwick University.

Østrup, Finn. 2010. "The Danish Bank Crisis in a Transnational Perspective." In *Danish Foreign Policy Yearbook 2010,* 75–102. Copenhagen: Danish Institute for International Studies.

Conclusion

George Philip, The London School of Economics

The contributors to this volume discuss a range of issues and realities in four different continents during the course of several different historical periods. There is evidently more to these works than can be discussed in detail in this short conclusion. It therefore makes sense to limit the discussion to two of the most important topics. One has to do with the ways in which economic policy making have changed under pressure of crisis; the other with how democracies, or semidemocracies, have responded to a prolonged period of financial adversity. How and why have democracies and their institutions mostly withstood this stress test on such a large scale?

SOME COMPARATIVE ASPECTS

The post-2008 recession, and its accompanying features, has probably amounted to the most serious threat that Europe's economies have faced since the Second World War. This is less true of Latin America and Korea, where the crises discussed in this book took place in somewhat earlier periods (in the 1980s and 1990s). It is also not the case with Russia. In the US, in contrast, the crisis has so far seemed manageable—so much so that there has been a tendency on the part of some policy makers to talk up the crisis in order to try to create more policy autonomy.

In Europe, however, there was no need to talk up anything. The crisis was quite serious enough. Nevertheless, as Heinrich and Kutter argue in their chapter, Europe's ability to crisis manage has also grown, even though it is too early to say that European anticrisis measures have succeeded. There is, however, a marked contrast between their chapter and the perspectives in Zartaloudis's chapter on Greece—a contrast which is reflected in the real-world differences of perspective within the Eurozone.

Many countries, however, that have already experienced crises have found ways of surviving them. Woodruff makes this point in respect to Argentina and Russia. Not only has there been life after debt, but also life after default. Default was only a disaster in the short term. In the long term, it increased the autonomy of the state and enabled defaulted governments to repudiate damaging contractual arrangements and renegotiate the economic rules of the game. Hopkin makes a similar point in a less dramatic way in the case of Southern Europe. Some degree of protectionism, Italian style, may be a better crisis response than Spanish-style orthodoxy. Jessop takes the argument further, and for him the triumph of economic orthodoxy in the 1980s and 1990s was the problem rather than the solution. The damaging outcome of earlier British crises was the strengthened role of the City of London and the banks.

DEMOCRACY AND ITS INSTITUTIONS

Given these divergent viewpoints about crises outcomes, it may be useful to re-define what we understand by failure. Democracy, and the survival of its institutions, may be more important in the long run than economic performance. It is certainly reassuring that no real parallel has emerged between Europe in the 1930s, with its Great Depression and triumph of dictatorship, and Europe today. Much of the same is true of Latin America, where the region's democracies have also thus far shown an ability to survive periods of stress. Although the post-2008 period has been quite positive for Latin America—growth has remained generally positive—the region has not been short of crises in a somewhat earlier period. There has been no open democratic breakdown in Latin America since the end of the 1970s despite some economic hard times. Meanwhile, the contributors on the US and Korea barely mention the possibility that democracy itself faces threats.

The enhanced role of international financial institutions (IFIs), backed by the US government in some cases and the EU in others, is surely part of the reason for the effective system maintenance since 2008. There is, however, something two edged about this. The IFIs may well have helped stabilize crisis-affected economies, but they have also in some ways shown themselves to be willing to take on policy making roles that would once have been regarded as legitimate areas of democratic governance. Ji's chapter discusses the way in which the IFIs were at least partly responsible for the triumph of market economics in Korea, and Philip makes a similar point about Mexico. Heinrich and Kutter develop this point in respect to the further strengthening of euro institutions. Zartaloudis's chapter also raises important issues about the double role of the international financial institutions in dealing with Greece. They wanted Greece to avoid shipwreck but also taught a hard lesson about financial responsibility. To put it mildly, this requires a degree of fine judgment.

Some Greeks certainly feel colonized by the EU, whether justifiably or not is another story. Yet, it is not only Europe that has seen greater economic integration. Mexico has gone a long way down the path of integration with the US. This began as a process of crisis management, but now things have gone much further, even though one cannot yet talk about shared sovereignty.

DIVERGENT RESPONSES TO CRISIS

Different countries have responded to globalization in different ways. Regional integration, which is one response, has probably gone the farthest in the Eurozone where there must be a legitimate question about whether traditionally understood national sovereignty today exists at all. Venezuela, in contrast, has up to now rejected the idea of closer integration with the US and has positively sought to maintain its distance. Russia, too, has rejected liberal institutions without suffering obvious harm. It may of course be significant that both Venezuela and Russia are oil exporters and have in recent years benefited from high prices.

THE SPECTER OF FISCAL POPULISM

So far, we can be cautiously optimistic about the politics of crisis, even though the story is certainly not over. Yet, while democratic breakdown seems highly unlikely in any of the countries being considered here, what does seem to be happening is some revival of what we may call (following Mexico's Miguel de la Madrid) fiscal populism. Fiscal populism can be defined as the rejection of both economic orthodoxy and institutionalized forms of politics, together with the acceptance of a majoritarian form of democracy. It often goes arm in arm with economic nationalism. While not necessarily negative, it can be risky.

It is noteworthy that that Mexico, which along with Argentina at one time appeared to be a natural home of fiscal populism, now seems to have comprehensively rejected it. However, there is a noteworthy politics of fiscal populism in both Latin America and Europe. In Latin America, Argentina and Venezuela responded to crises by electing fiscal populists whereas in Mexico and Uruguay the response was to reject them. In the case of Mexico, the pain inflicted by repeated economic crises and, in Uruguay, the experiences of its neighbors no doubt help to explain this divergence. In Europe, Zartaloudis sees some possibility of fiscal populism emerging in Greece, while Hopkin sees divergent outcomes in Southern Europe, with Italian economic nationalism proving more resilient and less vulnerable to populism than Spain's greater market orientation. This outcome, like several others in the book, would be unexpected. However, it is noteworthy that the Europeanists in this volume (Jessop excepted) are much more skeptical of fiscal populism than some of the contributors on countries outside the region.

SOME COMPARISONS AND CONTRASTS

Fiscal populism remains a possible option, but other political consequences of crises in our selected countries have varied from case to case. This variance has occurred for reasons that have had more to do with politics than with the inherent characteristics of the crises themselves. While there is probably some kind of relationship between the economic severity of a financial crisis and its political consequences, arguments for economic determinism are not persuasive. What matters more is how a particular set of circumstances comes to be interpreted by opinion formers of various kinds, which in turn will depend on historical and cultural factors. Issues of discourse are central to outcomes and are tackled in the chapters by Ji and Panizza in this book.

The political outcomes of the various crises discussed in the book will vary according to a wide range of circumstances. Yet, there are enough comparative issues to suggest that there may be some point in attempting a continuum of crises and their outcomes. Here we attempt such a continuum.

At the most extreme of the various possible outcomes (let us call it *A*) there is the specter of democratic collapse. Fortunately, this remains no more than a specter, but fears have been expressed—sometimes publicly but more often privately—that democracy itself is in danger in some crisis-ridden countries and that violent conflict could follow from the triumph of extremist politicians. At the extreme, there is talk of an institutional collapse of significant magnitude. Further down the scale of intensity, we have the outcome case (let us call it *B*) where crisis marks a real rupture from institutionalized democracy, but not to the point where authoritarian government looms. A significant degree of civil disorder may nevertheless occur, and the locus of power may for a time shift to the streets. Fiscal populism comes into play. If outcome *A* brings to mind the collapse of parliamentary government in Europe in the 1930s, a loose analogy for category *B* would be the collapse of the Fourth Republic in France in 1958. Institutions failed and were replaced, and economic structures may have changed, but democratic values survived in a meaningful way and may indeed have become stronger in some cases. The Revolution never came, despite significant unrest.

Outcome *C* is less radical. It involves the basic maintenance of the status quo, with some change but less than might be expected from the degree of economic pressure experienced. Under outcome *C*, democracies "muddle through," even under acute conditions. The possibility is not excluded that the outcome might be "reactionary" in the sense that fears of radical and unwelcome change may lead ultimately to the reinforcement of the status quo.

Finally, we have outcome *D*, which might best be summarized in the words attributed to British Prime Minister James Callaghan in 1978: "Crisis, what crisis?" In this case, securely institutionalized policy making limits both the positives and negatives of potential crisis situations. Opinion formers may try to talk conflict up rather than down, but nothing really happens. Category *D* fits the old joke of financial markets having predicted seven of the last two recessions.

Fortunately, no author in this work has unequivocally forecast outcome *A*. One contributor, Zartaloudis, does come close and sees a real danger that political extremists may end up doing irretrievable damage to Greece's democratic institutions. The parties of the center that had dominated Greek politics when that country seemed to be prospering have substantially given way to parties of the extreme right and left. International factors have acted, in part, as destabilizing influences both when the Greek economy was on the way up and on the way down. A period of excessive slackness in budgetary policy abruptly gave way to a period of what most Greeks regard as excessive tightness (Greece's creditors may not have seen it this way).

The European financial establishment has, in its own way, tried to protect Greek institutions, and it may not altogether have failed. While the toughness of the financial terms imposed on Greece may be resented, the survival of the euro and the institutions of the EU have been an overriding concern of European policy makers. It has also made Greek withdrawal from the main European institutions (the dreaded "Grexit") essentially impossible without a crisis in democratic institutionality. And, for as long as Greece remains within the parameters of Europe's complex institutions, democratic collapse is highly unlikely. Even if they somehow did come to power electorally, Greece's theoretically extremist parties would in office have to act like sheep in wolves' clothing or risk their period of governance becoming nasty, brutish, and short.

Then Latin American experience offers some intriguing contrasts to Europe because its international institutionalization is different and much weaker. It is true that there exist some international institutions in Latin America, but these are much weaker than those in Europe. We are also looking at a somewhat earlier period. Nevertheless, it is significant that the region's democracies have survived some significant crises. Some, particularly the Banco Latino crisis in Venezuela, were sufficiently serious to lead to a temporary collapse of at least some institutions, but not of democracy itself. The 2002 coup attempt may seem an exception to this, but the point is that it failed. Venezuela has experienced several military coup attempts since 1992 and none have succeeded. Even so, extrainstitutional forms of politics such as coup attempts are not unthinkable in Venezuela as they have been in Greece. Venezuelan policy following the collapse of the Banco Latino could also be seen as a (temporary) victory for populism.

In a broader comparative context, therefore, Venezuela (like Greece) might score somewhere between *A* and *B*, depending on whether one sees the rise of Chavez as involving a threat to democracy or as a deepening of the country's hitherto mainly formal democratic institutions. While Chavez is certainly an electoral democrat, he is also one of only a few coup leaders to have been elected head of a country whose democratically elected government he previously sought to overthrow. This is not encouraging from the perspective of institutional stability and fits in well with the notion of populism. Venezuela also provides us with an object lesson on not drawing conclusions too soon.

Argentina's response to the crisis of 2001–2002 shares some common features with Venezuela's response to the Banco Latino crisis. Both might be described as populist, but Argentina's institutions seem somewhat less insecure. The main contrast between the two countries is that Argentine political personalism is mediated via Peronism which, although in some ways institutionally weak, is not as individualized as Venezuela's Chavismo. Russian experience bears comparison with that of Argentina—Woodruff does indeed compare them. Both countries have to an extent overcome fiscal crisis, but at a cost to their political institutions.

The support for "everybody out" slogans in Argentina is, however, similar to that of Venezuela at the time of the banking collapse. The Argentine crisis of 2001–2002 decisively defeated one of the most determined market-reform experiments of Latin America and undermined the Washington Consensus in that country. Although Venezuela's market reformism was tepid by Argentine standards, it too was decisively undermined by banking crisis. Moreover, the disastrous character of the most recent Argentine military government—particularly its military defeat in the South Atlantic—has made a return to power of the military effectively unthinkable. Only Greece, of the other countries discussed here, has a similar record of failed military government, though Russia lost the Cold War, and the Soviet coup attempt of 1991 was a comprehensive bungle. In Venezuela, by contrast, the military retains a good deal of political prestige as it did under the old USSR.

Away from Greece, Venezuela, Russia, and Argentina, we move into calmer political waters where gradual change is more at issue than the reemergence of populism and institutional breakdown. Mexico would seem to fit outcome C (institutional muddling through) in the sense that democratic institutions are much more secure than they were in the early 1980s. Mexico is politically unusual in that its authoritarian politics (during 1940–1986) were themselves largely institutionalized. The authoritarian system rejected fiscal populism before democratizing. Today, Mexico's democratic institutions and its good relation with the US seem secure enough. It may be true that the "populist" left twice came close to victory in presidential elections in 1988 and 2006. Had they won, things might well have turned out differently in either case. However, the effect of both the 1982 and 1994 crises was to push Mexico in the direction of democracy and alliance with the United States. In Korea, too, democracy as such was not undermined by the crisis as was national capitalism. In both countries, liberal capitalism emerged triumphant.

A final Latin American case is provided by Uruguay, whose democratic institutions have largely remained secure during the 2001–2002 crisis. An important reason for this was the dominant political impulse distinguishing that country from Argentina. We see here a feature of many other countries in which major political change does not happen—namely, an unwillingness to become too closely associated with the politics of a neighboring country. This may be particularly significant in small countries with big neighbors. Uruguay's crisis may actually have strengthened institutions, which would make it an outcome D (as is the case of Denmark). Although there is no chapter here on Irish politics, a similar logic also applies to another small country that would rather be formally aligned with the euro than informally aligned with the British pound.

Then there are the various other European cases. Here Hopkin asserts a paradox. Spain is by common consent more democratically institutionalized than Italy. However, with the passage of time, this may be a source of weakness rather than strength. Some element of populism may be system maintaining.

Finally there is the exceptional case of the US. The US is evidently not immune to financial or other difficulties, but it is much less vulnerable to institutional problems than Latin America or Europe. This is largely because it is responsible for its own currency. Nevertheless, the US saw some spectacular failures of financial institutions in late 2008 and, even if economic issues probably did not cost the Republican Party the presidency in that year (one can argue that they would have lost anyway), they surely affected the margin of victory. They later played some role in reshaping political attitudes. Ashbee analyzes what he calls "liberal Keynesianism" and brings to mind a weaker version of the New Deal. As in the 1930s, however, budgetary issues have encouraged a new kind of militancy, but this time on the Republican Right. The US probably merits an outcome C. Political institutions in the US have not changed by much since 2008, but the mentality of its policy makers has indeed.

In general, financial crises are something like bloodless wars. They provide a powerful test for the political systems that have to cope with them. In some respects, the test will be arbitrary and perhaps even unfair, but crises responses are likely to be remembered more vividly and for longer than the smoother operations of politics as usual. They are also likely to matter more. Crises outcomes, too, will almost inevitably involve some element of the unexpected. This unexpectedness may be benign, as with some of our case studies, but in the worst of cases may be negative to the point of danger. It is this unexpectedness, though, that brings the study of politics to life. It reminds us that there is always more to learn about politics than can be reduced to formulae.

Index